DEADLY WINTER

DEADLY WINTER

The Life of Sir John Franklin

Martyn Beardsley

NAVAL INSTITUTE PRESS
Annapolis, Maryland

First published in Great Britain in 2002 by Chatham Publishing,
99 High Street, Rochester, Kent ME1 1LX

Published and distributed in the United States and Canada by the
Naval Institute Press, 291 Wood Road, Annapolis, Maryland 21402-5034

Library of Congress Catalog No. 2001099826

ISBN 1-55750-179-3

This edition is authorized for sale only in the United States,
its territories and possessions and Canada.

Manufactured in Great Britain.

Contents

Alas! no more shall he behold,
Nor friends nor sacred home. On very nerve
The deadly winter seizes; shuts up sense;
And o'er his inmost vitals creeping cold,
Lays him along the snow a stiffened corpse –
Stretched out, and bleaching in the northern blast.

From an unattributed poem in William Jerdan's
Men I have Known.

List of Illustrations

Between pages 112 and 113

John Franklin by Alfred Bock after L Haghe (Allport Library & Museum of Fine Arts, Tasmania)

Bellerophon (National Maritime Museum, Greenwich)

Matthew Flinders (Allport Library & Museum of Fine Arts, Tasmania)

Sketch of the young Eleanor Ann Porden (Derbyshire Record Office)

John Richardson (Anne Savours)

Akaitcho and son (From *Narrative of a Journey to the Shores of the Polar Sea in the Years 1819–20–21–22*, by John Franklin)

Junius and Augustus (From *Narrative of a Journey to the Shores of the Polar Sea in the Years 1819–20–21–22*, by John Franklin)

Expedition Doubling Cape Barrow (From *Narrative of a Journey to the Shores of the Polar Sea in the Years 1819–20–21–22*, by John Franklin)

Winter View of Fort Franklin (From *Narrative of a Second Expedition to the Shores of the Polar Sea in the Years 1825, 1826 and 1827*, by John Franklin)

The *Dolphin* Squeezed by Ice (From *Narrative of a Second Expedition to the Shores of the Polar Sea in the Years 1825, 1826 and 1827*, by John Franklin)

Esquimaux Encampment off Richard's Island (From *Narrative of a Second Expedition to the Shores of the Polar Sea in the Years 1825, 1826 and 1827*, by John Franklin)

Hobart Town (Allport Library & Museum of Fine Arts, Tasmania)

Old Government House (Allport Library & Museum of Fine Arts, Tasmania)

Lady Jane Franklin (Author's collection)

The Arctic Council (Allport Library & Museum of Fine Arts, Tasmania)

Sir John Franklin (National Maritime Museum, Greenwich)

Franklin Memorial, Westminster Abbey (The Dean and Chapter of Westminster)

The Breaking Up of the Ice (Dr Russell Potter)

The message found at Victory Point (National Maritime Museum, Greenwich)

SIR JOHN FRANKLIN
IN THE ARCTIC

80°W
70°W
60°W
50°W
40°W
75°N
30°W
GREENLAND
ELLESMERE
ISLAND
Smith Sound
Cape York
70°N
Baffin Bay
Croker Bay
Lancaster Sound
DISKO
65°N
Davis Strait
Ross Bay
Fury and Hecla Str.
BAFFIN
ISLAND
Melville Peninsula
Ross Bay
Gore Bay
Foxe Basin
Arctic Circle
SOUTHAMPTON ISLAND
Frobisher Bay
60°N
Ungara Bay
LABRADOR
HUDSON
BAY
55°N
80°W
70°W
60°W

~ Introduction ~

WHEN I was a small boy my grandfather had a collection of plastic model sailing ships in a display cabinet which he was unwise enough to let me play with whenever I visited. (I can only recall the *Golden Hind*, but I suspect the *Victory* and possibly the *Revenge* were among them.) By the time I reached my teens only the most skilful and ingenious of jury-rigging would have made those ships seaworthy once more. But like all good men-o'-war they had seen a lot of action, and maybe my grandfather appreciated this whenever he surveyed the gradual deterioration of his painstakingly constructed fleet.

And so as a child my heroes were not only Bobby Charlton and Dixon of Dock Green but also men like Drake and Nelson, and I became aware of their exploits, their sacrifices and their place in British history.

My daughter, who is more intelligent than I was at her age and on the verge of secondary education, has no idea who Drake and Nelson were or what they did, and I predict that future generations of adults will be in the same position as her. A contestant on a recent television quiz show was of the opinion that Rommel led the Allied forces to victory in North Africa.

It has not been a surprise, therefore, to be met with blank stares on telling people I was writing a book about Sir John Franklin. Franklin's exploits were the stuff of melodrama, and his achievements were not inconsiderable; but those achievements came mostly in the form of a gradual accumulation of scientific knowledge rather than one sudden, dramatic discovery with which to stamp his name indelibly in people's minds.

Another reason why Franklin and his ilk are less well known than they might be is the modern trend towards revisionist history. Much energy is now invested in searching for flaws in the characters of the heroes of previous generations (not a difficult exercise in the field of human behaviour) and in putting a modern and, in my opinion, anachronistic, slant on the actions and beliefs of people living in different centuries and different worlds. This kind of view brings its own agenda to whatever subject is under scrutiny, and as such is at least as biased as any earlier attempts at telling the 'truth'.

In his day, Franklin was a Neil Armstrong and a Colin Powell rolled into one. The publication of the account of his first overland expedition helped to cement his international fame. He was treated like a celebrity in France, the Empress Mother of Russia avidly followed his exploits and, with characteristic shyness, he felt it necessary to steer clear of Leicester Square before his North Pole voyage lest anyone should recognise him from the 'panorama' celebrating the expedition which was on display there.

Now, Franklin is better remembered in the parts of the world where he made his mark than he is in the country of his birth. In Canada, among other institutions bearing his name, there is a Sir John Franklin High School in Yellowknife, Northwest Territories, and a Sir John Franklin Junior High School in Calgary, Alberta. There is even a Sir John Franklin Karate Club in Manitoba! You can patronise the Sir John Franklin Hotel in Victoria, British Columbia, or the one in Kapunda, South Australia. (You could perhaps travel at a leisurely pace from one establishment to the other on the *Sir John Franklin* icebreaker ship.) But it is perhaps in Tasmania that the Franklin name rings out the loudest. Because of the fact that he was outmanoeuvred by men infinitely more cynical and ruthless than he was, memories of his governorship of that island are dominated by the events leading to his departure. But he and his wife Jane played a positive and major role in shaping that infant colony's future, and the people of Tasmania have never forgotten them. There is a Franklin town, village, national park and river. In the capital, Hobart, Franklin Square can be found, and Franklin's statue gazes upon the changing face of the city that was his home for seven eventful years. Tasmania boasts the oldest Royal Society outside England, founded by Franklin, and Jane is remembered in Jane Franklin Hall, a college of the University of Tasmania, and the Lady Franklin Museum, which she founded in 1842.

Franklin has been celebrated in song, verse and prose from the time of his death to the present day. *Lord Franklin* is a folk song whose origins are lost in the mists of time but which is still in the repertoire of singers in that genre. The poetry began with his own first wife, Eleanor Anne Porden, and was carried on by Tennyson, a relative by marriage, Swinburne and a host of other lesser-known poets. Fictional accounts of the Franklin story, particularly relating to the 1845 North West Passage expedition, still emerge at regular intervals. The latest known one was published in 1999, *North With Franklin*, by John Wilson (Fitzhenry & Whiteside), apparently inspired by, and partly based on, the last letters of Commander James Fitzjames who sailed with Franklin in the *Erebus*.

To the best of my knowledge, almost a generation has passed since the last full Franklin biography, Roderic Owen's *The Fate of Franklin* (Hutchinson, 1978). Interest in the historic struggle to complete the North West Passage remains as strong as ever, and Franklin's name figures prominently in those accounts. Those whose sole interest is in the debate and mystery surrounding this enigma will find little new in this book, and may even be disappointed at the lack of space I have devoted to the very many years of searching that went on in the second half of the nineteenth century. I have adopted this approach partly because the majority of the seemingly innumerable search vessels found precisely nothing. But also, from the very outset I decided that this was to be the story of Sir John Franklin's *life*. He lived in a time of discovery, adventure, invention and technological progress, yet also of poverty, social injustice and political corruption. Franklin was a warrior and explorer, and as a young man hankered after promotion and the money and prestige that went with it. But through it all his honesty and integrity remained intact, and it is my wish that the reader will come to a better understanding and appreciation of Franklin the man through the pages of this book.

Acknowledgements

I am very grateful for their help and permission to quote from archive material to the staff of the Nottingham Central Library,

Derbyshire Public Records Office, Lincolnshire Archives, Public Record Office at Kew, Royal Geographical Society (with the Institute of British Geographers), British Library, National Maritime Museum at Greenwich, and to Robert Headland at the Scott Polar Research Institute. Permission to reproduce material from the Flinders Collection was kindly granted by Mr R Perry and Lincolnshire Archives.

Thanks also to Professor Stuart Houston and Ernie Coleman for their pointers, and to Roderic Owen for his help and kind hospitality.

Finally, a very special thanks to Ralph Lloyd-Jones, whose guidance, knowledge and generosity have been indispensable during the writing of this book.

Notes on the Text

One of the hardest parts about researching this book was deciphering the handwriting of both John Franklin and his wife Jane. There is nothing that makes the spirit sink so low as to be faced, at the end of a long day of note-taking, with pages of crabby handwriting which is also cross-written (the nineteenth-century practice of saving paper – and thereby stamp duty – by filling a page then over-writing on the same page but at a right-angle to the original).

When I have been unsure of a word, I have, wherever possible, referred to already published versions for confirmation. In rare cases where the correct word is still in doubt I have placed it in square brackets [thus].

I have left the long and meandering sentences, idiosyncratic punctuation, and occasional misspelling exactly as I found it. Just occasionally for the sake of clarity I have drawn attention to an error in the conventional way – [sic].

Place names have been generally spelt in the modern way, except when in the context of a contemporary quotation.

I have used the term Eskimo instead of Inuit, which I realise bucks the modern trend. It is the appellation with which I believe most people are still familiar, and which appears so often from the mouths and pens of the time in question that my use of it provides some uniformity. As I understand it, the word 'Eskimo' means 'Eaters of Raw Flesh', which being, historically at least, a common and necessary practice among the people to which it refers could hardly be classed as derogatory. It is still usual throughout the world for one race to call another by a name with which they have become known for historical reasons, yet which is not the name by which they know themselves. This seems only natural and reasonable. Many peoples would not use the word 'English' when referring to my race, and I could not feel justified in insisting that they did so.

Nevertheless, I apologise to anyone who cannot go along with this line of reasoning.

MARTYN BEARDSLEY
Beeston, March 2001

~ 1 ~

Every Inch an Honest Tar

On 16 April 1786 the ninth child of the Franklins of Spilsby, Lincolnshire, came into the world. He was the fifth and last of their boys (they would have twelve children in all) and he was named John.

John Franklin was born at a time when a century of revolution in agricultural practices was in the process of being eclipsed by a nascent industrial revolution that would change the world forever. In Britain, the Enclosure system was at its height, radically affecting the lives of that vast majority of the populace which still lived and worked on the land. The population of London was well under a million and no other city had more than twenty thousand inhabitants, but the nation was well on the way to becoming the 'workshop of the world'. Modifications to James Watt's steam engine had opened up its range of uses in industry and transport, heralding changes in the way people lived and worked that previous generations could never have imagined. While all this was going on, the dark shadow of conflict loomed ever closer. The French Revolution broke out three years after Franklin's birth, and Napoleon was to seize power seven years later.

Despite the technological advances there were still many blank spaces on the world map as far as the insatiably curious Europeans were concerned: from Australia to Africa to the Polar regions. It was a want that would have a fundamental bearing on the life of the baby opening his eyes to the world for the first time, in a tiny room of a house that still stands today. (At the time of writing it serves as a bakery, though in a previous incarnation it was – more appropriately – a frozen food establishment!)

The Franklins were not poor, but it appears they had come down in the world somewhat. H D Traill, who in 1896 wrote the first comprehensive biography of John Franklin,[1] quotes a family tradition that the Franklins had belonged to the 'wealthy yeomanry', but that this wealth had been squandered by John's grandfather. Willingham, John's father, was a 'mere' merchant – but more than one of his children would go on to leave their mark in the world. Two of his other sons became army officers and one a successful lawyer. One of John's seven sisters was Isabella, later to become Mrs Cracroft; her daughter Sophia will figure in this story later on.

There is a statue of Franklin in Spilsby's market place. In a speech at the unveiling of this memorial in 1857,[2] his lifelong friend Sir John Richardson revealed the little-known fact that the young Franklin obtained the 'rudiments' of education at St Ives in the neighbouring county of Cambridgeshire. After this we know that he attended Louth Grammar school, about fifteen miles from home. It was a school in decline; there were seventy boys there in 1798 when Franklin was a pupil, but this number would dwindle to twenty over the next few years.[3] The school is perhaps more famous for later having been attended by Tennyson, who hated it; Franklin's sentiments have not been recorded. Many years later a schoolfriend from those days told Franklin's wife that he recalled his 'earnest, animated . . . countenance', flowing hair, and 'manly figure and bearing'.[4] Franklin himself, writing to his sister when a 'blooming youth' of nineteen, asked if she remembered the

> little mischievous, and with all dirty little boy… Do you not see me bolting into a room (sweetly smelling of brown soap) with fixed eyes, and open mouth, ready to catch the least syllable the company may drop; and occasionally put in a word, or two, by way of letting a light on a subject; contrary to the wishes and thanks of my mother and sisters…[5]

He used to be, he admitted, 'very imprudent and forward' (yet now, at nineteen, 'rather diffident') but also cowardly 'when challenged to box by other boys'.

At a very young age Franklin had made up his mind to go to sea. Early biographers have spoken poetically of this momentous revelation arising during a solitary walk to the coast. However it came about, by the age of fourteen the die was cast. There is a diary-style entry during 1800 in an accounts book of Matthew Flinders, father of the outstanding young sailor and navigator of the same name:

> On Friday, August 22nd Mr Willingham* Franklin and his brother John, made us a visit for a few days. They are accomplished youths, the first intended for the Church, and the latter every inch an honest Tar. I wish success to them both.[6]

It may well be that the exploits of Flinders junior provided Franklin with the inspiration to join the Royal Navy, and it would not be long before they were sailing together. Before this could come about, it is said that Franklin got his first taste of life at sea on a merchant ship plying its trade between Lisbon and Hull, but his future career really commenced around a month after he had so much impressed Mr Flinders, for just as the nation had recently acquired a new flag through the Act of Union, HMS *Polyphemus* had gained a new midshipman. It was something about which his father had misgivings. Britain's navy was fighting to counter the threat of invasion by Napoleon, and had recently found itself isolated after the break-up of the allied coalition, with Holland and Spain going over to the French side; it would not be unnatural for a father to hesitate to put his fourteen year-old son into a man-of-war. He had other ambitions for his promising boy, probably in commerce. But even if he were thinking along military lines, a career in the army was considered to be a socially superior and more prestigious path to take. Even for an officer, the navy was, as N A M Rodger points out in his detailed study of the Georgian navy, 'An arduous, dangerous and ill-paid profession'.[7]

Whatever the reasoning behind it, young John Franklin was assigned to this 64-gun warship under one Captain Lawford. Brother James was in London preparing the ground for John's venture. He wrote to their father in September reporting that the *Polyphemus* was expected in Yarmouth within days and suggested, with the approval of family friend Captain Epworth, that John should be sent to school until it arrived. It seems to have been the Flinders connection

---

* This was Willingham junior.

(Matthew the younger was married to John's aunt) which helped him secure his berth, since James wrote: 'I have this day wrote again to Miss Flinders wishing her to send up a Letter of Introduction to Captain L. for John to take down with him'.[8] He was, he said, sending up the outfits he had been busy procuring, which included checked shirts, blue jacket and 'trowsers' ('on which there must be Anchor Buttons'), flannel drawers and three pairs of thick worsted hose. Some readers will readily identify with James's sentiments when he adds wistfully: 'Never was I so tired of doing nothing and yet continually running after this nasty cloaths-buying business...'

Another family friend, Mr Allenby, saw young John onto the Yarmouth coach and provided him with £10 – despite James's valiant if enervating efforts there was still bedding and a sea chest to buy. Allenby remarked that the boy was in good spirits and seemed capable of looking after himself. He would need to be. Life on a man-o'-war was rarely easy even at the best of times, but before he had reached the age when modern children leave school, John would find himself in the thick of the historic and bloody battle of Copenhagen.

A generation earlier (but little had changed) when Horatio Nelson joined the *Raisonnable*, another 64-gun ship, as a 'middy', he spoke of the strangeness of this new environment he had entered: 'I could not think what world I was in, whether among spirits or devils...' He was bemused by the 'different language and strange expressions of tongue...'[9]

The midshipman was at the bottom of the pecking order of officers in the Royal Navy. Most were boys or teenagers, and were often referred to as the 'young gentlemen', though some were older men for whom the hope of promotion had long since faded. A Third Rate fighting vessel like the *Polyphemus* would have a complement of roughly 500 men, with around sixteen midshipmen. The younger middies might sleep in the gunroom on the lower gundeck, where, according to the writer and seaman John Masefield,[10] the gunner kept a 'fatherly eye' on them, looking after their feeding and clothing arrangements. Otherwise, the home of the midshipman, and especially the more senior members of that rank, was the cockpit, which was aft on the orlop deck. This was more or less below the waterline when the ship was fully loaded, with lanterns and candles providing the only light. Masefield vividly describes the 'continual pestilential stench' from the bilges, directly beneath the orlop, which mingled with the odour of 'rancid butter and putrid cheese' from the nearby purser's store, together with the 'tarry, musty smell of old rope' from the cable-tiers further forward. The table from which the midshipmen ate their food was used to lie wounded men on for surgery – mainly amputations and suturing – during and after battle.

A midshipman was in many ways an apprentice officer, and he would have to serve a minimum of two years before becoming eligible for promotion to lieutenant, for which the passing of an examination was necessary. There are many stories of the rigours of life for the midshipman: the conditions, the quality of the food, the bullying and rough horseplay. But larger ships would often have a schoolmaster, who in addition to routine academic subjects would introduce the boys to the skills necessary for progress in their new careers, such as navigation and trigonometry. On a more practical level, a boy like Franklin would have been assigned to a watch: most of the ship's crew were divided into two watches, with one watch resting while the other performed its duties. The watches changed every four hours, and as an example of the way in which everything at sea was different from ashore, the 'day' on a warship began at midnight or 4am, depending on which watch you were on. Midshipmen would often be expected to go aloft to be initiated into the arcane world of handling sails and rigging. Despite their junior position they had the privilege of access to the hallowed quarterdeck, and they would be expected to act as general messengers and dogsbodies for the lieutenants.

So this was the strange and uncompromising world in which John Franklin found himself; yet, judging from the cheery, optimistic letters he wrote during this period he seems to have been not in the least daunted by it all. The day before the English fleet under Admiral Sir Hyde Parker departed Yarmouth Roads, he wrote to his parents explaining that they were about to sail for the Baltic. It was thought, he said, 'that we are going to Elsineur to attempt to take the Castle, but some think we cannot succeed. I think they will turn their tail when they consider we have 35 sail of the line…'[11] One of which, he proudly points out, is the *St George*, 98, 'Admiral Nelson's flag'.

What is also clear from this letter is that, even at this early age, Franklin's thoughts tended more towards exploration than fighting. He realises his current duties make it unlikely that he will able to join Captain Flinders' forthcoming expedition to explore the coasts of 'New Holland', but: 'If we do return before the *Investigator* sails, I shall thank you to use your interest for me to go'. Did it even occur to the nonchalant neophyte that he might be one of the many men never to return from this attack on the formidable defences of Copenhagen?

On the way out, Franklin got a taste of the kind of conditions he would face on future expeditions: gales, ice, and snow on the masts and yards beset them in the Channel. The Danes had left the allied coalition and taken a position of 'armed neutrality'. Their ships and coastal defences commanded the entrance to the Baltic, whose ports provided raw materials essential to the naval powers; Britain felt it could not afford to allow French and Spanish ships the luxury of free access to this region. Diplomatic attempts were being made even as the fleet sailed, but Nelson soon decided that Hyde Parker was dithering and that the arrival of the powerful British fleet would persuade the Danes to see sense. The diplomacy eventually came to nothing and Nelson got his way. Instead of waiting for the enemy to come out and do battle, he would take twelve line-of-battle ships in on an audacious surprise attack: avoiding a treacherous sandbank, along a shallow channel, and sailing between the shore batteries of Copenhagen and a line of ships and floating batteries anchored offshore which outnumbered his squadron by more than two to one. Franklin's *Polyphemus* was one of those ships chosen to go in.

What followed was a victory which would be remembered as much as anything for the refusal by Nelson, who could see that despite the ferocity of the fighting the Danes were being battered into submission, to comply with signals to disengage sent by the distant Hyde Parker, who could not.

Sadly, if Franklin wrote anything down about his first sea battle, it no longer seems to exist. In action, armed midshipmen guarded the routes from the gundeck to the orlop in order to deter anyone whose nerve broke from seeking refuge in the safest part of the ship. They also acted as signals officers and messengers, and it is likely that Franklin's future role of Signals Officer started here.

By the middle of the morning of 2 April 1801, the leading ships were already fiercely engaged when the *Agamemnon*, which had been supposed to make for the *Prøvesteenen*, tried but failed to manoeuvre into position, and Nelson ordered the *Polyphemus* forward in her stead. The *Polyphemus* eventually found herself taking on two enemy ships simultaneously, one of similar strength and the other a rather more heavily armed opponent of 74 guns. After several hours of deafening, thundering gunfire and blinding smoke, the guns of the 74 fell silent and both enemy vessels were eventually boarded by parties from the *Polyphemus*. Her own log records thirty casualties, including six dead. The Danish defences were overpowered and after talks on board one of the British ships the dangerous alliance between Denmark and Russia was officially broken off. Nelson was a hero, and John Franklin had been blooded.

The *Polyphemus* got off quite lightly, taking into account the torrid nature of the battle. The traditional mode of combat was for two lines of ships to sail past each other like jousting knights, firing as they went; it often ended with individual ships locking horns (sometimes literally locking yards), blasting 32pdr cannonballs and other assorted hardware into each other, sometimes from point-blank range, until one could continue no longer. At its most brutal it could be rather like two heavyweight boxers with their boots glued to the floor, thumping each other's heads until one crumpled. Ships rarely sank from a pounding by the non-explosive cannonballs. The decisive factor was usually debilitating damage to either the ship or crew. It was not uncommon for even the victor to end the battle in a crippled state, but triumph when its adversary could no longer endure further casualties. This was brutal, but worked well for the British because it is generally agreed that they were superior in the area of gunnery and could maintain accurate fire at sometimes twice the rate of enemy ships. Nevertheless this standard tactic was nearly always costly against ships of equal power, and the leading ship in the assault, the *Edgar*, had over a hundred more casualties than the *Polyphemus*; the *Monarch*, which had come under extremely heavy fire from both shore and ship, suffered 220 casualties.

Franklin returned to England on the *Isis* to find that that *Investigator* had yet to depart – there might still be time for him to get a berth. He was very fortunate. Flinders had been ready to leave even before the battle of Copenhagen took place, but a combination of circumstances had delayed him. In his account of the voyage,[12] Flinders mentions that the *Investigator*'s complement included 'two young gentlemen more than allowed' for a ship of that class (a sloop), and it is almost certain that Franklin was one of those 'young gentlemen', squeezed in at the eleventh hour. And although it was a family connection that led to Franklin obtaining a berth, Flinders must have had faith in the boy's abilities, for he had carefully planned this venture and there was no room for make-weights. Only volunteers were taken – and there were far more of those than could be accepted. 'Such officers and crew as were aged, or did not volunteer for this particular service, were discharged', he declared.[13]

Flinders wrote to Franklin's brother Thomas, outlining what uniform and other gear would be necessary, but emphasising that John must be quick in getting to the ship if he were to join the expedition. He made it, and before long Matthew Flinders was relaying to Thomas a letter full of praise for this 'veteran' of Copenhagen. The boy was now studying the navigational aspects of astronomy, and his new captain considered that John would 'soon be my right-hand man in that way', and added that the First Lieutenant 'scarcely knows how to talk enough in his praise...'[14] Franklin's fighting career was far from over; there were still battles to be fought. But on 18 July 1801 the sails of His Majesty's Ship *Investigator* disappeared over the horizon, opening a chapter on a new career of exploration and discovery that would turn Franklin into Spilsby's most famous son.

✳

The *Investigator* was a sloop of around 344 tons, but she must have seemed more like a cutter after the months spent on board a line-of–battle ship. She had been overhauled and re-coppered, and was 'considered to be the best vessel which could, at that time, be spared for the projected voyage to Terra Australis',[15] according to Flinders. He had insisted on only the best. One of his first acts was to have all the ship's stores sent away and replaced with goods of a higher quality – and more of them.

This voyage had been the brainchild of the renowned Sir Joseph Banks, who had sailed on the *Endeavour* with Captain Cook. The chosen captain, Matthew Flinders, was an experienced and extremely talented navigator and explorer who had already been to Australia, and there were other esteemed men with him including Scotsman Robert Brown, a highly rated young naturalist, and Ferdinand Bauer, regarded as one of the best botanical artists of the day.

Despite Flinders' meticulous planning, the ship began to leak as soon as they cleared the English Channel.* When they reached Madeira, Flinders and the ship's carpenter went round her in a boat, and it appeared that water was coming in through the seams. They were caulked, but the leak worsened as they made their way to the Cape of Good Hope.

The Cape was sighted on 16 October, where Franklin noted that the colony was short of provisions and ships already on the station on two-thirds rations. Flinders recorded with some pride that he was following the dietary regime prescribed by 'the great Captain Cook' and he had not a single man on the sick list.

According to William Jerdan,[16] Franklin was one of two midshipmen whom Flinders chose to accompany him whenever he went ashore. Franklin wrote to his father from False Bay:

> Captain Flinders has instructed me in different points of navigation,† which tends to prepare me for promotion; he also when at sea prevents me from keeping day-watch purposely to attend him in working his Time-pieces, Lunar etc.[17]

He also enquired of his parents whether they had heard anything of the prize money he expected to receive from the 'Danish actions' –

---

* She had struck a sandbank on the way to Spithead before the voyage commenced, and although a subsequent inspection in Portsmouth Harbour had found no damage, it seems at least possible that this mishap contributed to the problem.
† And possibly also spelling, since although in later life he was to become quite accomplished with the pen, in this letter he refers to 'tuff' beef and being 'drest' in a 'lose' jacket etc.

the shared portion of the value of a captured ship being the prime way in which an officer could supplement his modest pay.

More repairs were carried out to the *Investigator*, and the voyage was resumed at the beginning of November. Franklin and his fellow officers trained their telescopes on that vast continent for the first time on the evening of 6 December, and the long and arduous task of charting her coast began. Franklin wrote to his mother, expressing a hope that his father was by now 'more easy about the situation of life I have chosen' (and so bright, breezy and confident does the sixteen year-old come across that it is hard to believe he was not):

> It was not either a youthful whim of moment, or the attractive uniforms, or the hopes of getting rid of school that drew me to it. No! I pictured to mind both the hardships and pleasures of the Sailor's life, (even to the extreme) before it was ever told to me... My mind was then so steadfastly bent on going to sea, that to settle to business would be merely impossible.[18]

In June 1802 the *Investigator* sailed, to Franklin's obvious relish, 'to the Northwards to tread in the steps of Captain Cook the famous navigator'.[19] Apart from his scientific duties with Flinders, he was reading up on French, Latin, navigation and geography, with some Shakespeare thrown in. There had been several deaths back home during his absence, and in October he was writing philosophically to his sister Eliza, 'Grim <u>death</u> minds not on whom he lays his clumsy paw...'[20] which attitude can be contrasted with the much more overtly religious interpretation he would put on such matters later in life. He also informed her, 'I have grown very much indeed, and a little thinner, so that I shall be a <u>spruce</u> and <u>genteel</u> young man...' Many years later, the clerk to Commodore Dance of the *Earl Camden*, whose path was soon to cross with that of Franklin, remembered him clearly at this age as 'a roundheaded, roundfaced boy with a most animated face and thick curly hair'.[21]

But before this, grim death would lay its ugly paw on the *Investigator*. G F Lamb, a Franklin biographer of the 1950s,[22] stated that his subject never committed to paper an account of his days on the *Polyphemus*, *Investigator* and his other early ships. That is more or less true – but during a reflective moment many years later he *did* scribble a brief note on an incident that occurred during that seminal voyage of discovery. It was common practice after such a venture for the commander of the expedition to write up and publish an account, and some forty years later Franklin blew the dust from his copy of Flinders' book and found his mind drifting back to another time as he flipped through its pages: 'I have been again reading the painfully interesting position of Capt. Flinders [*sic*] Narrative',[23] he mused, referring to an occasion in February 1802 when he and other officers were observing the return of the *Investigator*'s cutter as darkness fell. Fowler, the First Lieutenant, was standing beside him and suddenly cried out that the boat had vanished from sight. Fowler himself was sent out in a boat to search for the cutter, but could find no trace, although he did notice a strong rippling of the tide that had nearly capsized him. All 'glasses' were trained on the spot where it had last been seen, but it was getting too dark to see anything.

The search was resumed at daybreak, and after a time a boat returned towing the upturned, stoved-in wreck of the cutter – but the bodies of the master, midshipman and six seamen who had been on board were never found.* 'I have ever since retained in my mind the whole of the circumstances',[24] Franklin wrote, probably only too well aware that he could have been the midshipman in that cutter. It may well be, though, as was so often true in the navy at this time, that one man's loss was another man's gain, because before the end of the voyage Franklin was promoted, temporarily at least (he would revert to midshipman on his next ship), to Master's Mate.

Port Jackson came into view very early on Saturday 8 May 1802, and by afternoon a pilot had joined them and the ship was taken to anchor in Sidney Cove. The *Investigator* had not been letting in too much water on this leg of the journey, and only a little re-caulking was required. The crew were still in excellent health – several Port Jacksonians 'expressed themselves never to have been so strongly

---

* According to Flinders, Mr Thistle, the master, had told a tale at the mess-table of a visit to a fortune teller before sailing. He had been informed that he was going on a long voyage on which he would be lost. Furthermore, other crew members visited the same prophet of doom, and were told that they would be shipwrecked – but not on the ship they went out on – which turned out to be uncannily accurate.

11

reminded of England, as by the fresh colour of many amongst the *Investigator*'s ship's company', according to Flinders.[25] Tents were set up on shore, and Franklin was assigned to help Lieutenant Samuel Flinders, Matthew's brother, with astronomical observations. At some stage there seems to have been a falling-out between Franklin and Lieutenant Flinders: a later letter to Franklin from Matthew Flinders' wife refers enigmatically to 'the affair you allude to respecting Samuel',[26] which she has *some* idea of, but 'I do not think that it lowered you at all in his opinion'. There does not seem to be any surviving Franklin reference to the matter.

After a twelve-week stay, the *Investigator* left Port Jackson heading north along the coast, with the brig *Lady Nelson* in company as a tender. Hugging the coastline, they charted every nook and cranny, regularly going on shore to record, collect specimens and make contact with the native 'Indians'. The *Lady Nelson* proved such a bad sailer that she was sent back rather than risk losing her on the Great Barrier Reef. The *Investigator* picked her way through with no major incident, but by the time they entered Torres Strait on the north coast her leaks had become worse than ever, taking in up to ten inches an hour. Flinders had her careened once they had reached a suitable place in the Gulf of Carpentaria during the middle of November. It soon became apparent that the ship was in a more serious state than they had realised; the more the carpenters poked and prodded, the more rotten timbers they found, until it became 'quite alarming'. Their disconcerting final assessment was that the ship was totally unfit to sail in bad weather, but might last six more months if the conditions remained fine.

Flinders realised that a return to Port Jackson was necessary, but he faced a dilemma: should he continue heading west, where monsoons were expected, or return the way he had come, where seasonal storms were also due? His apprehension over re-negotiating Torres Strait and the Great Barrier Reef, together with his desire to continue his survey of the remainder of the coast while he was still able, led him to take a decision to press on.

The weather was kind to them, and they were able to continue their work for a further three months, but Flinders did not want to push his luck. By the beginning of March 1803 there was still a long way to go, and most of the crew were feeling the effects of the heat and lack of fresh food. Flinders himself had 'scorbutic sores', a symptom of scurvy, and although he does not specifically say so, it would be very surprising if Franklin and other members of the crew were not affected at least as badly. He decided to forsake the survey and make haste for Port Jackson.

Winds and necessity drove them to Timor, under Dutch control, where they spent a week replenishing their supplies. The leaks had not been so bad since re-caulking, and when examined the hull did not appear to have deteriorated to any great extent. However, by the time they left Timor ten men had come down with diarrhoea and others were developing similar symptoms. Flinders put this down to the effects of fresh fruit and vegetables after many weeks of abstinence, but it seems clear that their stay in Timor left them with a far more serious legacy. The boatswain 'breathed his last' on 17 May, and a few days later 'one of my best men' died from dysentery and there were fourteen others on the surgeon's sick list.[27]

Five men died before they reached Port Jackson at daybreak on 9 June, and four more succumbed during the next few days. The ship was given a thorough going over, and the final report stated that, 'she is not worth repairing in any country, and that it is impossible in this country to put her in a state fit for going to sea'.[28] It was the end of the road for the 'crazy old *Investigator*' as Franklin's future wife was to refer to the ship in years to come.

With the good offices of Governor King, a ship was procured to carry the men from the *Investigator* back to England, though not all would be going home. Apart from the sick men, a number of seamen chose to stay, whilst Brown and Bauer remained to study the region's natural history.

Flinders, Franklin and the other officers were to travel as passengers on the armed ship *Porpoise*, with the *Investigator*'s First Lieutenant, Fowler, taking command. It was an elegant name, but a far from elegant passage. Within a few days of setting out, as they passed through Torres Strait, the anxious cries of lookouts warned of breakers ahead – but it was too late. Desperate avoiding action could not prevent the *Porpoise* striking a coral reef, losing her foremast and smashing the underside of the ship so severely that the hold rapidly filled with water. Soon after that, the *Cato*, which had been accompanying them, met the same fate; a third vessel, an East Indiaman called the *Bridgewater*, managed to steer clear of trouble. By now it was nearly dark, so the stranded mariners were not too surprised to see the masthead lantern of the *Bridgewater* disappear – she would be standing off ready to come to their assistance at first light.

In the morning they could see the full extent of their predicament. The *Cato* was all but destroyed; Franklin's *Porpoise* was stuck fast but still in one piece. By a happy quirk of fate, there was a sandbank nearby large enough to accommodate the crews of both ships. They could also see the *Bridgewater*, and they waited.

And waited.

The *Bridgewater* sailed serenely away. The two crews were moved onto the sandbank, which Lamb aptly describes as 'an archetypal desert island', roughly the size of two football pitches and just a few feet above sea level, and they set to work transferring stores from the *Porpoise*. On the highest part of the bank a topsail yard was erected and the blue ensign flown upside down as a signal to the *Bridgewater*, which they still believed must return as soon as the wind moderated.

But the *Bridgewater* never did return, and worse still, when her commander, Captain Palmer, reached his intended destination of India, he wrote his name indelibly into the annals of treachery by giving a completely false account of the calamity to a Calcutta newspaper.[29] He claimed not to have been able to safely reach the stricken ships, whereas Flinders soon found there to be a perfectly good anchorage off the sandbank. Worse still, in saying that he would have been 'too late' to help anyway, Palmer was falsely implying that the crews of the two ships had perished.

Lest all this sounds too much like a one-sided attack on Palmer, it was not long before the third mate of the *Bridgewater*, unable to stomach the misleading account disseminated by his Captain, courageously went public with the true story: 'I did, for the first time in my knowledge, neglect my duty and gave a contrary account'.[30] This led to 'many words' and, for his honesty, Mr Williams (his name deserves to be recorded) forfeited his employment, his pay and some of his clothing.

Back on the sandbank, and faced with a mixture of two crews and a potentially life-threatening situation, both Fowler and Captain Park of the *Cato* readily assented to the highly respected Flinders assuming overall command. When it became clear that the *Bridgewater* had deserted them, it was agreed that Flinders would take one of the *Porpoise*'s cutters and head for Port Jackson. Enough food and water had been salvaged from the ship to last Franklin and the ninety-three other men on the sandbank three months, even at full allowance.

The cutter, christened the *Hope*, ventured forth on 26 August 1803 with fourteen men aboard and provisions for three weeks. As they embarked on their epic voyage of 750 miles in an open boat down the eastern coast of Australia, a seaman ran to the flagstaff on the beach, hauled down the blue ensign and hoisted it again the right way up. This act, symbolic not only of faith in their leader but also of contempt for the *Bridgewater*, moved Flinders deeply.

A month passed by, and Franklin and the other inhabitants of the desert island began to fear the worst. Then, on 7 October, six weeks after his departure, the cavalry arrived in the shape of the *Cumberland*, with Flinders on board, together with the *Rolla* and the *Francis*. Franklin and Flinders now parted company, and their lives took very different paths. Flinders was taking the *Cumberland* to England, but the little schooner could not carry everyone, and Franklin, along with Lieutenant Fowler and Matthew Flinders' brother Samuel, was one of those allocated to the *Rolla*, which was bound for China, where he would await a passage home.

Flinders was forced to land on the French-held island of Mauritius for urgent repairs, unaware that war had broken out once more between France and England. He did have his 'passport', a convention specifically designed to protect explorers on both sides, but the island's governor pedantically and spitefully decided that this was only valid while he was in the *Investigator*, and he was placed under arrest.* Matthew Flinders spent six and a half miserable years on Mauritius. Many accounts give the impression that he was cruelly treated and his health broken during this time (he died only a few years after his return to England) and that he was released only when the British re-took the island. In fact, he was under a sort of 'house arrest' for most of the time and free to roam widely. He experienced some ill-health while on Mauritius, but this was partly as a result of his privations while at sea, combined with a long-standing complaint (never positively identified) which seems to have eventually claimed his life once back in England. His release, long overdue and granted with great reluctance, came some time before the British attack on the island.

Flinders' imprisonment was a fate that could so easily have befallen Franklin, but instead he found himself seeing in the New Year of 1804 in Canton, awaiting a passage home. By the end of the month he was stowing his few remaining possessions on board the *Earl Camden*, one of a fleet of sixteen merchantmen and twelve smaller ships of the East India Company under Commodore Nathaniel Dance – but the southern hemisphere was still not ready to let go of the boy from Spilsby.

Dance had been worried at the prospect of guiding a highly lucrative fleet of tea-ships through waters known to be patrolled by a French squadron under Admiral Linois, and he must have been somewhat relieved to have a group of battle-hardened Royal Navy officers and men land in his lap. The naval officers were distributed among three of the merchantmen, which they set about reorganising along the lines of a Third Rate man-o'-war (albeit with only a fraction of the available armament) and possibly even making some cosmetic external alterations to make the vessels look a little more like warships.

After a couple of weeks the small fleet found itself in the clutches of a squadron of French warships consisting of a line-of-battle ship, two heavy frigates, a sloop of war and an 18-gun brig. The merchantmen had superiority of numbers, but this was meaningless when they could nowhere near match the firepower of the French

---

* Terence Grocott, in *Shipwrecks of the Revolutionary and Napoleonic Eras*, claims that Flinders took soundings on entering the harbour and should instead have requested a pilot, thereby implying that he was the author of his own downfall. However, Flinders makes it quite clear in his published account that a pilot *was* requested at the earliest opportunity, and one eventually joined them. The truth is his mere arrival off the coast flying the blue ensign had been enough to arouse deep suspicion.

squadron. A line-of-battle ship like Linois' *Marengo* (84 guns) ought in theory to have been capable of swatting them away like flies, and even the heavy frigates alone might have fancied their chances. Yet in one of the many 'Boy's Own' style incidents from this period, Dance took a course of action worthy of that supreme exponent of bluff and bravado, Thomas Cochrane. He and Fowler ordered the convoy to form line-of-battle. The French Admiral (who would be visiting Mauritius while Flinders was still there) had received news of Dance's preparations and kept his distance for the rest of that day. The following morning Dance raised his colours; Franklin himself was in charge of signals on the *Earl Camden*'s quarterdeck. Linois responded and began to close on the merchant fleet – it is said with the intention of cutting off some ships from the rear of their line. Seeing this, and perhaps advised by Fowler, Dance manoeuvred his ships to bear down on the French. There was a brief exchange of gunfire; Dance's leading ship, the *Royal George*, bore the brunt of this and lost one man and sustained one other casualty. Despite this, the French gunnery was found to be largely inaccurate. And then, apparently unnerved by the rumoured strengthening of the merchant fleet and the bold and well-performed battle manoeuvres performed by them, Linois was sufficiently discouraged to turn tail, with the merchantmen having the temerity to *pursue* the French squadron for two hours, a pack of hyenas snapping at the heels of a pride of lions, before resuming the voyage home.

In August 1804, Franklin caught sight of the English coast for the first time in just over three years. While the *Earl Camden* was still off Beachey Head he was writing to his father about

> a voyage which has been attended with many fatigues, but more pleasures…dampened by the detention of Captain Flinders at Mauritius. He is a Prisoner of War after a Wreck on a reef in the schooner *Cumberland*.* [31]

He recounted losing most of his clothes when the *Porpoise* was foundered, entailing the expense of obtaining more in China, but in

---

* A number of writers have repeated Franklin's erroneous belief that Flinders was wrecked, but as we have seen, he sailed into Mauritius for badly needed repairs.

spite of everything, he reported laconically, he had 'gained some knowledge and experience'.

When news of their encounter with the French reached shore, *The Times* (11 August 1804) was moved to declare that the action of these heavily laden, unescorted merchantmen represented perhaps 'the most complete triumph that British sailors have ever enjoyed over the enemies of this country…'

Franklin corresponded with, and indeed met Flinders after his return, despite the latter's worsening health problems, and was kept posted on the progress of Flinders' narrative of the voyage. Robert Fowler, the *Investigator*'s First Lieutenant, with whom Franklin also kept in touch after their return, wrote to Franklin in July 1814 to say that he had seen Flinders two months ago 'looking miserable. I don't think long for this world'.[32] He died that same month.

In peacetime, Franklin would no doubt have had the leisure to make a tour of friends and relatives, basking in the light of attention whilst recounting to them the many and varied adventures that had befallen him. But the war was hotting up, and he was immediately assigned to another ship. He had a few weeks to catch his breath before she arrived back in England.

~ 2 ~

Bellerophon – Death or Glory

THE *Bellerophon*, known to the tars as 'Billy Ruff'n', had a proud history and was famed as a formidable 74-gun fighting ship. She had played the leading role at the Glorious First of June (with a young Matthew Flinders on board), and on her quarterdeck Napoleon would, in time, make his formal surrender. Soon after Franklin joined she had been assigned to play her part in an important, if less than glamorous, blockading operation directed at the crucial French ports, with the aim of stifling the movement of supplies and keeping enemy warships penned in. Such was Britain's naval supremacy that the presence of her fleet was enough to keep the French at anchor for most of the time. But it was boring work, and must have seemed doubly so to Signal Midshipman Franklin, with all of his recent adventures fresh in mind and the restless spirit of an explorer never far from the surface. It could also be dangerous, though the danger came more from the elements than from enemy action. Storms and strong tides posed a constant threat in the Bay of Biscay where the *Bellerophon* spent several weeks, and some ships were unlucky enough to be driven onto the rocks.

In one of Franklin's own logs, kept while serving on the *Bellerophon*, there is an account of a late summer storm:

> A violent explosion of electric fire took effect in several parts of the ship at the same instant…the maintop gallant mast except the heel and yard totally disappeared and the rigging burnt to pieces… Another ball of fire struck the mizzen topmast and shivered it to pieces. Descending down the mizzen mast it broke several of the hoops and injured the mast badly in all parts…from thence it descended through the Quarterdeck breaking all the glass in the cabin and compasses in the binnacles and afterwards took an oblique direction through the Bulk Head of the wardroom where it

stunned several and materially injured a Boy in one of the officer's cabins…there was much smoke and fear of fire…[1]

The *Bellerophon* had been assigned to the Channel Fleet under Admiral Cornwallis, and was involved in the blockading of Brest, at that time France's principal naval port on the Atlantic coast, and also for a time the naval port and arsenal of Rochefort. In May 1805, Franklin wrote to tell his mother that his ship had been victualled and stored for six months so that they would be ready to chase the Brest fleet should they venture out.[2] Maybe she found this reassuring, because at this time there was a great deal of anxiety – even panic – at the thought of Napoleon's all-conquering army reaching Britain's shores, and with some justification. Semaphore stations and beacons were arrayed between London and the coast, the army was mobilised and food stocks were prepared against the worst. But first he had to cross the Channel, and the navy was certainly not panicking.

'I don't say the French won't come', the First Lord of the Admiralty declared. 'I just say they can't come by sea.'[3]

Franklin was under a new Captain, John Cooke, who had not been on the *Bellerophon* long himself. He had made his mark as a frigate captain in those seas, and has been described as genial and kindly, but firm and efficient in the running of his ship. In action, it was said, his men would do anything for him. Franklin found him 'very gentlemanly and active. I like his appearance very much'.[4] His main gripe was that the tedium of blockade duty was driving his messmates to practise on their flutes and other instruments, and the din was beginning to get on his nerves.

Then came the news that Admiral Villeneuve, commander of the combined French and Spanish fleets, had slipped out of Toulon with a large number of ships. The *Bellerophon* and the *Dreadnought* were immediately sent to a new location. Writing to his father at the end of July, Franklin said that their ultimate mission was a secret. He surmised that they were preparing for a landing in Egypt 'in case Napoleon should advance on our Indian settlements'.[5] In fact, they were bound for Cadiz, both to keep an eye on any remaining ships, and to be ready to join Nelson in his hunt for Villeneuve.

Around this time the crew of the *Bellerophon* found a diversion when they took under their wing one Peter Johnson, a 'Sweed' who had been on board an English man-o'-war (there were men of many nationalities in English ships) and had then been wrecked and made a French prisoner of war, which after Flinders' fate must surely have aroused Franklin's sympathies. Johnson had escaped to Turkey, only to be made a slave, followed by two years in prison. He was released only in order to serve in their army. He had lived on bread, water and two ounces of rice a day. The 'Billy Ruff'ns' fed him, shaved his 'mustacheos and tufted head' and put him in a fine set of sailor's clothes.[6]

As summer gave way to autumn, Admiral Villeneuve, who had led Nelson a merry dance across the Atlantic and back, returned – almost taking the *Bellerophon*'s little detachment by surprise. When the squadron of three battleships, together with a frigate and a bomb vessel, found themselves faced with a thirty-strong battle fleet, discretion was the order of the day. Although Villeneuve detached sixteen ships to go after the British, the chase was not a determined one and soon the whole combined French and Spanish fleet of over thirty-three ships of the line was stuck in Cadiz with the British, marshalled by Nelson, waiting for them to make a move.

Napoleon was by now growing impatient with his admiral. He temporarily gave up on the idea of invading England, and instructed Villeneuve to take the French and Spanish soldiers based in Cadiz to Naples. On 19 October, reluctantly but under pressure to exonerate himself in his Emperor's eyes and at loggerheads with his Spanish allies, in whom he had no confidence, Villeneuve took his fleet out to sea.

The following morning Franklin's captain, John Cooke, was preparing to join Nelson for dinner on board the *Victory*. Before he had a chance to leave, his First Lieutenant, Pryce Cumby, caught sight of a signal from the *Mars*, the nearest ship to them:

Enemy is Coming Out.

The *Victory* gave the signal for 'General Chase, South East', and the *Bellerophon* became a hive of activity.

Most people who know anything about the battle of Trafalgar are aware that Nelson's battle plan was innovative and unorthodox. Instead of the usual strategy of the two lines of ships passing each other firing as they went, the naval version of a medieval joust, he intended to send two columns of ships on an almost perpendicular course to Villeneuve's line in order to break through it, then isolate and overpower a portion of his fleet before the rest could come to their aid. In fact it was novel, but not the first time a tactic like this had been employed, and Villeneuve had guessed that Nelson might do something of the sort. The drawback of the plan was that the leading vessels of the two British columns would have to endure heavy punishment from several enemy ships before they could bring the greater part of their guns to bear on the enemy. The British fleet moved to intercept Villeneuve for the rest of that day and throughout the next.

At just before 6am on 21 October 1805, as they at last closed on the enemy, a signal from the *Victory* ordered the planned splitting of the fleet into two columns to be put into effect. The *Bellerophon* was allocated to the division under Collingwood, Nelson's second-in-command, and was the fifth ship in his line. Captain Cooke ordered the ship beat to quarters and cleared for action, and the brisk roll of the drums sent the crew scurrying about their tasks. A British man-o'-war could be cleared for action in under twenty minutes. This was a major transformation which involved every man on board and included taking in all but 'fighting' sails, erecting anti-boarding netting, lowering boats containing livestock and furniture, clearing the captain's cabin of bulkheads and furniture to make way for extra guns and their crews, and distributing supplies of gunpowder from the magazine below – a task carried out by boys nicknamed 'powder monkeys'. Wet sand was spread over the decks to give some protection against fire and some grip for bare feet, and buckets of water were placed behind every gun – salt water in case of fire and fresh water to quench the thirst of the men. The tightly secured guns were released and prepared, gun ports opened, and each team set out the tools of their trade beside the gun. Members of the gun crews who were assigned to join boarding parties at a later stage of the battle stuffed pistols and cutlasses in their belts.

Franklin, as Signal Midshipman, was posted on the poop deck with his team, along with numerous marines, and men on standby to trim the sails or fire the powerful poop carronades. He it was who

22

noted Nelson's 'England expects...' message, copied it onto his slate and took it to Cooke on the quarterdeck. The Captain then made a tour of his ship, informing his crew of Nelson's message, and telling them what *he* expected; he received a loud cheer from the gun crews, who chalked *Bellerophon – Death or Glory* on their cannon.

Ahead of them in their line they could hear bands on the *Belleisle* and the *Tonnant* playing *Hearts of Oak* and *Britons, Strike Home*; to their rear, the crews of the *Dreadnought*, *Swiftsure* and Franklin's first ship, the *Polyphemus*, cheered each other all the way into battle. Old hands, many by now stripped to the waist and with their scarves tied around their heads to soak up the sweat and hopefully keep out some of the noise from the guns, leaned out of the gun ports and pointed out to their mates enemy ships they had come up against in past encounters.[7]

Just before noon the leading British ships began to receive the first long-range fire from the enemy. Before the British ships opened fire one of Franklin's middy colleagues accidentally trod on a rope attached to the lock of a gun, causing it to go off; it was believed that the enemy took this as evidence that the *Bellerophon* was the flagship sending a signal, and that this explained in part why she subsequently came in for such close attention.

As the British fleet bore down on the enemy, Franklin's ship came under heavy fire, losing men and incurring structural damage during the agonising wait to open up with their own guns. Just after midday the *Bellerophon* broke through the enemy line, pouring such devastating carronade and broadside fire into the Spanish ship *Monarca* that she soon struck her colours. In such an encounter, the smoke from hundreds of guns very quickly prevented the gunners from seeing what they were firing at and those on the quarterdeck from seeing where they were heading. Above the swirling fog of war the topgallants of another ship were spotted looming towards them – but not soon enough to prevent a collision. The *Bellerophon*'s foreyard became entangled with the mainyard of *L'Aigle* (74), which despite carrying the same number of guns as the *Bellerophon* was a much larger and more heavily armed and crewed ship. Her sides, which towered over the *Bellerophon*, were lined with soldiers, and there were more aloft, many throwing grenades and firing explosive shells from mortars.* To make matters worse, the *Bellerophon* was soon coming under fire from no fewer than four other enemy ships ranged around her.

In less than twenty minutes the soldiers on *L'Aigle* had wreaked havoc upon her enemy's upper decks. Out of fifty-eight men stationed on the quarterdeck only eight remained standing, including Cooke, firing away with his pistols, and his First Lieutenant Cumby. Where Franklin was on the poop there was a similar slaughter. Franklin remained unharmed for now, but this sudden and ferocious onslaught must surely have shaken his confidence; Copenhagen was hot work, but the *Polyphemus* had taken nothing like such a battering as this. Down below, however, a different story was unfolding.

The respective gun crews were in such close proximity that they could snatch at each other's ramrods. The effect of cannon fire at this range can scarcely be imagined, and the superior British gunnery wreaked terrible destruction on the hull and gundecks of *L'Aigle*. But all this time the other ships were sending broadside after broadside into the *Bellerophon*; topmasts, yards and rigging came crashing down, and the rudder was destroyed; she became unmanageable. For the *Monarca*, the sight of the enemy ship which had earlier humiliated her now in such a parlous position was too much to resist; she hauled her flag back up and closed in, joining the *Bahama*, *San Juan Nepomucento* and *Swiftsure* (a British ship captured by the French years before) who were all pouring fire into the *Bellerophon* from the opposite side to *L'Aigle*.

In a scene reminiscent to one being played out on the *Victory*'s quarterdeck, Lieutenant Cumby was warning Cooke that his gold captain's epaulettes made him a prime target for the numerous enemy snipers.

'It's too late to take them off,' the Captain reflected. 'I see my situation; I can only die like a man.'[8] He sent Cumby down to order the guns to be elevated in an effort to give the soldiers on *L'Aigle*, who were making repeated attempts to board the *Bellerophon*,

---

* Nelson discouraged the use of snipers in the 'tops' of his ships, because of the serious risk of them setting fire to their own ship's sails and rigging.

something else to think about. It was an order that possibly saved the ship; but before Cumby returned, Captain Cooke had fallen – it is said around the same time as Nelson. He had been reloading his pistols, having earlier shot a French officer who had made it onto his quarterdeck, when two musketballs thudded into his chest. A quartermaster rushed to his fallen Captain's side and asked him if he wanted to be taken below.

'No', Cooke replied. 'Let me lie quietly one minute; tell Lieutenant Cumby never to strike!'[9] He died soon afterwards.

A fellow midshipman had been shot dead while Franklin and he stood together in conversation, and Franklin himself had to dodge the musket balls of a sniper who was targeting him from the foretop of *L'Aigle*. An interesting episode concerned one of Franklin's signals team called Beaty. The *Bellerophon*'s ensign had been shot away twice and replaced – it was a matter of honour to replace it since to remove or lower it signified surrender, or 'striking'. But it was dangerous – almost suicidal – work in the heat of close battle. When Beaty saw that the flag was down again, he declared, 'Well, that's too bad: the fellows will say we have struck', and he took a Union Jack and scrambled up the rigging with it. This made him an easy target for the many snipers perched just yards away in *L'Aigle*'s rigging, and normally his chances of survival would have been almost nil. On this occasion it appears the enemy were so impressed by his courage that they held their fire until he had fastened the flag in place and returned to the deck.

When Cumby came back up he found himself in command. His first decision was to gather everyone still standing on the poop deck and send them to the relative safety of the covered half-deck ready to repel boarders. Franklin must have been one of this group. But down below the English ship's gunners had virtually pounded their opposite numbers into silence, and following Cooke's order were training their guns on the upper decks of *L'Aigle*. This soon persuaded her crew to divert their efforts into disentangling themselves and getting clear, which they were eventually able to achieve – only to come under fire from the *Defiance* and eventually strike her colours. This fight had lasted about an hour. The *Bellerophon*'s main and mizzen topmasts were hanging over the side, and she had lost her jib boom, spanker boom and gaff to enemy fire. She was crippled, but still more than holding her own against the other ships engaging her. The hapless *Monarca* struck her colours to the *Bellerophon* a second and final time, and a prize crew were sent to this ship and also the *Bahama*; the other ships drifted out of the battle.

Such was the ferocity of the multiple engagement that there were soon too many casualties for the cockpit, and the valiant late captain's cabin was commandeered for the grizzly work of amputation. Although Franklin had escaped without serious injury, the thunder of the guns left him partially deaf for life. According to Lamb, Franklin was officially commended for his 'very conspicuous zeal and ability' during the battle.[10] The *Bellerophon*'s casualties were twenty-six dead and 126 wounded out of a complement of around 540. The bone-weary crew managed to jury-rig mizzen-top and main-top masts, and it was a tribute to their efforts that the ship was not only able to keep a prize, the *San Juan*, in tow, but ride out the storm that followed Trafalgar. They and others were, however, blown towards Cadiz, where a number of unscathed enemy ships came out to take advantage of what they believed were helpless enemy vessels – they were soon disabused of this notion and driven off.

The *Bellerophon* limped into Gibraltar, and after repairs was given the honour of escorting the similarly shot-up *Victory*, carrying Nelson's body, back to England for his funeral. When she made it to Plymouth Sound in early December, Franklin learned that all the newspapers were saying his ship in particular had been 'warmly engaged'. 'I fear you have been much alarmed for my safety since the late action on the 21st Oct.', he wrote to a sister,[11] reassuring her of his fortunate good health, despite 'the arduous action of that day'.

In later, quieter times Franklin's duties took him back to that region:

I had been fondly hoping that we should pass…over the very spot where the Battle of Trafalgar was fought…[conditions prevented this]. All the recollections of that day were brought back to my mind… I saw the unfurling signals of *England Expects that Every Man Will Do His Duty* and *Close Action* waving before my mind's eye – heard the order for the first discharge of our guns and the dreadful carnage that followed, traced in fact each event in succession to the last close of the day – when even the sight of the nineteen prizes scarcely sufficed to console us for the ever lamented loss of our Commander in Chief and the havoc which Death had made among our companions...[12]

But there was to be no hero's homecoming yet for Franklin and many others. In April the following year he wrote to his sister in Lincolnshire from off Vigo, where the *Bellerophon* was keeping an eye on an enemy squadron. He was looking forward to returning soon, and maybe getting his hands on some prize money; but he could not resist expressing his annoyance at the First Lord of the Admiralty, who had taken command and promptly rewarded the victors of Trafalgar by banning shore leave and visits to other ships:

> Earl St Vincent is very unpleasant and being nearly the greatest man in power over naval affairs – he enjoys himself by fatiguing and annoying everyone around him, in whatever rank or station they may be...[13]

In the lull after Trafalgar, the *Bellerophon* seems to have gone through a transitional phase and, according to Franklin's certificates of service,[14] she was presided over by several temporary captains. Lieutenant William Cumby, who took command of the ship after Captain Cooke's death, sent Franklin's certificate of service to brother Thomas with an accompanying letter saying that he was 'sincerely hoping his meritorious conduct may soon meet the reward of promotion'.[15] But after Cumby moved on, and perhaps the adrenaline had settled down, Captain Rotherham, not a 'Billy Ruff'n' at heart, let things slide. 'I sincerely wish to get clear of the ship for she gets more disgraceful every day', Franklin told his sister in the New Year of 1807. Things had got so bad that the admiral had 'publicly expressed his dissatisfaction by signal'. The new captain would no doubt be inviting Franklin to dine with him that evening. 'I shall enjoy seeing him chew his quid of tobacco – a delicious repast, surely! Don't you envy me?'[16]

He chided his brothers – via his sister – for not having replied to his recent letters. He was hoping that Willingham in particular, with his London contacts, might be able to help in some way with his career advancement, and we are treated to a rare and uncharacteristic example of Franklin self-pity: 'Nothing has transpired about my promotion... I am however not so very sanguine as to expect every thing to work for my immediate promotion; that perhaps would be thwarting the usual luck of the <u>Franklins</u>'.[17]

On 14 October the *Bellerophon* was anchored in Cawsand Bay, Cornwall, from where Franklin wrote to his brother-in-law, still sounding thoroughly fed up:

> We are once more near old England in the old ship after a tedious, tiresome cruise of five months... But whats more gratifying to my feelings, thanks be to goodness, we have a prospect of not taking the old heart out again.[18]

The word was that much of the crew was to be paid off from the *Bellerophon* and transferred to the *Bedford*, 74, 'a most gay event for me as by that step I shall get out of so detestable a ship'.

On 25 October 1807 he did join HMS *Bedford* at Plymouth; it was a ship that was to be his home for a number of years, and where he found himself under Captain Walker whom he rated a 'smart and active officer'. He was now Master's Mate. It was only one small step up from midshipman, but human nature being what it is one can easily imagine more senior colleagues pumping this young man for a few tales from two of the most memorable battles in British naval history.

As a Master's Mate, Franklin would have had a wide range of duties, from keeping the log up to date to heaving the actual, physical log* overboard, but it was only a matter of weeks before he found himself elevated once more: 'The First Lieutenant has been kind enough to acknowledge his approbation of my conduct, and has promised to solicit the Admiral to give me an order as Lieutenant of the *Bedford*'.[19] On 11 February 1808 his promotion came through officially.

There would have been four lieutenants on the *Bedford*, which

---

* It was paid out on a line with a series of knots tied in it to measure a ship's speed – hence the 'rate of knots'.

was a 'third-rater', the preponderant type of battleship in this era. He was now a deputy of the captain, and no longer required to stand watch at night. His duties might require him to lead a press gang ashore, and in action at sea he could be in command of a battery of guns. He would have worn a blue, long-tailed coat with white trimmings and gold buttons, white breeches down to the knee and white stockings. It was usual for a sword to be hung from a belt worn over the shoulder, and to top it all was a three-cornered hat with a cockade.

The *Bedford* was assigned to escort duty for the Portuguese royal family, fleeing to Brazil from Napoleon who had overrun their country for daring to trade with Britain. Their Highnesses were shown around Franklin's ship, and he got to kiss the royal hands. By now his mood had changed. 'Believe me, Willingham', he wrote to his brother from San Salvador, 'I am happy as man can be on board a ship. The *Bedford* possesses every good quality…'[20] He was getting as 'fat as any foal', he told his sister, and 'brown as any tawny…you may meet in your tramps to London Bridge or elsewhere'[21] – but he was perpetually short of money thanks to his paltry pay.

Just before Christmas 1808 Franklin wrote to tell his sister Betsey that he was cruising off Rio de Janeiro waiting to convoy some ships back to England. He added an afterthought that will strike a chord in the hearts of all Franklin researchers: 'I have some doubts whether it will be legible. Indeed, it often strikes me that you cannot read my letters…'[22]

By September 1810 Franklin was back in Portsmouth and applying hopefully for leave, but before long the *Bedford* was again underway, cruising in the North Sea. It was the dreaded blockade duty again – a French naval base in the Texel. This was followed by a trip to the West Indies escorting a merchant convoy. At this time he was corresponding with a young nephew who was full of questions about his exploits. In one letter, written on board the *Bedford* off the coast of Suffolk, he first counselled the boy, Tom, to 'continue…to apply with every care and attention to your learnings…' Franklin then went on to answer Tom's questions:

How do you like the West Indies? - Very well; I had however but a cursory view while passing near them. The scenery was generally picturesque. Many spots were most beautiful... We arrived at Barbadoes after an eight week voyage... I landed on Barbadoes, Granada and Jamaica, but had not much time to see about them... The ground is tilled by negroes, who are unhappily slaves to their Proprietors. They are generally well treated...the [idea] however is dreadful. Every Englishman ought to feel proud that by his law the further importation of them is prohibited. You know I suppose those unfortunate people were brought from Africa and exposed in their voyage to many cruelties...[23]

By now Franklin was keen to move on. He had nothing against Captain Walker, but he wanted to broaden his horizons and in doing so increase his chances of further promotion. The best way of achieving both goals, he decided, was to get himself posted to a frigate. Heavy battleships like the *Bellerophon* and *Victory* might get the glory, but set-piece battles were comparatively rare; action of one kind or another was much more common on board a frigate, whether it was chasing down privateers, enemy merchant shipping or other warships. Frigate captains were more likely to be given the freedom to use their own initiative and make a name for themselves.

Captain Epworth, who helped Franklin before he had joined the old *Polyphemus*, wrote to him from his new command, the frigate *Nyaden*, saying that although his First Lieutenant was senior to Franklin, it might be possible that his Second Lieutenant could 'be disposed of to advantage' so that John could replace him. Epworth correctly predicted that war with America was in the offing, and thought it would be good for Franklin to be in place before it started (the Americans had no line-of-battle ships and frigates would feature prominently). Robert Fowler tried to put in a word for him, and in addition to these moves Flinders let him know that if he got another ship 'you are the first to whom an offer of going would be made'.[24]

The problem was that Captain Walker of the *Bedford* did not want to lose his talented young officer, and put a block on the move. When Epworth was moved to another frigate, the *Nymphe*, Franklin wrote congratulating him and at the same time fishing for a position – even Second or Third Lieutenant would do. Franklin's brother Willingham, something of a legal high-flyer and later to be appointed a judge at the Supreme Court of Madras, had some Parliamentary contacts and was also acquainted with George Warrender on the Board of the Admiralty. Whilst these were by no means decisive connections, big brother did his best to help Franklin achieve his aims. He wrote directly to Lord Melville seeking a place for John on the *Nymphe*, saying that although Walker's motives were good (he was still declining to let Franklin go), and might be seen as complimentary to his brother, refusing him such an opportunity might be 'prejudicial to his interests' – and even those of the Service: robbing a promising officer of beneficial experience.

It was a nice try, but a long shot. 'I do not know one man who is at all acquainted with Lord Melville',[25] Willingham admitted. His Lordship's reply said that he would forward Franklin's name to the Board as a candidate for removal to a frigate. Willingham thought the letter 'civil', but he passed it on to his brother, who knew 'better how to interpret Admiralty letters than I do and will be able to say what may come from it'. Nothing did, and twenty years were to pass before Franklin got his frigate.

Soon after this, and while war in Europe continued, the *Bedford* and her crew became involved in a conflict of a different kind, as predicted by Captain Epworth. It was a brief squabble that tends to be overlooked because of the greater events happening elsewhere in the world at the time. Britain's relationship with the United States had been in an increasingly fragile state for some while. Among other things, Britain was wary of America's acquisitive intentions regarding Canada, while the Americans were getting fed up with having their citizens illegally pressed into Britain's navy* and their ships being harassed when attempting to visit ports in countries under Napoleon's control.

The *Bedford* was sent to New Orleans to take part in a joint army/navy operation against that city. It was one of those episodes with which British military history is littered: an almost suicidally courageous attempt to achieve a strategically dubious objective. The

---

* A more complicated affair than one might imagine. A distinctive 'American' accent had yet to develop, and the system of American sailors carrying documents exempting them from impressment was, not unnaturally, widely abused.

31

only approach was by rowing boat, and Franklin was among a force of around a thousand which had to run the gauntlet of American gunboats and other vessels. At great human cost the British force defeated their opponents, only for it later to transpire that the soldiers who were to approach from a different direction were defeated by the terrain and enemy fortifications, and the operation fizzled out. Franklin, however, distinguished himself. Not only did he collect his badge of honour – a shoulder wound according to Roderic Owen, a more recent biographer[26] – he created a good impression among his superiors:

> We were employed during the whole of that unfortunate expedition against New Orleans. Unfortunate, I may say, for had its termination been otherwise, I might have hoped from the nature of my employment thereon, to have obtained Promotion.[27]

This was to Robert Brown, the naturalist who had been with Franklin on the *Investigator*, and with whom Franklin kept in touch for the rest of his life. He told Brown that his actions had been noted by the generals leading the attack, and they had written to the Admiralty with a 'strong request' that he and another naval officer involved be promoted;[28] he had heard nothing on the matter since.

Two things seem to have been at the forefront of his mind at this time: the above-mentioned desire for promotion (to the rank of Commander), and a yearning to go exploring again. Before the *Bedford* had sailed for New Orleans he had written to Brown about the death of their old captain, Matthew Flinders, which he had learned of in the newspapers. He felt deeply the loss of the man who had given him his first taste of adventure, but he also had concerns of a more practical nature. He had been counting on Flinders' published account of the expedition impressing the Admiralty enough for their Lordships to hand out promotions; Flinders was now gone and as far as he knew the book remained unpublished. Even though the navy scored better than the army when it came to talented men gaining advancement on merit rather than influence, it still helped to have a guardian angel, and 'interest I have none', Franklin reported ruefully.

Brown reassured Franklin that Flinders had managed to complete his account before he died, and that it was published just a few days before he passed away.* He could not say whether or not it would aid his chances of promotion, and he himself had no great influence at the Admiralty. But he promised to put in a word where he could, letting it be known that Franklin had been one of the most promising young gentlemen on the quarterdeck of the *Investigator* and of whom he had since heard favourable accounts. Furthermore, he knew that Flinders had his promotion 'very much at heart'.[29] (All of which seems to be overlooking the small point that Franklin *had* actually already been promoted since his Flinders days – from Midshipman to Lieutenant by way of a brief flirtation with the post of Master's Mate.) Franklin was grateful, but feared that too much time might have elapsed for Flinders' account to sway the Admiralty very greatly.

The *Bedford* arrived at Spithead at the end of May 1815. The promotion list came out in June, and Robert Fowler wrote to say, 'I am sorry to find your name omitted'.[30] He was transferred to the *Forth* where he was First Lieutenant – a promotion of sorts. But within a month the battle of Waterloo was fought, and the outlook for naval officers soon changed dramatically.

It has been estimated that the navy in peacetime had up to ten times the number of officers it could gainfully employ. Within months, Franklin found himself back at home in Lincolnshire and, like many others, on half-pay and with no idea of what the future held in store for him. He made some use of his time by studying marine surveying, and he considered the possibility of a post at the naval college in Portsmouth. But he really wanted to explore. He had recently met the legendary Sir Joseph Banks, and discreetly enquired about the possibility of joining a ship he had heard of which was soon to sail for the Congo to find where the River Niger went. The vessel was called, rather unimaginatively, the *Congo*. Banks thought (correctly) that Franklin was too late to obtain a passage. The best advice the venerable old gentleman could give was that Franklin keep

---

* There seems to be some confusion surrounding this. Most writers on Franklin and Flinders say that it was published the day Flinders died. What seems to have happened is that Flinders received his advance copy on or around the day of his death, which means that the account itself would have been actually published some time later.

up his studies in order to prepare him for future expeditions. He would in time have cause to be relieved at missing out on this trip: there was horrendous illness and suffering; yellow fever and malaria claimed the lives of every single officer.

He was twenty-nine years old and he had been at sea for around half his young life, with a mere few weeks ashore during the whole period. The future must have seemed bleak, but he would not have to kick his heels for too long. Now that there was no war to be fought, the Admiralty, in the interests of both scientific advancement and national pride, was indeed turning its attention to filling in the blank spaces on its charts – and Franklin's name figured prominently in their plans.

~ 3 ~

The Most Northern Point

FAR from being put off exploration in Africa by the lingering deaths of so many men, Franklin was, typically, keen to go out and take up where they had left off. He wrote to Joseph Banks putting his case:

> Sir,
>
> I consider it to be my duty, after the kind attention you have honored me with, by mentioning my name to Mr Barrow on the subject of the Expedition to the Congo…conceiving it possible their Lordships might have it in contemplation to fill up the Vacancies and complete the object of the Expedition, I took the liberty of writing to Mr Barrow to offer myself for any appointment therein which their Lordships might be pleased to confer upon me… it will be a cause of great gratification to me if this [petition] should meet with your approbation. I have felt ever since I had the honour of being introduced to you desirous, and indeed your goodness and attention in conversing then with me, on subjects connected with any [professional] claims on my part, [great] anxiety to merit your approbation… I hope you will permit me to solicit your assistance in the furtherage of my work and beg you to be assured that I shall [feel] gratefully obliged. I was happy to find the reports we learned of your state of Health were Much exaggerated. I most sincerely hope you are perfectly restored To good Health and Spirits.
>
> I have the Honor to be Sir
> With great respect and esteem
> Your much obliged servant
> John Franklin[1]

We will never know what kind of impression he had made on Banks when they met, but it must have been a good one for him to have been noticed at all when one considers the number of unemployed naval officers, not to mention scientists and gentleman adventurers, who were jostling in the same queue as him. The letter itself reads like a transparently obsequious blandishment to the modern eye. The idea of the now corpulent, gout-ridden man in his mid-seventies being restored to perfect health was rather preposterous. But this kind of deference was then commonplace – expected, almost – and Franklin was playing his cards well. He knew perfectly well that he was unlikely to get anywhere without soliciting the interests of figures such as these and, besides, Banks was known to respond well to such flattery.

The Congo idea did not come to anything, but the chain of connections, tenuous though it in some ways was – from Robert Brown on the *Investigator* who knew Banks, who knew Barrow at the Admiralty – did lead to an appointment of a very different kind within months.

It is an often overlooked point on the part of more recent Franklin commentators – and particularly his modern critics – that the numerous references to the young Franklin impressing all and sundry must have been more than mere routine and vacuous praise. For him to have got where he did without a genuine patron and in the face of stiff competition, there had to have been some substance to the glowing testimonials to his character and intelligence.

His efforts to get himself noticed paid off. In January 1818 he was writing to a sister from lodgings near Bedford Row to tell her that he had been appointed to command a brig called the *Trent* on a forthcoming expedition. 'I have to jaunt down to the dock every day', he enthused. 'It has been decided that I am to be attached to that division which goes directly to the Pole under the Command of Captain Buchan'.[2]

To the Pole? By ship? It must be borne in mind that vast areas of the globe beyond the northern shores of mainland Canada were unexplored, and no one really knew what to expect at the North Pole. The idea of a navigable sea in the extreme north was considered perfectly feasible at the time – but even supporters of this theory were aware that ships hoping to reach this mythical sea could expect to encounter impenetrable ice *before* reaching such a latitude. One believer in the 'temperate sea' scenario was John (later Sir John) Barrow, referred to already in Franklin's letter to Banks about the Congo. Barrow was the Second Secretary to the Admiralty, close to Banks, and enthusiastic about exploration. He is often referred to as the 'father of Arctic exploration' but he was a promoter of discovery in both hemispheres; the reason why the north began to look a more attractive prospect was the possibility that changing climatic conditions might make passage through the frozen seas a reality (a possibility being mooted again in modern times but, sadly, for different and more disturbing reasons).*

However, the Admiralty had evinced little interest in the Arctic for many years, and much of Barrow's time in office had been dominated by the war with France. The whalers were the ones with their fingers on the pulse in these regions, plying their trade each season between Scottish and northern English ports and the seas between Greenland and northern Canada. One whaling captain in particular is credited with inspiring this particular expedition: the intrepid William Scoresby, who, while Franklin had been on post-Trafalgar blockading duties, advanced further north by sail than any other and had witnessed dramatic changes in the ice field which sound uncannily familiar to the modern ear. Vast areas of ice were breaking up and dispersing, giving rise to the tantalising prospect of a long-awaited breakthrough – literally – in Polar exploration.

To reach the North Pole would be mainly a matter of scientific interest and national pride at being the first. Both of these factors applied to the North West Passage, the other Holy Grail of northern geography, with the added bonus of possible benefits to trade: a 'short-cut' to the East. It has been said that Britain's only interest in the North West Passage was to be the first, since even if a ship were to force its way through during these exceptional circumstances it could never become a regular trading route. Scoresby knew this, but while so much of the region remained unexplored, some were unwilling to let go of the more profitable scenario; including, it seems, Barrow. Banks and Barrow were the kind of men who would want to discover the North West Passage just because it was there,

* See Appendix Four.

but the latter had to persuade his political masters and keepers of the purse strings that there was at least a possibility of the nation getting some of its money back in the long run. This hope was not quite dead, and probably played more of a part in the decision to put resources into this and future ventures than is given credit for.

And so, Franklin spent the early months of the New Year preparing for this expedition. It was the first such venture for many years, and captured the nation's imagination. The swarms of visitors to Deptford, where the ships were being fitted out, hindered the preparations, and Franklin, for once, was feeling rather out of his depth:

> It seems quite ridiculous to find myself placed among these parties, when I consider how little I know of the matters which usually form the subject of their conversations. At present, however, the bare circumstance of going to the North Pole is a sufficient passport anywhere. What a fortunate person must I, therefore, consider myself to have it, and thankful to my good friends who procured it for me![3]

By a strange quirk of fate, two of the people given a guided tour of the ships were to become Franklin's first and second wives, respectively. One was a young poet called Eleanor Anne Porden, who was moved to compose a verse about the expedition – of which we shall hear more later; the other was Jane Griffin, a young lady with a tremendous appetite for knowledge and an urge to travel and explore that easily matched that of Franklin. It is not known whether either of them met Franklin at this point, though it is quite likely that they would have been introduced to any officers who happened to be present at the time of their visit. Of the two, Eleanor is much less likely to have met him because the ships she specifically mentions visiting did not include the one Franklin was to command. The two converted whalers Eleanor saw were the *Isabella* and the *Alexander*, heading for the North West Passage; bound for the North Pole were the *Dorothea* and Franklin's smaller *Trent*.

However ingenuously optimistic the venture might seem from the modern perspective, it was no naïve, tally-ho escapade. The vessels had been much strengthened and modified inside and out at the Shadwell dock, equipped with ice saws, ice anchors and other aids; there were many seamen from whaling ships in both crews, and an Eskimo interpreter. Scoresby himself had been offered a position as pilot, but refused; he had envisaged, as the one who had brought the news of the clearing ice and put the plan to the Admiralty, that he would be appointed to lead the expedition. He considered himself snubbed, if not betrayed, by Barrow. But notwithstanding any machiavellian behaviour on Barrow's part, the Royal Navy was a professional body, and the most realistic compromise would seem to be the one that was on offer: its own officers to head the expedition supported by experienced pilots.

The North West Passage ships were commanded by Commander* John Ross, with Lieutenant Edward Parry as his second-in-command. The Pole vessels were under the leadership of Captain David Buchan with Franklin as his second. Parry and Franklin, both Arctic virgins, were to become two of the leading figures of the age in this branch of the Royal Navy's operations. *The Times* of 26 March reported that the sailing of the expedition had been deferred for a few days, allowing Lord Melville, First Lord of the Admiralty, to inspect the ships and also witness the canoeing exploits of the Eskimo interpreter, who had become quite a celebrity in his own right:

> The officers of the expedition [said *The Times*] seem quite confident that the *Dorothea* and the *Trent*, under the command of Captain BUCHAN, destined for the discovery of the North Pole, will attain their object; but they are by no means sanguine of the success of the *Isabella* and the *Alexander*, under Captain ROSS...

Yet despite the thronging crowds and the way the venture seemed to have captured the nation's imagination, approbation was not universal. The following day's *Times* carried a letter from a 'practical seaman' astutely questioning the thinking behind the whole business – particularly the supposed trade route through the North West Passage: 'Now, Mr Editor, what will commerce, navigation, or

---

* In some accounts Ross is described at this juncture as 'Captain'. Whoever commanded a ship might be termed the 'captain' though they had not yet attained the permanent rank of Post-Captain. Lieutenants and Commanders regularly skippered smaller vessels such as these.

science gain by such a discovery? Nothing!' Shortly afterwards the same newspaper ran an article 'From a French Paper':

> Some English writers have already indulged themselves in illusory conjectures on this enterprise; they describe Greenland as bursting from the icy barrier which surrounds it. They repeat the traditional reports of the last century, respecting some whale-ships, said to have reached the Pole, and even to have passed on the other side of it…and even flatter themselves that commerce will be carried on in a direct route from London to Canton, by the Pole…
>
> The gratitude which the English Government merits from every friend to science ought not to prevent us from examining upon what foundation their hopes of success in this enterprise rests. It is even an advantageous justice due to the commanders of the expedition, to point out to them beforehand, the immense obstacles against which they have to contend…[4]

It is very likely that Franklin would have read these negative views before setting sail; nevertheless, he wrote with cautious optimism on 1 May to tell his sister that they had safely arrived at Lerwick on Scotland's Shetland Islands:

> I am addressing you directly from the most Northern point I ever obtained… Our hopes are yet alive of reaching the Pole…we are fully prepared to meet obstacles and indeed calculate on them but we hope to be enabled to meet them.[5]

They would need to be fully prepared, for the *Trent* was already leaking like a colander. They had left the Thames carrying provisions for two years on 25 April 1818, but almost as soon as they cleared the river, what had once been a minor trickle quickly became a cause for concern. At Lerwick the little *Trent*, 250 tons, was beached and inspected. Repairs were effected using some of the extra timbers that had been brought along (no doubt with the idea that the expedition would have made it rather further north than Scotland before they were needed).

In the same letter to his sister, Franklin makes the first explicit reference to what appears to be a new-found zeal for the Christian faith: 'May that Almighty Power protect and guide us who can order all things and doth as seemeth best to his Infinite wisdom'. Being a

Christian was part and parcel of being an English gentleman (or lady) at that time, and although a certain amount of hypocrisy is only to be expected, Christian faith and values (as interpreted in that age) guided the lives of many Europeans in a way that has largely disappeared and is perhaps difficult for us to appreciate fully. That said, Franklin's sudden burst of archaic Biblical invocation sounds like the proclamation of a recent convert. Perhaps during his three years' enforced leave from active service, he first came into contact with the small circle of fairly radical Christians who were to shape and influence his views in the time to come.

The sight of the brig lying on the beach like a collapsed drunk, accompanied by the sound of sawing and hammering, did nothing for the proposed recruitment drive at this port. Ten officers and twenty-eight crew eventually set sail for the island of Spitzbergen, well inside the Arctic Circle, their first staging-post; but whatever was causing the worst intake of water had not been found, and seamen found themselves spending as much time at the pumps as performing their normal duties.

Franklin and his fellow crewmen had been transported to a different world: of midnight sunshine, glaciers, icebergs, walruses and strange optical effects. One of the first things to strike many of the crew after they crossed the Arctic Circle on 14 May was the permanent daylight. Initially it was such a novelty that some were reluctant to turn in for the night, but the combined effects of hard work and sleep deprivation soon cured them of their curiosity. Before reaching Spitzbergen, Franklin encountered pack ice for the first time in his life, and then when a mild south wind gave way to a cold blast from the north, heavy snow fell upon the decks – even the curiously shaped flakes were different to the ones they were accustomed to seeing – and ice began to build up on the rigging and hull of the brig.

As they approached the southern tip of Spitzbergen the channels through the ice became narrower and trickier to navigate. When they gratefully emerged into a stretch of open sea, it was only to encounter a fierce gale that parted the two ships. Every time the bow of the *Trent* plunged into the sea a fresh layer of ice encased her sides and decks, and the tons of extra weight incurred by this phenomenon had to be countered by seamen hacking the stuff away from the bows with axes. Other crewmen were employed in beating the rigging with sticks in an effort to prevent ice building up and making the ship unworkable. There were signs that they were entering ice fields again; conditions and visibility were so atrocious that Franklin decided to heave-to. It turned out to be a shrewd decision: the ship soon became enveloped in fog, and when it cleared he discovered that they were right into the main pack ice, and would probably have been wrecked had he carried on regardless.

They met up with Buchan's *Dorothea* again as they approached the pre-arranged rendezvous point of Magdalena Bay on Spitzbergen's north-west coast. From their position they could see the pack ice, and it was clear that there was at present no route through it. Buchan decided to anchor in the bay and survey the region. After a few days' respite in that sheltered position, charting and exploring, the ships went out to try the ice again.

It was no better than before, and after nosing into a narrow channel that had opened up, only for it to close behind them, they found themselves trapped. All they could do was secure their vessels to large pieces of ice and hope for the best. The *Trent* was still leaking, and one night while they were thus imprisoned the Assistant Surgeon thought he could hear the rush of water beneath where he lay, and declared he might have discovered the site of the problem. A number of men rushed down to the 'spirit-room' and cut away the special lining at the spot from where the sound seemed to be coming. Water immediately gushed in, quickly reaching waist-height and beyond. But they had solved the mystery – a bolthole had been left open by lazy or incompetent shipwrights, and the problem was quickly and easily remedied.

But the ships were still stuck in the ice, huge blocks of which jostled around the puny vessels and threatened to crush them. At one time the *Trent* was forced four feet into the air by the pressure beneath it. After almost two weeks like this the ice opened up and they took their chance to escape. In early July they made another attempt to press further north and, with the help of sailors on the ice hauling on ropes, they were able to make some progress through narrow channels. It was valiant, but slow and backbreaking work, and eventually had to be abandoned. They had reached approximately 80° 34' north.

Neither Buchan nor Franklin published an account of this expedition, and much of our knowledge of it comes from the *Trent*'s Lieutenant Frederick Beechey, who remedied the situation many years later.[6] It was Beechey who pointed out how unlucky they had been in 1818 – British ships would subsequently achieve higher latitudes without even entering the ice.

Buchan did not give up without a fight – he had the ships literally dragged along using a combination of ice anchors, windlass and pure brute force. But, frustratingly, the ice was drifting south at a faster rate than they could progress north: in effect they were like men walking slowly up the 'down' escalator. Both ships again suffered in the powerful grip of the ice – particularly the *Dorothea*, but even Franklin's *Trent* was at one point so forcefully twisted by the movement of the surrounding ice that all her cabin doors flew open. It took three weeks of non-stop toil to extricate themselves and reach open water. Even now Buchan gave it one last shot, heading west to see if the ice in the direction of Greenland looked any more promising; but a terrific gale, during which the ships were buffeted by massive blocks of ice as if in some gigantic pinball game, put paid to any hope they had.

Franklin impressed Beechey during this crisis. He ordered a massive cable to be cut into lengths and hung over the sides to give some protection against collision; extra ropes were rigged to secure the masts, and hatches were nailed shut:

> I will not conceal the pride I felt in witnessing the bold and decisive tone in which the orders were issued by the commander of our little vessel, and the promptitude and steadiness with which they were executed by the crew.[7]

They returned to the anchorage at Spitzbergen to lick their wounds. There was hardly a timber on the *Dorothea* that was not broken, and Beechey figured that if she had not been given her extra inner lining she would certainly have sunk. There was some debate among the officers over what to do next. Buchan's instructions ordered him to carry on in the second ship if one were disabled, but with the *Trent* also in a far from healthy state, he thought this was too risky. Franklin volunteered to continue the mission in the *Trent*; it was a commendable attitude, but possibly inspired more by a sense of duty than realism. It is hard to believe he expected to be given permission, and Buchan duly turned the idea down on the grounds that it was far too dangerous for the stricken *Dorothea* to attempt the homeward journey alone. It was decided that they could do no more than patch up the ships before returning to England.

While this work was being carried out, Franklin and Beechey went out by boat surveying the coast in the vicinity of their anchorage, hoping to improve the rather hit-and-miss Admiralty charts for the area. They also found the time to assist Fisher, the expedition's astronomer, who had set up an observatory on shore. On one occasion Franklin and Beechey were in a boat inspecting a cavern at the bottom of a glacier when, the latter recorded, they heard a 'report as if of a cannon'. A massive piece of ice had broken away and plunged at least 200 feet into the sea. It disappeared beneath the water, leaving only the ominous 'boiling' of the sea and spray on the spot where the impact had taken place. Then, just as suddenly, it exploded above the surface like a leaping whale. Franklin and Beechey hurriedly turned the head of their boat to face the oncoming succession of rollers. It was just as well, for the wash was powerful enough to tip over the *Dorothea*, being careened some four miles away.

Another occasion, mentioned by Beechey by way of light relief, was an escapade by a seaman called Spinks, determined to be first back from a hunting party in the mountains. He set off down the precipitous snowy slope on his backside, using his heels to keep his speed to a safe rate of knots. Despite his best efforts, the route was so steep that he soon lost his balance and control, and shot down the mountainside at an alarming and ever-increasing speed. Franklin, Beechey and the onlooking sailors were genuinely afraid for his life, particularly when they lost sight of him behind a crag. His anxious comrades raced at the spot where he landed, expecting to find a battered corpse. Instead, a grinning Spinks emerged from the deep snow: sore and bruised, but in one piece – which was more than could be said for his clothes. He had, commented Beechey, worn away 'two pairs of trousers and something more…'[8]

The repairs were finished by the end of August, and after a brief detour to see if there was any favourable change in the ice, they headed home. The two ships sailed into Deptford on 22 October 1818.

*

Two weeks later the *Isabella* and *Alexander* came home. Although not achieving the North West Passage, Ross's explorations had gone some way towards improving knowledge of the likely approach, and he was optimistic that it was an attainable goal. But a more controversial aspect of the voyage has long tended to overshadow the successes.

On pushing into Lancaster Sound from Baffin Bay in thick fog, he decided that he could make out, during a temporary clear spell, a ridge of high mountains barring any further progress in that direction. We know with hindsight that whatever he saw it was not mountains: Lancaster Sound leads into Barrow Strait and is, in fact, the only viable opening for a ship wishing to complete the North West Passage. Once they were at home Ross came under attack from several quarters, and mostly in an underhand way. Parry's negative opinion soon trickled out, and Barrow, who seemed to take the failure personally, wrote an almost childishly spiteful article about Ross's 'failure', which was published anonymously. There were other attacks, and Ross's reputation never quite recovered. He was made up to captain the same year, but this may have been an attempt to keep him quiet, being, as he was, quite capable of speaking up for himself and stirring things up. But the promotion could not save his career, and he would never pace the quarterdeck of a Royal Navy ship in his new rank.

The second-in-commands of both expeditions, however, had made their marks; for them, doors were beginning to open.

~ 4 ~

Akaitcho

AT some stage after arriving home that winter, John Franklin read a poem written to commemorate the recent arctic adventures in which he had been a player. The young poet had written *The Arctic Expeditions*[1] after visiting the ships at Deptford before their departure, and it was published while he was away. In her introduction she stated that the idea of a passage to the North Pole* had fascinated her for years, and that her visit to the ships had re-awakened this interest and inspired the verse.

Like all of her published poetry, *The Arctic Expeditions* was part verse, part scientific treatise, with copious explanatory footnotes. By this means she displays her knowledge of Icelandic culture, Scandinavian mythology and meteorology – among other subjects – and this was one of her shorter poems! One line reads,

Darkling you ply your saw with fruitless toil…

And she points out for the benefit of the reader that this is 'In allusion to the ice-saws with which the vessels destined for these expeditions are provided'. (The 'fruitless toil' proved to be only too accurate a prediction.) The poem ended with an additional discourse on the problems and theories regarding ascertaining the Magnetic Pole. It may have been this scientific angle to the poem, more than the verse itself, flattering though it was, that impressed Franklin enough to prompt him to wangle a meeting with the writer.

Her name was Eleanor Anne Porden. She was twenty-three years old; he was now thirty-two. There seems to have been an immediate mutual attraction. Eleanor would later tell her friend Jane Griffin that an 'eye witness of their first interviews…saw at once how their

---

* And also the possibility of finding a 'lost colony' on Greenland, a theory which seems to have been in circulation at that time.

acquaintance was likely to end'.[2] They could both be reserved and awkward in company, which may in itself have given rise to each recognising a kindred spirit in the other; he was something of a minor hero and may have been wearing his impressive blue and gold lieutenant's uniform; she was short, dark and pretty,* witty, and possessing a lively, enquiring mind. But she was also something of a celebrity herself, being a published and critically well-received poet. *The Veils*,[3] written when she was sixteen, had come out in 1815 and led to her being elected a member of the Institût de Paris. She was a leading light of a literary society called the Attic Chest, which met regularly at the Porden house on Berners Street in the heart of Marylebone's artistic and literary quarter. She lived there with her mother and father. The latter was an architect of some renown, and the education of Eleanor, his youngest daughter, had been undertaken privately and primarily under his own direction.[4]

A lot of what we know about Eleanor and her relationship with Franklin comes from their surviving letters, but much of the fine detail is provided by the journals of her new acquaintance, Jane Griffin. Jane first met her at a dinner party at the Disraeli's† house in early 1819 (probably after Eleanor had already come into contact with Franklin), having already received a copy of *The Veils* from Miss D'Israeli. When they got talking Eleanor told Jane she recalled seeing her at the home of their mutual acquaintance, the Rogets, as well as at the Royal Institute, of which they were both regular attenders:

> She [Eleanor] is a plain, stout, short woman, having rather a vulgar, tho' a very good-natured countenance and I saw nothing of pedantry or pretension in her manner, but rather some embarrassment and timidity of manner. She has dark hair and eyes, and a reddish, coarse face, and appears about or near 30 years of age tho' she is said not to be more than 23.[5]

Hardly the stuff of a blossoming friendship. Those interested in conspiracy theories might wonder whether Jane herself had already

---

* Beauty is in the eye of the beholder! A less flattering assessment follows; mine is based on the only portrait we have of her.
† The family home of the future prime minister – Benjamin would have been around fifteen years old at this time.

met Franklin (not at all unlikely) and knew of his attachment to Eleanor; it would not be hard to read jealousy into her brusque assessment. But these were objective first appearances recorded in a private journal, and in fact a friendship between the two did quickly develop; Jane's kindness would be one of the last things Eleanor spoke of in her final days, and if she did look older than her years it was almost certainly due to the as yet undiagnosed illness that dogged her during her short life.

During the evening in question a couple of young ladies approached Eleanor for her autograph, and Jane noted that her father seemed 'not a little vain at his daughter's talents...'[6] They met on several subsequent occasions during the coming months, and Jane was eventually invited to dine at the Porden's home. She discovered that Mrs Porden was confined to her room by ill-health, little knowing that she would have cause to make the very same observation about her new friend within a very few years:

> On our retiring to the drawing room we talked and joked with Miss Porden on her universal talents. She makes all her own clothes, preserves and pickles, dances quadrilles con amore, belongs to a poetical book club, pays morning visits, sees all the sights, never Denies herself to any body at any hour, and lies in bed or is not dressed till 9 o'clock in the morning.[7]

Eleanor had a very rich inner world. Three years earlier she had scribbled down some thoughts: '...if but to show me, at some future time, how far my present opinions have been confirmed or changed by experience'.[8] These doodlings show that Eleanor suspected she possessed some form of clairvoyance (which would probably have triggered an alarm with the straight-laced Franklin, had he known of it). She recalled an instance when, being about to accompany a friend into a room, she felt a strange urge to hold back. She later discovered that a person she strongly wanted to avoid was in that room:

> Some persons will perhaps think me an enthusiast for the Second Sight, and I own that I have some faith in it.[9]

On one occasion she was woken by servants who thought there was a robber in the house, and she experienced not so much fear as the 'thrill of danger', and insisted on tip-toeing from one room to another until finally 'disappointed to find that their alarm was without foundation':

> I never hear thunder but wish to hear it roar louder.[10]

She had a long talk about Gothic legends with a friend, who urged her to write a 'Legendary Tale' of her own. It would probably have been an ideal vehicle for her talents, but she never pursued it. (At virtually the same time someone called Mary Shelley was having similar thoughts, and her *Frankenstein* was published the year Franklin and Eleanor met.)

This, then, was the young woman to whom Franklin was drawing inexorably closer as the preparations for his next venture got underway.

❖

The Admiralty had decided on a speedy return to the Arctic. The Pole and its supposed temperate sea, which Buchan and Franklin had not come even close to discovering, were put on the back burner; there was to be a combined land and sea attack on the North West Passage. Parry was selected to take the *Hecla* and *Griper* back into Lancaster Sound and demolish Ross's mythical mountains. Franklin was given leadership of an expedition which was to make its way overland to the northern coast of Canada and then push eastwards by boat, hopefully joining up with Parry and completing the Passage.

Franklin was perhaps a little fortunate to be given command of this expedition, though there were not really any other naval officers familiar with land-based exploration in this region. If Barrow wanted to establish a base from which to build an arm of his service with the necessary experience to take Arctic exploration further in the coming years, one way to go about it was to send keen, promising young men who had proven themselves in other areas, and match them up with local people who did know the environment. Pierre Berton in *The Arctic Grail*[11] suggests that Franklin got the position because 'he came from a well placed family', which is odd because he did not. The fact that 'a niece would later marry the poet laureate, Alfred Tennyson'[12] is hardly a powerful argument to support this theory. But it has to be said that Berton – from whom many readers and subsequent commentators on Franklin will have gained their impression of him – does not seem to like Franklin or the Royal Navy for some reason. The picture he paints of Franklin – 'reckless ambition…hunger for fame…simple, plodding, run-of-the-mill naval officer…'[13] – would not have been recognised by most of those who met him, nor any of his biographers proper, as presenting a true representation of his character or abilities.

In any event, Franklin was commanded to sail to York Factory in Hudson Bay, trek to the Great Slave Lake, and then on to the Coppermine River where he was to follow it to the sea and 'determine the Latitude and Longitude of the North West Coast of America, and the trending of that coast from the mouth of the Coppermine River to the eastern extremity of that continent'.[14] For the first part of the journey there would be fur trading posts where he could find accommodation and provisions, but eventually he would have to strike out into the unknown. The last exploration in the region had been thirty years ago, but he was to go further than any white man had ever been.

First, there were preparations to be made. Franklin was to be accompanied by two midshipmen: George Back, who had been on the *Trent*, and Robert Hood. Both were artists and would record pictorially the various stages of the journey. Scot John Hepburn was one of two ordinary tars who would act as attendants to the officers; the other would not last the distance, but Hepburn would prove himself a rock. Writing after the event, John Richardson (see below) would remember him as being 'worth 3 or 4 people'.[15]

Franklin mentioned another addition to the party in a letter to his sister: 'There is a surgeon, Dr Richardson who combines a general knowledge of the subjects of natural history with his professional requirements'.[16]

Richardson was an excellent choice. Jane Griffin described him as a middle-sized man of about Franklin's age, who 'looks like a Scotchman, as he is', with broad, high cheek bones, a wide mouth, grey eyes and brown hair. 'Thoughtful, mild and pleasing…he has a pretty strong accent.'[17] These were the days when men commonly excelled in more than one discipline, and both of the talents mentioned by Franklin, together with his strength of character, were of great value to the expedition. A telling remark in the same letter to his sister showed that Franklin had learned a lesson from the North Pole voyage: 'Experience has taught me never to indulge in too sanguine hopes of either success or reward'.[18] He would be sailing out on a Hudson's Bay Company ship, the *Prince of Wales*, and expected to be away for around two and a half years.

Arrangements had been made for the expedition to be assisted by the two fur companies who had posts throughout the region: the already mentioned Hudson's Bay Company (HBC) and the North-West Company. The problem was that the rivalry between the two had erupted into virtual warfare. Simon McGillivray, the North-West Company's agent in London, had to write to his operatives telling them to expect Franklin, emphasising that neither he nor the expedition had anything to do with their territorial disputes with the HBC – he was travelling on one of their ships only because it provided the most direct route.[19] Some time after the expedition had set off, McGillivray made some prescient remarks in reply to a request for details of the expedition by the MP Henry Goulbourn. They would not, he said, be able to carry a great deal in the way of provisions, and so would be relying on the natives:

> who are themselves very precariously supplied. One of the officers employed says in a letter which has been published, that the difficulties of their progress has been greatly exaggerated, but this was before he had encountered any of them, and I fear that by him at least they have been greatly underestimated...[20]

Parry set sail first. The *Hecla* and *Griper* struggled through the ice and then triumphantly navigated Lancaster Sound, pressing on to Melville Sound before the ice became simply impenetrable and they were forced to turn back, frustrated and disappointed.

Before Franklin left he was seeing quite a bit of Eleanor. In fact, they had fallen in love, but a combination of factors led to things being left hanging in the air: stuffy nineteenth-century social etiquette, the long and dangerous mission he was about to undertake, and perhaps more than both of these things put together, their own respective awkwardness when it came to discussing their feelings face to face rather than in writing. They met to say their farewells two days before he was due to sail. Franklin had not quite a proposal in mind, but he did want to let her know how strongly he felt about her. The only way he felt able to venture into this unexplored realm, which probably scared him more than any number of French three-deckers or icy seas, was to drop a few hints and hope she would take it from there. Lovers were supposed to have an almost telepathic understanding, were they not? There can be few who will not recognise the stomach-tightening nervous tension Franklin must have experienced on that spring day as he waited for her to pick up on the hints he was dropping and help him out.

She did not, even though she did have an inkling of the way he felt. It was neither callousness nor indifference on her part. It *was* only an inkling she had, and although in correspondence she was noticeably more open and direct than Franklin, in the flesh she was no more skilled than he in such matters. Eleanor later claimed she could not even be sure, with so much still hidden beneath the surface, that he would remember her once the rigours of the voyage had begun to occupy his mind.

She was wrong. During the coming hardships she would often be on his mind, and he on hers.

*

The *Prince of Wales* left Gravesend on Sunday 23 May 1819, in company with the *Eddystone* and the *Wear*, and reached her first port of call, Stromness in the Orkneys, just over a week later. Franklin wrote to tell his father that they were detained there by 'contrary winds' but had found accommodation and had used the time in trying out the various scientific instruments they had brought with them.[21] The plan was to obtain hired hands here, but there were problems. First, he discovered that the 'great demand for them at home affords full occupation'. A group of Orkney boatmen assembled to hear details of the venture: most thought they would rather stick to their usual, relatively safe occupation; a few said they would sleep on it. Only four were taken on 'after much hesitation':

> I was much amused with the extreme caution these men used before they would sign the agreement...such caution on the part of the

Northern Mariners forms a singular contrast with the ready and thoughtless manner in which an English seaman enters upon any enterprise without enquiry, however hazardous, without enquiry, or desiring to know, where he is going, or what he is going about.[22]

Franklin has been portrayed as a weak and even naïve leader by Berton and others, many of whom seem to have taken their lead from him. Fergus Fleming[23] describes Franklin as hesitant and 'abnormally' sensitive. Franklin was never a hesitant leader. His *judgement* can be debated, but that is another matter. I suspect the 'hesitancy' tag comes more from the record we have of his courtship of Eleanor – but how many of us would like our character to be judged on the way we handle our love lives? The main evidence quoted of his being 'abnormally sensitive' is that he did not like floggings (nor did Nelson – discipline was never a problem on either of their ships) and that he once remarked that he preferred to blow flies away instead of crushing them! If there was an area where he betrayed any naïveté it was demonstrated in the above remarks from his *Narrative* of this expedition. He had only ever really known life from the perspective of the Royal Navy. Sailors, and particularly British sailors of the day, were a world apart from the rest of society; they had a culture that set them away from others every bit as much as if they were inhabitants of the most remote, exotic nation on earth. There is an account of old sailors coming across a much loved former captain; on crossing the street to greet him it is said that they automatically placed themselves on his leeward side – the captain has to be able to gauge any change in the wind.

The Orkney boatmen had no need to risk their necks in some wilderness if they could make their livings closer to home. They probably had wives and families, and were used to weighing up the risks and fending for themselves. This was a novelty to Franklin.

Also while they were at Stromness a brig carrying missionaries anchored, and Franklin and Richardson were able to obtain some 'rudimentary information on the Esquimaux languages' and an 'Esquimaux' translation of St John's Gospel.[24]

On 16 June they set off across the North Atlantic for Canada.

One would not necessarily jump at the chance of sailing with Franklin. Something always seemed to *happen*. On 5 August they were in Davis Strait between Greenland and Baffin Island; there was thick fog and they were unable to take soundings. Suddenly they saw 'a barren rugged shore towering over the mastheads'. The ship hit a rock, displacing her rudder. The swell pulled them back off the rocks, but the current was now carrying them into a small bay and more rocks – 'The prospect was most alarming'. They struck another rock – which knocked the rudder back into place, allowing them to steer away from this danger, only to be driven again by the current into a huge iceberg, badly holing the ship. Franklin later wrote to his sister that they were 'apprehensive of keeping the vessel afloat'[25] and had to keep pumping and bailing for thirty-six hours non-stop until the carpenters and their crew from both the *Wear* and the *Eddystone* could at least partially fix the leak. Even then it took three days of desperate pumping before the battle was won.

It was shortly after this that Franklin met his first Eskimos. A number came on the ship to barter, and he was struck by the way in which they would lick any item they had obtained in order to 'finish the bargain'. He also noted the surprising extent to which these natives of the region were affected by the climate. Most had sore eyes, all seemed of 'plethoric' habit, and several suffered with nosebleeds.[26]

The *Prince of Wales* anchored at York Flats on 30 August, and Franklin was met by the Governor of the HBC post, a Mr Williams. Here they found that several men of the North-West Company were under arrest, and Franklin began to fully appreciate the 'state of violent commercial opposition' between the companies. Nevertheless, the prisoners freely gave him helpful advice for his coming journeys. Seeing how sensitive the situation was, Franklin wisely gave his own men instructions to refrain from being drawn into any internecine disputes.

On 9 September the party set off to an eight-gun salute and three cheers from the 'fort', as many of these trading-posts were known. There was a string of them between here and the Great Slave Lake – more miles away than they would have even cared to contemplate at that stage. After that, they would be living off the land. They could not fit all of the provisions into the boat provided for them by Mr Williams, but he promised to forward the rest the following season.

He and some of his men accompanied the expedition on the first stage of its journey.

By 19 September they had reached Hill River where, Franklin mused, 'The beauty of the scenery, dressed in the tints of autumn, called forth our admiration and was the subject of Mr Hood's accurate pencil'.[27] Franklin was always more comfortable with a sextant in his hand than a pen, and this is about as poetic as he gets. He was full of praise for the Orkney boatmen, who regularly had to jump into the freezing water to lift the boat over rocks. At Oxford House, a deserted HBC post, they came across some Cree Indians 'miserably dejected' and suffering from measles and whooping cough; they would later discover that this was not an isolated case. After a month of toil on the part of the boatmen,* but in generally good weather, they reached the mouth of the Saskatchewan at midnight. There was evidence of people having camped here, and the HBC men who had accompanied them went around armed and on the alert until satisfied that they were not going to be ambushed.

On 22 October, when they reached Cumberland House, the margins of the lake on which it stood were already freezing over. This, combined with the first hard frosts and heavy snowfalls of winter, led them to conclude that it would not be possible to travel further by water until the spring, and they accepted Governor Williams' invitation to winter with him.

As winter set in, Indians began to arrive at the settlement. As well as suffering from disease, they were starving. One of the Franklin myths is that he was foolish not to 'go native'; the Indians knew the land and how to survive. There were skilled hunters among the Indians, and they would be vital to the expedition, but Franklin found that the use of the bow and arrow had died out; hunting was done with guns, for which the Indians relied completely on Europeans for powder and shot. In addition, there is little the best hunters in the world can achieve if nature is unkind and there is

---

* Officers did not stoop to this kind of labour. This seems a ridiculous waste of human resources to us now, but it was the way things were done then. The one thing that can be said in mitigation is that it meant the officers were free to perform the scientific and artistic duties for which they were there in the first place.

nothing to be hunted. These factors would come into play, yet have been conveniently overlooked by many. Little did Franklin know how much he would be able to sympathise with these people when he was told that 'Men and women are yet living who have been reduced to feed upon the bodies of their own family to prevent actual starvation...'[28]

One facet of the cultural dissonance that the British newcomers would never get used to was the Indian response to bereavement:

> It is much to be regretted that these poor men, during their long intercourse with Europeans, have not been taught how pernicious is the grief which produces total inactivity, and that they have not been furnished with any of the consolations which the Christian religion never fails to afford.[29]

Haughtily put, but he did have a practical point. Not only did the peoples of the region become paralysed, as it were, by the death of a family member, but many went so far as to destroy what paltry possessions they had – even their hunting weapons and the tents they lived in – as a demonstration of the depth of their grief. Practices which might have seemed very selfless and noble in ordinary times must have led to many more additional and unnecessary deaths when maintained during the ravages of famine and epidemic.

The New Year of 1820 was welcomed in with a volley of muskets, as was the custom in those parts. They had a celebratory meal of beaver, which Franklin found 'extremely delicate'. Although he had intended to spend the winter at Cumberland House, it became clear that a journey north into the Athabasca region would be necessary. Not only would he be able to obtain there useful information on what to expect once they ventured beyond the Great Slave Lake, but it was also the only place where guides, hunters and interpreters were to be found. He decided to go with Back and Hepburn, leaving Richardson and Hood at Cumberland House. Only one of the doughty men of Orkney was prepared to go any further, and the second seaman, one Samuel Wilks, 'proved to be quite unequal to the fatigue of the journey. I directed him to be discharged in the Spring, and sent to England by the next ship'.[30]

Dr Richardson used the time while Franklin and the others were away to observe the Cree more closely. They were 'constantly exposed to fatigue and famine' and he could not help but notice the way in which they had been exploited by the white traders. They had a practice of applying fat or marrow to their hair and faces. It was supposed to help protect them from the cold and keep their skin soft – but any budding entrepreneur who smells a potential profit here should also sniff the product first:

> It renders their presence disagreeable to the olfactory organs of an European [sic], particularly when they are seated in a close tent and near a hot fire...[31]

Franklin, Back and Hepburn were accompanied by several HBC men. The mercury in their thermometer had by now retreated into the bulb and frozen, and the deep snow, together with feet unaccustomed to snow-shoes, made the going arduous. One night when they were halfway to Cumberland House, Franklin writes that wolves 'serenaded us through the night with a chorus of their agreeable howling',[32] but the concert was interrupted when Back, who had been sleeping a tad too close to the fire in an attempt to combat the bitter cold, found that his buffalo robe had caught fire, and on jumping up the heat from his toasted shoes made him hop in Chaplinesque fashion out into the snow to cool his feet.

They reached Carlton House on 31 January, a journey of 263 miles, which had left Franklin with painfully swollen ankles. There were Cree Indians here, and both Franklin and Back overheard an elderly member of that race talking about the Indians killing all the white people in the area, quickly qualified with the rueful comment: 'A pretty state we shall then be in, without the goods you bring us'.[33]

Once Franklin's ankles were sufficiently recovered, they were on the move again. The snow was still deep, though the temperature was milder. After a few days they spotted a small owl watching them from a tree over a deserted Indian hut. Some thought it was a bad omen.

By 19 March they reached a North-West Company station where the officer in charge expressed doubt as to whether any more Canadian voyageurs (boatmen) would be persuaded to go to the sea because of their dread of the Eskimos. Fort Chipewyan was reached a week later; they had travelled 857 miles, mostly in deep snow. After getting used to the snow shoes, Franklin found the worst part of the journey to have been the

> wanton and unnecessary cruelty of men to the dogs, especially the Canadians, who beat them unmercifully and habitually vent on them the most dreadful and disgusting imprecations.[34]

As for themselves, the dogs would hover on the fringes of the camp, 'snatching at every kind of food that happens to be in reach'.

They stayed at Fort Chipewyan for several months, waiting for the snow and ice to melt, and making preparations for the next leg of their journey. They were brought news from the Great Slave Lake that the chief of the Copper Indians and some of his hunters had been engaged on their behalf by a Mr Wentzel of the North-West Company. The Indians were optimistic about the venture:

> They had no doubt of our being able to obtain the means of subsistence in travelling to the coast. This agreeable intelligence had a happy effect upon the minds of the Canadian Voyagers [sic], many of their fears being removed: several now seemed disposed to volunteer...[35]

By July one of the birch-bark canoes they would be using was finished. It was just over thirty-two feet long. The voyageurs were as well versed in handling these vessels as Franklin was in the ways of a square-rigger – and 'handling' was often what they literally had to do. Many 'portages' were necessary along the rivers: stretches made unnavigable by rocks or other hindrances where the men had to haul the boat out of the water and carry it for a distance. 'They often run with it', Franklin noted in admiration.[36] There was a trial on the lake, where particularly stormy conditions gave them some idea of what to expect when they reached the coast: 'We had the satisfaction that our birchen vessel proved an excellent sea boat'.[37]

Soon after this Richardson and Hood were warmly welcomed back into the fold, and they had brought with them two more canoes and some provisions – though, worryingly, not nearly as much as had been planned. Ten bags of pemmican* at one of the North-West Company posts was found to be mouldy, and at an HBC post a group of hungry voyageurs had eaten all the food set aside for Franklin's expedition. This meant that they would be setting out with only a single day's provisions, but there was no advantage in waiting any longer since there was little enough food to support them at Fort Chipewyan.

Richardson and Hood also brought ten 'zealous' voyageurs with them, which meant that when they set off early on 18 July 1820 there were sixteen voyageurs altogether, who, much cheered after imbibing their 'customary dram', sang paddling songs as they went.

Franklin had been assured of the Canadians and their boats that 'it rarely happens that any incidents occur...' On the second day out, one canoe smashed off the bow of another in a coming-together; after this was repaired another was dropped onto a rock during a portage and broke in two.

On 24 July they reached Moose Deer Island where they engaged an interpreter called Pierre St Germain, and a few days later at Fort Providence they were joined by their second interpreter, Jean Baptiste Adam. A fire was lit on a hilltop to announce the expedition's arrival to the Indian chief and his hunters; Franklin was informed by Mr Wentzel of the North-West Company, with twenty years' experience in the region, that first impressions were of great importance when dealing with the Indians, so uniforms and medals were donned, and the Union flag hoisted on one of their tents.

The following day a flotilla of canoes arrived. The Copper Indian chief disembarking with a 'grave aspect' from the leading boat was called Akaitcho. As represented in a painting by Hood, he looks younger than one might expect of a chief. He was shown into the fort, where he went through the ritual of smoking his pipe, and partook of some spirits and water with his hunters. Then he gave his speech. He loved the white men upon whom his people relied so much, he said, and was more than happy to carry out what was required of him. He would do his utmost to provide them with 'the means of subsistence' right to the end of their journey; his only trepidation being the threat presented by the dreaded Eskimos they could expect to encounter. These fine words would in time come

* Dried and pounded buffalo meat mixed with melted fat.

back to haunt Franklin and his men. Digressing slightly, Akaitcho enquired about Franklin's medicine chief – whose powers were so great, he had heard, as to be able to bring the dead back to life. 'The prospect of seeing his departed relatives had enlivened his spirits', Franklin remarked with an unintended pun. It was diplomatically explained to him that Dr Richardson's powers did not go quite *that* far…

Franklin told Akaitcho that he was here on behalf of the 'greatest chief in the world', under whose dominion all the trading companies fell. He outlined the route that Wentzel had proposed they take, but one of Akaitcho's guides came up with an alternative which he said was not only shorter, but would provide more opportunities for hunting along the way; he sketched it out in charcoal on the floor. Franklin was sufficiently impressed to adopt this suggestion, and the meeting was concluded by the British officers handing out medals and other more practical gifts to the Indians.

Franklin was impressed with Akaitcho, whom he thought 'evinced much penetration and intelligence, which gave us a favourable opinion of his intellectual powers'.[38] The Indians set out first, assuring Franklin that they would meet up with him at the mouth of the Yellow Knife River. Only once they were gone were the stores for the journey packed, 'as they are in the habit of begging for everything they see'. They took with them an array of weapons for hunting and self-defence, and provisions for approximately ten days. A further voyageur was hired, making it a total of twenty-eight people setting out the day after the Indians. The wives (and children) of three voyageurs were coming along to make clothes and shoes once they reached their projected winter quarters. There were three canoes for the main party and the women had their own smaller one. Everyone was in high spirits, 'heartily glad to be heading for the Coppermine River and through country not previously visited by any European'.[39]

They soon reached the Yellow Knife River and the appointment with Akaitcho and a fleet of seventeen canoes: several of which were in the charge of women

who proved to be noisy companions, for they quarrelled frequently, and the weakest was generally profuse in her lamentations, which were not at all diminished, when the husband attempted to settle the difference by a few blows with his paddle...[40]

The voyageurs must have been envious at the portages – of which there were many – of the Indians with their lighter and unburdened canoes. At every such obstacle the Canadians had to go back and forth four times for every one by the Indians. On the river, Back 'delighted and astonished' the Indians by his success in fly-fishing.

But after a few days the mood began to change. Food supplies had dwindled alarmingly. Akaitcho's hunters were sent out to find meat, but his prediction that the lakes on the expedition's route would provide plentiful fish to supplement their now meagre diet proved overly optimistic. Impressive though it was, Back's skill with the rod was not going to fill the bellies of a small army of men engaged in the daily slog that was their lot. The voyageurs were starting to grumble, and Franklin feared that if no food was obtained soon they would be unable to continue. Soon all that was available was 'portable' soup and arrowroot, 'but this food is too insubstantial to support their vigour under their daily exhausting labour...'[41]

On 11 August an Indian arrived with the news they had been hoping for – he had spotted a distant fire, a signal by the hunters that they had been successful in catching reindeer. This at first boosted flagging morale, but when after two more days they had not reached the Indian hunters

> our Canadian voyagers, who had been for some days past murmuring at their meagre diet, and striving to get the whole of our little provision to consume all at once, broke out into open discontent, and several of them threatened they would not proceed forward unless more food was given to them. This conduct was the more unpardonable, as they saw we were rapidly approaching the fires of the hunters, and that provision might soon be expected.[42]

He had been forewarned that they would be likely to push him as far as they thought they could get away with, and gave them a strongly worded lecture on the necessity of maintaining discipline. But he was not immune to their plight: 'Their present hardships were of a kind which few could support without murmuring…no one could witness [it] without feeling a sincere pity for their sufferings'.[43]

They were rewarded for their grudging patience the following day, when the first hunters were encountered. Fortunately for the party, the weather had not added to their woes: it was a warm 77° Fahrenheit. Akaitcho now went on ahead to Winter Lake in order to get food in ready for the arrival of the main body of the expedition. With food inside them, the voyageurs found their voices once more, and resumed the paddling songs which had been curtailed by hunger and misery.

On the afternoon of 20 August, Franklin says:

> We read divine service and offered our thanksgiving to the Almighty for his goodness in having brought us thus far on our journey; a duty which we never neglected, when stationary on the Sabbath.[44]

They had arrived at the spot earmarked by the Indians as a suitable winter encampment, having travelled 553 miles from Fort Chipewyan: mostly in the boats. The men had tackled just over 21 miles of portages – but since the boats and cargoes could not be managed all in one go, each portage entailed the voyageurs making three trips with loads of 180lb and one 'light', thus Franklin estimated that they had actually walked around 150 miles in this way.

Akaitcho turned up during the last week of September – but he was not a bringer of good tidings. First, he had only managed to store up fifteen reindeer. St Germain told them that news of the death of Akaitcho's brother-in-law meant that they had spent several days 'bewailing his loss' instead of hunting. But worst of all was Akaitcho's declaration that he would not be accompanying them on their descent to the Coppermine River. He believed that there were signs of winter setting in already, and that anyone going on such a journey would lose their life. Franklin pointed out that this was a complete contradiction of what he had been telling them up till now; Akaitcho's defence was that he had not previously realised how slowly they travelled. Franklin tried to reassure him: with all the baggage being left behind, they would be able to step up their pace – and they could turn back if the weather started to deteriorate. 'Well', replied Akaitcho, 'I have said every thing I can urge, to dissuade you from going on this service, on which, it seems, you wish to sacrifice your own lives, as well as the Indians who might attend you...' He would not let it be said that the Indians had left them to die, so he would send some of his younger men, but 'From the moment they embark in the canoes, I and my relatives shall lament them as dead'.[45]

Franklin left it at that for the time being, but he soon heard about what might have been an ulterior motive for Akaitcho wanting to renege on his agreement: the Indians were keen to go off after deer skins to provide winter clothes for themselves and to sell to the Canadians. Franklin heard from Wentzel that Akaitcho intended to return to Fort Providence. 'I came reluctantly to the determination of relinquishing the intention of going any distance down the river this season...'[46]

The officers all agreed that a descent to the sea would cause a complete breakdown of their relationship with Akaitcho, and suggested the compromise of dispatching a reconnaissance party to the river. Franklin, and later Akaitcho, agreed. Back and Hood would take a light canoe to explore the Coppermine with two of Akaitcho's hunters; the rest of the Indians would go hunting to build up provisions for the expedition.

Akaitcho had heard Franklin and the others talking about a forthcoming eclipse and quizzed Franklin about it. He was amazed that they knew exactly when it would happen, and remarked, 'that this knowledge was striking proof of the superiority of the Whites over the Indians. We took advantage of this occasion to speak to them respecting the Supreme Being...'[47] In the event, the predicted eclipse was lost to view in heavy snow.

On 29 August Back and Hood set off with St Germain, eight voyageurs and one Indian hunter. On the same day Akaitcho also departed, leaving two hunters behind, along with old Keskarrah, the guide, and his family. Those left behind with Franklin began work on building their winter quarters. By early October Back and Hood had returned and the house – Fort Enterprise – was finished. It measured fifty feet by twenty-four, divided into a hall, three bedrooms and a kitchen; the walls and roof were plastered with clay, and deerskin parchment covered the windows. Back went on his travels again – to

Fort Providence to arrange for more of their stores to be sent from Cumberland House. But soon after this Akaitcho came in reporting that the deer had gone south. The arrival of such a large group placed a serious strain on supplies. There was not enough ammunition for them to go out hunting; Franklin knew that ordinarily the Indians would resort to fishing and the use of snares under such circumstances, 'yet on the present occasion they felt little inclined to do so, and gave great scope to their natural love of ease, as long as our store-house seemed to be well stocked'.[48]

Belanger, who had been with Back, turned up at Fort Enterprise one day so encased in ice and snow that they barely recognised him. He told of a strenuous journey to Fort Providence, resulting only in the discovery that part of their supplies were missing. An HBC officer had been transporting them from York Factory, and had come across some North-West Company canoes. He decided this was a good time to lighten his load, and demanded that as this was 'in the service of the government' they should share his burden. When they refused, having other duties to perform, the HBC officer simply dumped 'their' half, including ammunition and tobacco for the voyageurs, on the beach, 'and departed without any regard to the serious consequences that might result to us from our want of them'.[49]

The only good thing to come out of it was a package which, once thawed out, was found to contain newspapers and letters from England. Franklin had been corresponding with a brother-in-law, a man of the cloth, and seemed to find in this friendship the perfect vehicle for giving expression to his now profound faith in the Christian religion. In a letter written at this time he speaks of receiving

> hope, comfort and support from religious books and especially the Bible during this season of leisure...I am amazed at the state of ignorance under which I laboured with respect to it blessed contents.[50]

This long letter virtually becomes a sermon: obviously not aimed directly at his relative, whom we can safely assume was not in need of one, but more in the nature of an outpouring of spiritual ardour to a like-minded soul. Significantly, he mentions Lady Lucy Barry and her circle, and the gratitude he owes her. Lady Barry headed a group of Calvinists and would later be described as a fanatic by Eleanor Porden, a view probably shared by much of London society. Franklin guardedly described himself as inspired by – but not belonging to – her fellowship, but the tone of this letter makes one suspect that her ladyship was personally responsible for his 'seeing the light'. Not all of the letter is taken up with matters of the soul. He describes Fort Enterprise as being in a pleasant situation on the banks of a small river where numbers of reindeer pass close by. He announced himself 'entirely free from my constant companion in England – the teasing cough'.

The newspapers brought news of the end of the long reign of King George III, and the accession of George IV.

When the Indians who had been to Fort Providence with Belanger arrived, they brought troubling rumours. Mr Weeks, who was in charge there, appeared to be spreading a rumour that Franklin and his comrades were charlatans. Far from being intrepid representatives of His Majesty's Government, they were a band of opportunists who were merely there to live off the kindness of the Copper Indians – who would never receive the promised recompense for their troubles. Reassured by Franklin, and no doubt considering that it was an improbably time-consuming and dangerous method of obtaining a free lunch, Akaitcho had the good sense to ignore the stories.

A small amount of ammunition had been sent, which was passed on to Akaitcho along with the hint that his party of around forty people was depleting reserves of food at a worrying rate. The chief promised to leave as soon as their snow shoes and sledges had been prepared. 'Under one pretext or another, however, their departure was delayed until the 10th of the month...'[51] When they did go, old Keskarrah was left behind. Not only was he in no fit state to hunt, but he was also nursing his sick wife. Keskarrah's daughter was called Green Stockings, 'considered by her tribe to be a great beauty', and Hood made a portrait of her which worried her mother, who was afraid that her beauty 'would induce the great Chief who resided in England to send for the original...'[52]

During their enforced winter inactivity, the officers wrote up their journals, read the few newspapers and magazines from home 'again and again' and in the evening joined the voyageurs in various games till late at night. During this period Richardson noticed that sometimes at night 'the moisture of the breath freezes with a considerable crackling noise...'[53] Axes were regularly broken in the attempt to chop down frozen trees. Franklin saw in the New Year of 1821 surprised that the rest of the Canadians had not arrived from Fort Providence – they were renowned for putting on an extra spurt when inspired by the prospect of alcoholic reward. What he did not know was that they had stopped along the way to have their own little celebration, which lasted all of two days. When they did arrive at Fort Enterprise and partook of the belated party laid on for them there, the conscience of one of the Indians who had been with them got the better of him, and he told Franklin what had happened:

> I felt for their privations and fatigues, and was disposed to seize upon every opportunity of alleviating them, but this, combined with many instances of petty dishonesty with regard to meat, shewed how little confidence could be put in Canadian voyager when food or spirits were in question.[54]

Wentzel arrived on 27 January with two Eskimo interpreters. In their own language their names translated as 'The Belly' and the 'The Ear', but they had been given the Anglicised (or perhaps more correctly 'Latinised') names Augustus and Junius.

The following week some of Akaitcho's men came for more ammunition, and revealed that their chief, having heard yet more negative reports about Franklin and his expedition from Fort Providence, 'his faith in our good intentions was somewhat shaken'. Franklin sent him a soothing reply. Eventually, Weeks wrote strongly denying responsibility for any of the stories that were in circulation, but one Indian assured Franklin that he had personally heard Weeks defaming him.

By the time Back returned in March from Fort Chipewyan, having trekked for over a thousand miles, the stock of reindeer meat was used up, and pounded meat reserved for making a summer supply of pemmican had to be issued. They received a welcome communication from 'The Hook', the Copper Indian chief second only to Akaitcho. He offered to provide them with dried meat on the banks of the Coppermine at the start of summer.

There were other problems for Franklin to consider: 'several circumstances having come lately to my knowledge that have led me to suspect the fidelity of our interpreters, they were examined closely upon this subject'.[55] He suspected that St Germain and Adam had influenced the Indians into deliberately being less successful in their hunting than they might have been, in order to provide an excuse for not proceeding further. St Germain, whom Franklin describes as 'artful', denied the main charge in a 'very dogged manner', but did admit to telling Akaitcho that Franklin had treated the chief shabbily, and 'affronted' him by the small amount of rum given to him. Franklin had no doubts as to St Germain's untrustworthiness, but needed his services and could only threaten him with a trial in England if the expedition were to be jeopardised by his actions. St Germain replied, 'It is immaterial to me where I lose my life, whether it is in England, or accompanying you to the sea, for the whole party will perish'.[56]

Akaitcho arrived at Fort Enterprise at the end of March, and gave his full assent to the plan put before him. He would go with them to the Coppermine and maybe even further – in order to meet the Eskimos and perhaps go some way towards patching up the uneasy relationship between them and the Indians. Akaitcho's people were short of food themselves by now, and Richardson did his best to administer to the many sick women and children among them:

> When we beheld them knawing [*sic*] the pieces of hide, and pounding the bones, for the purpose of extracting some nourishment from them by boiling, we regretted our inability to help them, but little thought that we should ourselves be afterwards driven to the necessity of eagerly collecting these same bones from the dunghill.[57]

Franklin was not employing artistic licence. Within a matter of months he would be picking up the actual bones, now being discarded by starving people as having served their purpose, in a desperate effort to extract yet further traces of nourishment from them. For now, he managed to take their minds off their plight in some small way by getting up a sledging event. The officers seemed particularly adept at falling off, to the great delight of the Indians ('These vehicles descended the snowy bank with much velocity...'[58]), and after one such mishap Franklin found himself buried in snow, when 'A fat Indian woman drove her sledge over me, and sprained my knee severely'.[59]

Commencing on 23 May there were several heated conferences with Akaitcho, who was attacking on a number of fronts: Weeks was not honouring payment notes given to him by Franklin; the rum they had given to him was weak; the clothing and other presents offered to him were inferior to those normally offered to him each spring at Fort Providence. Franklin replied that he could not comment on Weeks' behaviour at this distance; the rum was of the milder kind favoured by the 'great men' in England; as for the clothing and gifts, it was simply impracticable for them to provide more owing to the nature of their expedition. Now it was Akaitcho's turn to listen to Franklin's grouses. What about the dried meat that the chief had promised to supply and was vital to the success of their mission? Were not his complaints a mere tactic to divert their minds from his failure to meet the terms of his engagement?

Akaitcho then 'shifted his ground' and reminded them of his prophecies of doom concerning the venture:

> This part of his haranguing being an exact transcript of the sentiments formerly expressed by our Interpreters induced us to conclude that they had prompted his present line of conduct by telling him that we had goods or rum concealed...[60]

But it was becoming clear that Akaitcho was not supported by many of his people – even his own brothers, who accused him of avarice; eventually realising how isolated he was becoming, Akaitcho conceded that Franklin was not withholding any hidden goods from him. He spent the next day in his tent, 'ashamed to show himself', and finally agreed to take his party to the river once the weather improved. The snow was too deep for travelling at present, and there was almost constant daylight. Franklin recorded that it was sometimes lighter at midnight than at midday.

It was not until 4 June that Franklin moved out of Fort Enterprise. The weather was warm now, and they were pestered by mosquitoes swarming in from the marshes. His group met up with Richardson, who had gone on ahead, and Akaitcho, at Point Lake which fed the Coppermine River. Richardson and two hunters with him had prepared 200lb of dried meat – 'our sole dependence for the journey'. The reason for this was that Akaitcho caught nothing, choosing instead to give away most of his ammunition to members of his tribe who had nothing to do with the expedition. Franklin resolved in future to give him only powder and shot in proportion to meat obtained. They all set out on 25 June 1821, with three canoes initially mounted on sledges, and the officers treating Akaitcho 'distantly' to show their disapproval of his behaviour. Progress was painful, thanks to rain 'honeycombing' the ice and making sharp and jagged ruts which ripped their moccasins and cut their feet, but on 1 July they at last reached the Coppermine River.

~ 5 ~

Que Nous Sommes Maigres!

THE Coppermine was around 200 yards wide, up to ten feet deep, with a powerful current. They ventured forth in bright sunshine, and it was a picturesque setting, with the rocky river banks giving way to gently sloping wooded hills; but the first rapids they encountered taught them to respect the power of the river and appreciate the fragility of their craft. After losing a dog which ran off after a reindeer, they descended a series of rapids past the mouth of the Fairy Lake River. Franklin thoughtfully reported for the benefit of future travellers in the region that

> the Northern Indian fairies are six inches high, lead a life similar to the Indians, and are excellent hunters. Those who have had the good fortune to fall in with their tiny encampments have been kindly treated, and regaled on venison.[1]

Before long, they were met by some hunters who, on finding the missing dog, had decided that the whole party must have drowned and promptly discarded all their baggage and meat. They discovered their error when they met up with Akaitcho's slave, but not before they had come too far to retrieve the meat. The Indians were 'much ashamed of the panic into which they had been thrown'.[2]

After this Franklin came upon 'The Hook' and his people, who had heard that the expedition was short of provisions and had been waiting for them with the little food he had been able to obtain, commenting on the 'unusual scarcity' this season. 'We are too much indebted to the white people, to allow them to want food on our lands, whilst we have any to give them',[3] he said. Franklin gave him a medal.

By 11 July they had reached the foot of the Coppermine Mountains from which Akaitcho's people got both their name and, formerly, the copper they used to make their utensils. Now they used the iron goods obtained from the white man's trading posts. The party was coming into Eskimo country, and when they came across the remains of an old Eskimo encampment it was deemed expedient to set up a system of watches. Augustus and Junius, meanwhile, gamely volunteered to try to make contact with the Eskimos, and went off with beads, mirrors and suchlike as gifts. When they did not return the following day, Franklin notes with some exasperation that 'Akaitcho, ever ready to augur misfortune, expressed his belief that our messengers had been killed, and that the Esquimaux, warned of our approach, were lying in wait for us…'[4]

The truth could not have been more different. Augustus and Junius returned with all limbs intact having spotted Eskimo tents. On 15 July* they went back and made tentative contact – but the arrival of others from the party frightened them away. Franklin's group did, however, come across an old man in hiding, petrified and too feeble to flee with his fellow countrymen. He had never seen a white man before. Once they had allayed his initial fears and suspicions, he was able to tell them that they would find plenty of food en route: there were lots of reindeer near the coast in the summer, fish were plentiful at river mouths, seals and musk ox would also be in abundance. They camped here, at Bloody Falls, where fifty years ago almost to the day Samuel Hearne had looked on helplessly while his party of Indians massacred a group of Eskimos out fishing. The ground was still strewn with skulls.

On 17 July, Franklin records:

> The fears which our interpreters, St Germain and Adam, both entertained respecting the voyage, were now greatly increased, and both of them came this evening to request their discharges, urging that their services could be no longer requisite, as the Indians were going from us.[5]

St Germain tried to claim that he had been hired to stay only as long as the Indians were with them – but he had to concede defeat on this myth when Franklin read back to him his written terms of

---

* Incorrectly designated 'June' in Franklin's published narrative.

engagement. With the Indians leaving, Franklin was more concerned about their hunting, as opposed to linguistic, skills. He heard a rumour that they had a plan for 'eloping', causing both the officers and the voyageurs, who knew their own safety was at stake, to keep a wary eye on St Germain and Adam.

On 18 July the Indians left, reassuring Franklin that they would provide a store of food at Fort Enterprise and caches along the Coppermine ready for the expedition's return. Wentzel also took his leave of them here, and with him went four voyageurs they felt they could manage without to ensure that there were fewer mouths to feed. Franklin's party of twenty men clambered into their canoes and commenced the journey to the sea; it was noted that the water already tasted salty, and ebbed and flowed during the day by four inches:

> Our Canadian voyagers complained of the cold, but they were amused with their first view of the sea, and particularly with the sight of the seals that were swimming about near the entrance of the river, but these sensations gave place to despondency before the evening was out.[6]

Their fears returning, the interpreters again begged to be released, although only one of the voyageurs was of a similar mind. Franklin hoped that the longer they went on, the calmer they would become. On Thursday 19 July 1821, they reached the Arctic Sea:

> The manner in which our faithful Hepburn viewed the element that he had been so long accustomed to, contributed not a little to make them ashamed of their fears.[7]

They had travelled around 334 miles from Fort Enterprise. With fifteen days' worth of dried meat, they 'launched upon the element, which was more congenial with our habits than the fresh water navigations, and their numerous difficulties and impediments we had hitherto encountered…'[8]

In the distance, they could see ice twinkling in the sunlight, and a small berg. As they paddled along the coastline, Franklin named a group of islands after Vice-Admiral Lawford, who as a captain had given him his very first opportunity in the Royal Navy on board the

Polyphemus. They passed numerous traces of Eskimo activity as they progressed, but if anyone was around they were keeping well out of sight. There was also little evidence of the 'plentiful' fish along this 'sterile and inhospitable' shore. Ice became a problem the further they went, as did the usual bugbear: food. On 28 July they were dismayed to discover that two precious bags of pemmican had turned mouldy, and their beef had been 'so badly cured, as to be scarcely eatable... It was not, however, the quality of our provision that gave us uneasiness, but its diminution, and the utter incapacity to obtain any addition'.[9] Even the ubiquitous mosquitoes, which they had assumed would be unable to survive in the cold sea air, would not leave them alone.

By 30 July they were down to eight days' food. They had reached a region where, according to the old Eskimo, they might obtain assistance from his countrymen; additionally, they had spotted reindeer and there was a river that promised good fishing. Augustus, Junius and Hepburn were sent out with gifts in search of Eskimos, while the rest of the party set fishing nets. This provided them with a paltry single salmon and five white fish, and even the return of Augustus and Junius with a brown bear they had caught did not signify a change in their luck. Having heard tales of this gigantic, fearsome creature from the Indians, their trophy proved to be a skinny, sorry looking specimen:

> Our fastidious voyagers supposing, from its leanness, the animal had been sickly, declined eating it; the officers, however, being less scrupulous, boiled the paws, and found them excellent.[10]

The mood of the party grew gloomier as each day passed with little success in catching anything to eat; the voyageurs became openly rebellious, and Franklin and the other officers suspected that the interpreters St Germain and Adam were stirring much of this up, and worse, intentionally sabotaging their own hunting forays in the hope that lack of food would put an end to the journey. They were by now paddling into the teeth of a fierce northeasterly,

> which raised the waves to a height that quite terrified our people...
> We were obliged, however, to persevere in our advance, feeling, as

73

we did, that the short season for our operations was hastening away...[11]

After a few days of this the canoes had sustained a good deal of damage. Franklin had been thinking about turning back for some time. It was apparent to him that the season was breaking up; they were down to their last three days' pemmican, and although they could see deer on the shore, the land was so flat and featureless it was impossible to get close to them. He put his thoughts to the other officers:

> We were all convinced of the necessity of putting a speedy termination to our advance, as the hope which we had cherished of meeting the Esquimaux and procuring provision from them, could now scarcely be entertained; but yet we were desirous of proceeding, until land could be seen trending eastward; that we might be satisfied of its separation from what we had conceived, in passing from Cape Barrow to Baths Inlet, to be a great chain of islands.[12]

It was decided that they would give it four more days, a decision which was 'joyfully received' by the men. Setting out the following day, Franklin named a group of islands *The Porden Islands* after the young lady (or at least her family) who waited for him in England, and a cape henceforth bore the name of Flinders. The wind had not let up – indeed, it was worsening: 'The Canadians had now the opportunity of witnessing a storm at sea; and the sight increased their desire of quitting it...'[13]

On 18 August, with the conditions so bad as to prevent them embarking, their sea journey was over, and the spot where their great adventure met its end was given the appellation Point Turnagain.

When a naval commander failed to achieve an objective, no matter how unrealistic the goal or extenuating the circumstances, there was always an unspoken sense of 'guilty until proven innocent' about it. This, coupled with the hostility encountered by John Ross after his premature return from seeking the North West Passage, may well have been in Franklin's mind when he summarised the reasons for the termination of the venture:

When the many perplexing incidents which occurred during the survey of the coast are considered in connexion with the shortness of the period, during which operations of the kind can be carried on, and the distance we had to travel before we could gain a place of shelter for the winter, I trust it will be judged that we prosecuted the enterprise as far as was prudent, and abandoned it only under a well-founded conviction that a further advance would endanger the lives of the whole party, and prevent knowledge of what had been done from reaching England.

Our researches, as far as they have gone, seem to favour those who contend for the practicality of the North West Passage...[14]

To back up this view, he gave several reasons: the general line of the coast appearing to run east–west and evidence of whales pointing to open seas; a connection with Hudson Bay indicated by the appearance of fish of the kind found there; the ice they had encountered appearing not to be bad enough to prevent the passage of a sea-going ship.

They had intended to return the way they came – via the Coppermine River – but that route would entail retracing their lengthy and risky sea voyage along a stretch of barren coastline, and their supplies had already dwindled almost to nothing. Franklin decided to put into Arctic Sound in Bathurst Inlet, and from there make his way inland up Hood's River. Gales prevented them from setting off for several days, but on 22 August, homeward bound at last, the Canadians paddled away from Point Turnagain 'with the utmost alacrity'. The calm conditions did not last for long, and soon the waves were high enough to prevent the occupants of one canoe from seeing the masthead of the other, even though they were within hailing distance. At various points along the coast they at last managed to kill enough deer to boost their depleted provisions, and during the evening of 25 August they finally reached Hood's River and left the sea behind them:

Here terminated our voyage on the Arctic Sea, during which we had gone over 650 geographical miles. Our Canadians could not restrain their expressions of joy at having turned their backs on the sea, and they passed the evening talking over their adventures with no little exaggeration...[15]

75

Dr Richardson, however, hit the nail on the head when he noted that 'The most painful and certainly the most hazardous part of the journey was to come...'[16]

✼

After a few days' journey the river became so shallow that it was decided to break up the canoes and use the materials to make smaller, lighter ones. Anything that was not needed for the journey was now left behind, and from here on the officers would themselves carry as much as they could manage. On 2 September they left the river to strike out overland in as direct a route as possible for Fort Enterprise. The pemmican was soon all gone, and by the morning of the 7th the weather turned much colder, with a biting wind: 'We were in a very unfit condition for starting, being very weak from fasting, and our garments stiffened by the frost'.[17]

On emerging from the relative comfort of his tent into the unimaginably harsh and raw conditions, Franklin fainted. He at first refused an offer of soup to help him recover, knowing that this was now all they had left; but at the insistence of the men he gave in, and soon recovered enough to make a start. The snow was a foot deep and the lakes were beginning to freeze over. The marshes over which they travelled were covered with ice, but it was only a thin layer and regularly gave way, leaving them knee-deep in freezing water. The canoe-carriers were blown over time and again by the force of the wind, and after a little of this treatment one of the vessels was broken beyond repair. Suspicion immediately fell on one of the carriers, Benoit, who had been heard to say that he would deliberately smash one of the canoes as soon as he got the chance – though when this was put to him he naturally protested his innocence. The worrying part about the 'accident' was that the remaining canoe had inadvertently been built too small, it was feared, to get them across the Coppermine when the time came. As if this were not enough, their only reward after three days without food was soup supplemented with arrowroot – and thus their food supplies were completely exhausted.

From now on they took to walking single file so that the leading man forged a path through the snow, making it easier for those following. They were obliged to resort to gathering lichen, which the Canadians knew as *tripe de roche*, along the way. This disgusting stuff was unpleasant to eat and eventually proved almost indigestible for some members of the party; yet without it, Franklin and a number of others would probably have perished during the harrowing days still to come.

Three days later they spotted a musk ox through the fog, and the best hunters were sent after it. So desperate from hunger to catch it were they, and so fearful of revealing themselves and scaring the beast away, that they stalked it for an agonising two hours while the rest of the party looked on with 'extreme anxiety'. The hunters opened fire; one ox was hit, but not fatally, and it managed to lumber away. A second musketball found its target, and to the relief of all the animal went down, turning the snow red around it:

> The contents of its stomach were devoured upon the spot, and the raw intestines, which were next attacked, were pronounced by the most delicate amongst us to be excellent... This was the sixth day since we had had a good meal.[18]

Snow and strong winds were still hampering their progress, and to make matters worse, on the 13th they unexpectedly came upon a large lake* barring their path; its shores stretched as far as the eye could see. That night the whole party shared a single partridge, mixed with the dreaded *tripe de roche*: 'This unpalatable weed was now quite nauseous to the whole party, and in several it produced bowel complaints'.[19]

Hood seemed to be affected by it more than anyone else. Worse was to follow. With every man growing weaker by the day, it was now discovered that the voyageurs had dumped three badly needed fishing nets on leaving Hood's River. These men, though working like Trojans throughout the journey, seemed incapable of thinking beyond the present moment, and now they were without their main means of obtaining food. In order to preserve stamina as far as possible, everything except ammunition, clothing and essential navigational instruments was abandoned.

* It was Rum Lake.

While they were encamped on the shores of the lake, trying to work out how to get across and continue their journey, and at a time when the voyageurs must have occupied an extremely lowly place in the estimation of Franklin and his fellow officers, there occurred an unexpected interlude. The shivering officers were huddled together around a fire when they were approached by St Germain, who

> presented each of us with a small piece of meat which he had saved from his allowance. It was received with great thankfulness, and such an act of self-denial and kindness, being totally unexpected in a Canadian, filled our eyes with tears…[20]

Their crossing was eventually effected across a fast-flowing river entering the lake, but it was a tricky and highly dangerous business. Belanger was almost lost, and Franklin's journal and scientific observations disappeared when the canoe capsized. The expedition leader himself was rescued by St Germain, whose immense efforts saved many lives that day.

By 19 September the men were faint from hunger. Some days there was not even *tripe de roche* to be found, and the practice of singeing hide in order to make it edible was begun. Franklin describes a typical day during this period:

> The first operation after encamping was to thaw our frozen shoes, if a sufficient fire could be made, and dry ones were put on; each person then wrote his notes of the daily occurrences, and evening prayers were said; as soon as supper was prepared it was eaten, generally in the dark, and we went to bed, and kept up a cheerful conversation until our blankets were thawed by the heat of our bodies, and we gathered sufficient warmth to enable us to fall asleep. On many nights we had not even the luxury of going to bed in dry clothes, for when the fire was insufficient to dry our shoes, we durst not venture to pull them off, lest they should freeze so hard as to be unfit to put on in the morning…[21]

They were now encountering hilly terrain, making the going even harder; Hood was suffering the most, but Franklin was having difficulty keeping up too. The voyageurs were threatening to throw down their packs and make their own way, but Franklin was not unduly worried since he knew they needed the officers to navigate the route to Fort Enterprise. Richardson was too weak to continue carrying the plant and mineral specimens he had collected, and at one point he and Franklin became separated from the rest of the party as the conditions and the differing reserves of stamina of each man caused the 'Indian file' to become more and more strung out. When they did catch up with the rest, they found that Peltier and Vaillant no longer had the canoe, vital for the crossing of the Coppermine – it had, they said, been broken in a fall and would be impossible to repair. 'The anguish this intelligence occasioned may be conceived, but it is beyond my power to describe it…'[22]

After a meal of old shoes* and scraps of leather, supplemented by a little *tripe de roche*, the starving and weary group trudged on until, on 26 September, they reached the Coppermine River – only about forty miles from Fort Enterprise. At first, the voyageurs did not, or could not, believe it truly was the Coppermine; when the officers finally managed to persuade them, and they realised that they would now have to find some way to get across, 'they deplored their folly and impatience in breaking the canoe…'[23] which makes Franklin's suspicions about the earlier incident sound about right. A search commenced for suitable material to make a raft.

In the meantime, any change of heart Franklin might have had regarding the scruples of the voyageurs was given a setback when two of them stole the officers' provisions. It was all the more galling because the Canadians knew, and Franklin freely admits, that the officers, less hardened to both the climate and such physical hardships, were faring worse than the voyageurs. Richardson records that by now discipline among the Canadians had virtually broken down. To the officers' credit, however, their *inner* strength had not faltered, and it never would.

On 27 September they had to make do with a putrid deer carcass for breakfast, and the next day they set to work building a raft. Once

---

* Franklin has been tagged as the Man Who Ate His Own Shoes, an epithet that tends to bring Charlie Chaplin to mind. But as Professor Stuart Houston points out in *Arctic Ordeal*, Franklin is referring to moccasins made from untreated leather, and so of some small but welcome nutritional value.

finished, it proved buoyant enough to take no more than one man at a time – but they hoped it would do. Spurred, if not by team spirit, then by a reward Franklin had offered, Belanger and Benoit, 'the strongest men of the party', attempted to cross the river with a line for hauling the raft back and forth. When they failed, Richardson volunteered to swim across with the line tied around his body. He was tantalisingly close to the opposite bank when he lost the use first of his arms, then his legs in the breathtakingly freezing water, and there was great consternation from the river bank as they watched him go under. They dragged him out of the river in an 'almost lifeless state' and endeavoured to warm and revive him. When they removed his wet clothes, all were appalled at the skeleton they beheld. The voyageurs cried, 'Ah! Que nous sommes maigres!'[24] ('How thin we are!'). The stark evidence of Richardson's condition aroused not only sympathy; it was as if he had held up a mirror to them all, revealing a terrible truth that their own conscious minds had tried to avoid.

By 1 October the wind was too strong to attempt a crossing, and the fare was no better – the antlers and backbone of a deer which had died the previous summer, scavenged and discarded by the wolves and birds, but still of great interest to these desperate, starving humans, who managed to extract some spinal marrow which, 'although putrid, was esteemed a valuable prize'. With their lips still sore from the acrid marrow, they set to work burning the remaining bones in order to make them edible. The following day, the voyageurs refused to pick *tripe de roche*, 'choosing to go entirely without eating, than to make any exertion'. A snowstorm lasted all that night and the following morning. One man who stands out at this time is the redoubtable Hepburn, one of the true heroes of this story. With the officers too weak to collect more *tripe de roche* and the voyageurs refusing, Hepburn came to the rescue, and went out gathering the lichen on his own. Unfortunately, Hood, even though 'reduced to a perfect shadow', was so debilitated by the effect the stuff had on his digestive system that he could no longer tolerate it even to save his life. This cut no ice with the voyageur who stole a partridge that had been put aside for him. They had all reached the ominous stage of no longer experiencing the feeling of hunger.

They managed to cross the river on 4 October, but they were one man short. The Eskimo Junius had gone missing several days earlier, and despite searches he was never seen again. On this day, Back was sent ahead with St Germain, Solomon Belanger and Beauparlant to try to find the Indians. The crossing of the Coppermine raised the spirits of the voyageurs, but now there was no *tripe de roche* to be gathered even if they had a mind to, and the party retired without eating that night. In the morning their stiffly frozen tents and bedclothes took an age to pack before they could make a start, and it was a bedraggled, ghostly bunch of men who pulled their reluctant feet through the deep snow. Of the officers, Hood was still in the worst state, and brought up the rear with Richardson; but Credit and Vaillant, who like Hood suffered worse reactions than most to the *tripe de roche*, were going downhill fast. At noon on the 6th, with the group strung out and many out of sight of each other, Semandre made his way to the officers to report that Credit and Vaillant had come to a halt. Richardson went back for them, but he could only find Vaillant; the voyageur was too weak to rise and the Scotsman was in no condition to physically lift him. The 'stoutest men in the party' were urged to try and retrieve their fallen comrade; not only did they refuse, but wanted to drop their own baggage and set off for Fort Enterprise on their own.

It now became clear that things could not go on like this, and a council of officers was held. It was decided that the ailing Hood, together with Richardson and Hepburn, would find a suitable place to camp, while Franklin would press on to Fort Enterprise to get food and assistance. It was a decision Franklin took with reluctance:

> I was distressed beyond description at the thought of leaving them in such a dangerous situation, and for a long time combated their proposal; but they strenuously urged, that this step afforded the only chance of safety for the party, and I reluctantly acceded to it… I separated from my companions, deeply afflicted that a train of melancholy circumstances should have demanded of me the severe trial of parting from friends in such a condition, who had become endeared to me by their constant kindness, and co-operation, and a participation of numerous sufferings.[25]

Franklin himself was in not very much better shape than Hood, and his party made only four and a half miles through the snow before being obliged to camp. Even carrying the tent became too much of an effort, and it was cut up so that some strips of canvas could at least be used to cover them at night. But after a meal of fragments of burnt leather, washed down with a 'country' tea made from local herbs, they found it impossible to sleep in the freezing conditions that night.

The following morning, J P Belanger and the Iroquois Michel, who had been begging Franklin since the previous day to let them return to Richardson's camp, finally got their way. Then later the same day Perrault and Fontano were overcome with dizziness and other symptoms of exhaustion and fatigue. The rest of the men began to say they could not go on any longer. Franklin knew that to falter now would be suicide:

> I now earnestly impressed upon them the necessity of continuing our journey, as the only means of saving their own lives, as well as those of our friends at the tent; and after much entreaty, got them to set out…[26]

But it soon became clear that Perrault could not carry on, and he was sent back to the camp; while they were attending to him, Augustus carried on alone. The Italian Fontano was the next to succumb and be sent back. Now they were five: Franklin, Adam, Peltier, Benoit and Semandre.

They had been subsisting for several days on scraps of leather and country tea, with the odd 'meal' of the awful *tripe de roche* if they were lucky. Augustus had not been found, and their only hope was that he had somehow found his way back to the camp.

Finally, they staggered to the threshold of Fort Enterprise: their Grail, the hope of succour that had kept them, on the brink of starvation and collapse, from giving up and lying down to die. But when they got there, they were devastated.

There was no food; there were no Indians.

~ 6 ~

The Throne of Mercy

ALL Franklin found at Fort Enterprise was a note from Back saying that he had been here two days previously and was now out in search of the Indians:

> The whole party shed tears, not so much for our own fate, as for that of our friends in the rear, whose lives depended entirely on our sending immediate relief from this place.[1]

It must have seemed like the end. They were broken men: sick and starving, frozen, too weak to hunt. The temperature was dipping as low as –20 °F, and Franklin noted how much earlier winter had set in than when they had been here the same time last year. Then, there had been hardly any snow, the Winter River had been free of ice, and there were hundreds of deer in the vicinity; now the snow was two feet deep, the Winter River was two feet thick in ice, and few deer were to be seen.

Franklin and the other survivors were compelled to make one room of the fort their living quarters and commence chopping the rest up for firewood, though it must have crossed their minds that they were only postponing the inevitable. For sustenance, they collected bones discarded during their last stay here and even ate the parchment from the windows. The only consolation for them was the unexpected arrival of Augustus.

On 13 October, Solomon Belanger arrived at Fort Enterprise with a note from Back which did nothing to assuage their misery: so far he had been unable to find the Indians. Franklin reckoned that they must have gone to Fort Providence, and bravely but unwisely took it upon himself, despite his pitiful state, to go there too. He did not get very far. Already emaciated and suffering from swollen legs, he made painfully slow progress, and before long he broke his snowshoes in a fall and was compelled to return.

He must have been in the very depths of despair on arriving back at the freezing, desolate fort, having failed in what he probably believed was their last chance of surviving. Even so, on finding that Semandre's condition had worsened, and since both of them were now too weak to work, Franklin stayed beside the voyageur and tried to keep up his spirits:

> We perceived our strength decline every day, and every exertion to be irksome; when we were once seated the greatest effort was necessary in order to rise, and we had frequently to lift each other from our seats.[2]

Peltier was virtually the only man who could perform any manual work, and when he had hacked as much wood from the main house as he dared without causing it to collapse, he started work on the outbuildings. But even for him it was a marathon struggle to bring the wood a mere twenty yards back to their quarters. By the end of October the soup they had been making from rotting bones was making their mouths so sore that even in their desperate state they could take no more, and they resorted to boiling deer skins. When a reindeer passed close to the house they were too feeble to go after it, let alone hold a gun steady enough to fire it.

On the evening of the 29th they heard noises outside. For a moment they allowed themselves to speculate that rescue had arrived at last – but it was Richardson and Hepburn. The former was dismayed by the scene that met his eyes, and the 'wretchedness of the abode, in which we found our commanding officer',[3] while for his part, Franklin was 'shocked at beholding the emaciated countenances of the Doctor and Mr Hepburn…'[4] After waiting for over two weeks, the doctor and the seaman had decided to make for Fort Enterprise. And they had a story to tell.

✳

It may be remembered that Richardson's party originally included Hood and Hepburn. J P Belanger (not to be confused with Solomon Belanger who had gone with Back) and Michel had been sent to join them, as had Perrault and Fontano. Perrault and Fontano never made it, adding two more names to the inexorably lengthening list of fatalities.

Michel turned up at Richardson's camp reporting that Franklin had sent him back; they had, he reported, lost the track along the way, and in the confusion Belanger had gone missing. In spite of this, not only was he able to tell them that he knew of a better place to camp, he was able to take them directly to it. Only in the light of subsequent events did this sudden familiarity with the area in which he had supposedly been lost take on a more sinister mien. Michel also told them that he had left a gun and ammunition on a nearby hill (Franklin was now able to inform Richardson that Perrault had the gun when he left his party).

They moved their camp to the spot suggested by Michel – but the Iroquois then disappeared without any explanation. Hood was now worryingly sick, suffering from dizziness, impaired vision and other distressing symptoms of starvation. Michel turned up again later that day with meat, saying he had found a wolf which had been gored to death by a deer. They ate it, not suspecting in their physically and mentally debilitated state that the flesh they were consuming might not have come from a wolf at all…

Over the next few days, Michel's demeanour became increasingly surly and hostile, not to mention suspicious. Why did he want the hatchet for his forays, when the hunters only ever used knives? Why would he not let Richardson go hunting with him? And why was he so evasive when asked about his activities? It soon reached the point where he refused to hunt or help with any work around the camp.

Hood could manage no more than one or two spoonsful of *tripe de roche* because of the 'constant griping' it caused him, and barely had the strength to sit up by the fire. At night, Richardson lay close to provide his comrade with additional warmth – 'but the heat of the body was no longer sufficient to thaw the frozen rime formed by our breaths on the blankets that covered him'. Yet in spite of it all, 'We were calm to our fate, not a murmur escaped us, and we were punctual and fervent in our address to the Supreme Being'.[5]

On 20 October Richardson tottered out to gather some *tripe de roche*, leaving Hood arguing with the recalcitrant Michel. After a time, a shot was heard. There was no immediate alarm; Hepburn assumed a gun had gone off while being cleaned. But after 'a considerable time had elapsed', they heard Michel calling – Hood was dead.

At first Richardson thought it must have been suicide; the poor midshipman's lifeless body had a hole in the centre of the forehead. But when the doctor – by now deeply mistrusting of Michel – examined the young man more thoroughly, he made a significant discovery. The hole in Hood's forehead was the *exit* wound. He had been shot in the back of the head and his nightcap bore the telltale burn marks of a point-blank range discharge. Michel strenuously denied having anything to do with it. Richardson and Hepburn knew there was no other possible explanation than that Michel had murdered Hood; Michel knew that *they* knew this. But this was all unspoken, and the tension must have been almost palpable as they held a funeral service for their fallen friend.

The decision was taken to join Franklin at Fort Enterprise, and they set out on 23 October. Michel would not let Richardson and Hepburn out of his sight, and as they walked he muttered threats and expressed his hatred of white people. Richardson was convinced that the only reason he had not killed them was that he needed their navigational skills in order to reach Fort Enterprise, but it seemed highly unlikely that he would allow them to tell their story at the fort, and the closer they got to their destination the more their lives were in danger. Michel, who had almost certainly been living off human flesh, was stronger than both of them put together, and more heavily armed; they had not even the energy to flee, let alone take him on.

In the afternoon, Michel finally went off to gather some *tripe de roche*, and for the first time since Hood's death Richardson and Hepburn were able to compare notes. They had both reached the same conclusion: if they did not seize the initiative and kill Michel, they would never live to see Fort Enterprise.

Hepburn immediately said he would do it, but Richardson felt he had to shoulder the responsibility himself:

Had my own life been threatened, I could not have purchased it by such a measure; but I considered myself as intrusted also with the protection of Hepburn, a man who by his humane attentions and devotedness, had so endeared himself to me, that I felt more anxiety for his safety than for my own.[6]

When Michel returned, Richardson approached him with a pistol and shot him in the head.

It seemed they acted not a moment too soon: the Iroquois had not collected any *tripe de roche*, and they guessed that he had been preparing his weapons ready for the final attack.

Over the next few days they survived on *tripe de roche* and putrid marrow from the spine of a deer they stumbled across. Richardson was continually collapsing and somehow hauling himself back to his feet, and when they saw deer Hepburn was incapable of holding the gun and taking aim. In this miserable state they finally reached Fort Enterprise to tell their story.

*

Bedding made from deerskins, left to rot by the Indians the previous winter, was now on the menu with a soup of pounded bones. It took Franklin all day to drag no more than three skins the twenty or thirty yards to the house. On 1 November Peltier, who had been unable to eat any *tripe de roche* that day, slumped onto his bed and was later heard making a throaty, rattling sound. He died in the night. Semandre's spirits appeared to sink rapidly and visibly at this loss, and he too was gone before daybreak. It must have seemed that the Grim Reaper was spinning the agony out: picking them off one by one, slowly but surely. No one had the strength to bury them, and their bodies were moved to the far end of the house.

The next few days were perhaps the most harrowing, as with energy and life sapping inexorably away, each man did what little he could to keep going. Most of them now had grotesquely swollen limbs – Richardson had to make an incision in Adam's leg to drain off some of the fluid to relieve the pressure. Franklin was virtually unable to rise. For the first time, the desolation began to get to them and they began to bicker about trivial things, leading Hepburn to remark, 'Dear me, if we are spared to return to England, I wonder if we shall recover our understandings?'[7] It is a credit to their characters that not only did they recover their 'understandings', but that the bond between them would be stronger than ever and unbreakable.

Just over a week after the arrival of Richardson and Hepburn at Fort Enterprise, Franklin heard a loud bang, and feared that part of a house had fallen in on his comrades chopping wood.

Then Richardson came in, bringing the news: *the Indians had arrived*. All were overjoyed except Adam, who by now was in such a bad way as to be virtually senseless. Franklin estimated that he himself would have died within hours had not help arrived, and the rest of them within a few days. Franklin and Richardson in characteristic fashion 'immediately addressed thanksgiving to the throne of mercy'.[8]

Three Indians had been sent by Back, having found them at long last; for speed they carried just a small amount of dried deer's meat, fat and some tongues – but it was enough to give the Britons severe indigestion from over-indulgence:

> Dr Richardson himself repeatedly cautioned us to be moderate; but he was himself unable to practise the caution he so judiciously recommended...[9]

Adam fared better, being hand-fed because of his collapsed state of health. One young Indian was sent back to fetch more food, but in the meantime his remaining companions were particularly uncomfortable about the two dead bodies they were sharing the house with. Franklin and Richardson dragged them outside and covered them with snow, while the Indians tried to make life more comfortable by cleaning the room and making a fire:

> The Indians set about everything with an activity that amazed us. Indeed, contrasted with our emaciated figures and extreme debility, their frames appeared to us gigantic, and their strength supernatural.[10]

Over the next few days, taking care not to over-eat, they gradually began to regain strength – though their sufferings were not yet over. Adam surprised everyone with the speed with which his health and strength returned, but Franklin and Richardson were still finding digestion a painful process, and the emergency rations brought by their saviours were dwindling fast. When, after six days, there was no news from their comrade, the remaining two Indians set out for Akaitcho's camp to get more help. Thus, Franklin and the others were left without food once more – but this time 'with appetites recovered, and strongly excited by recent indulgence'. Two days later Hepburn was out chopping wood when he came across a group of Indians. With them was Benoit, one of the voyageurs who had gone with Back, bearing a note from their comrade letting them know that he was on his way to Fort Providence.

Franklin was itching to go too, and boosted by the arrival of more food they left Fort Enterprise for the last time. Although they had recovered somewhat they were far from being in robust health, and progress was slow – Richardson's swollen legs in particular hampering their speed. The Indians did everything they could to make life easier for them: cooking for them, feeding them, giving them their snowshoes, and picking them up when they fell. Franklin was saved from frostbite by the Indians rubbing warmth into his face and hands.

On 26 November 1821 they arrived at Akaitcho's camp. These were no longer the same men whom Akaitcho's people had known some months before, and their wraithlike appearance was met with silent, shocked stares. Akaitcho personally cooked a meal for them – an activity he never normally deigned to perform for himself or anyone else. Though not openly expressing it, perhaps it occurred to Franklin that guilt was at work here as much as sympathy. After a few days the whole party began to move south, and along the way they were met by Belanger. He had brought supplies from Fort Providence, together with news from the outside world. Hostilities between the Hudson's Bay Company and the North-West Company had been ended by a merger between the two rivals. Letters from home told them of Parry's voyage – and of promotions for Franklin, Back and Hood.

Another unexpected, and no doubt highly welcomed, bonus was that they were able to change their 'linen' for the first time in over three months. The goods Franklin had ordered for Akaitcho in the spring had not been sent, causing both puzzlement and embarrassment. This time, though, when they all met up again at Fort Providence a few days later, Akaitcho's attitude was markedly different to what it had been when they had last met. He made a speech exonerating Franklin from any blame, and even managed to bring some levity to the occasion, remarking, 'It is the first time white people have been indebted to the Copper Indians...'[11]

Franklin was particularly pleased that Weeks, whose lies to the Indians in the spring had caused so much damage, was here to hear this – though he makes the characteristically conciliatory observation that Weeks had probably only been acting on a 'mistaken idea that he was serving the best interest of his employers'.

The horror of the past few months was at last really over. Franklin and Richardson, accompanied by Belanger, Benoit and Augustus, bade their fond farewells and set off with sledges to recuperate at the HBC post on Moose Deer Island. Adam decided to stay with the Indians.

They arrived at Moose Deer Island in the middle of December and settled down to enjoy the hospitality of Mr McVicar, the chief trader. It was over two months before Franklin's swollen limbs returned to something like normal, and at least two more before he had recovered his 'ordinary state of body'. It was 26 May before they were ready to go, and they arrived back at York Factory on 14 July 1822. Their return to the place where it had all started must have been a poignant one; they had last been here nearly three years ago, fresh, fit and full of optimism. It must surely have seemed like a lifetime had passed by since then:

> And thus ended our long, fatiguing voyage, and disastrous travels in North America, having journeyed by water and by land (including our navigation of the Polar Sea,) five thousand, five hundred and fifty miles.[12]

Franklin would be feted a hero for having done his duty and led his handful of survivors out of a long dark tunnel into the light at the other end. But the modern mind is not nearly so inclined to leave unturned the stones that mark the exploits of celebrated historical figures.

✻

The heaviest criticism levelled at Franklin is always centred on this expedition because of the heavy loss of life. Some of the criticism seems to be motivated by political correctness: an Englishman, a representative of the wicked British Empire, wandering around in someone else's country, lives lost – Franklin is the perfect target for the revisionist historian. (It is a small but, I believe, telling point that Professor Stuart Houston in *Arctic Ordeal*[13] talks of Akaitcho's 'servant', consciously or otherwise, in a meticulously researched account, avoiding Richardson and Franklin's more accurate term, 'slave'[14] – he had been abducted from another tribe.)

The problem with this is that the image of Franklin has drifted further and further away from the factual until he has become a sort of cartoon-character buffoon, with few skills, who set out one fine morning and headed north to conquer the Arctic with a map and an extra pair of woolly socks. Criticism of either the voyageurs or the Indians is rare or even absent in these writings.

Let us look first at Pierre Berton's assessment of Franklin's 'wobbly' leadership.[15] The testimonies left by those who were impressed by his leadership qualities would make a chapter in themselves, and in fact the charge of indecisiveness directly contradicts one of the other major criticisms often levelled at this expedition – his determination to press on. This latter point is a more valid complaint, although even then it might be justly filed under The Benefit of Hindsight. For example, a crucial time for the expedition was during the journey along the Arctic coast when the decision was taken to turn back. Berton says that Franklin 'dallied', and 'wasted five days on the Kent Peninsula vainly seeking an Eskimo settlement where he hoped the expedition could winter'. Professor Houston's commentary on Richardson's journal says that Franklin promised to turn back if they did not find an eastward trend of the coast in four days, and that he broke his promise.[16]

To put Franklin's predicament into perspective, a number of points need to be borne in mind. He had seen, and been told to expect, signs of Eskimo activity all along the coastline and had every right to expect to make contact at some stage. Additionally, the expedition was caught out, as anyone might have been, by the unusually early start to winter that year. Regarding the timing of the return journey, the decision to give it four more days was taken on 15 August. On the 18th Franklin clearly states in his *Narrative* that a gale prevented them embarking; it continued until the 22nd, when they started back (not the 23rd as Berton says).

Franklin did not dally and he did not break his promise. Of course, there were several points at which he might have given up. He could have arrived in England with no lives lost – and nothing to show for his caution. It is too simplistic to judge him without regard to the historical context. It is completely misleading to extract him from the twin forces of the early nineteenth-century sense of duty *and* the even more implacable *naval* concept of duty. He would hardly have been human had he not been influenced by the reaction to Ross's premature return to England, while modern critics would no doubt have decided he simply was not 'up to it'. He might have turned back before the 15th; he might have decided the coastal journey was too risky even to consider. He might even have stayed at home and not gone to the Arctic at all…

Eleven men died altogether. Only one of them was an officer, and even his demise was not from 'natural' causes. The officers did not carry heavy burdens, like the voyageurs, and they did not have the skill to hunt, like the Indians. Franklin 'exerted himself the least', claims Berton, yet was 'the first to faint'; from 25 September he 'couldn't keep up'. George Simpson of the HBC said that Franklin 'has not the physical powers required for the labor of moderate Voyaging in this country; he must have three meals p diem, Tea is indispensible [*sic*], and with the utmost exertion he cannot walk more than *Eight* miles in one day…'[17]

Critics make it sound as though the officers treated the voyageurs almost like slaves, whereas they were simply doing the job for which they were specifically hired and paid. It was the kind of work they did on a daily basis, except now they were doing it with Franklin instead of on their normal fur trading routes. The officers were there to carry out and record scientific observations, collect specimens and, in pre-photographic days, provide an artistic record of their journey. There is absolutely no basis for claiming that Franklin 'exerted himself the least', and to make an issue of a starving man in extreme conditions fainting (the one and only time) is, frankly, fatuous. Franklin was quite open about the officers not being as physically hardy as the voyageurs. On 20 September he and Hood dropped to the back of the group because they could not go as fast as the others[18] – but they did 'keep up'.

Simpson clearly despised Franklin* (and Back, who was pestering him for more supplies). His accusation simply does not ring true of someone who had spent far more time at sea than on land since the age of fourteen. Afternoon tea was not, and to the best of my knowledge still is not, an integral part of Royal Naval tradition.

There is a good case for saying that the expedition should have consisted of a handful of men travelling light and finding their own food, but this was a brainchild of the navy, so for them to send a number of their most promising young officers on a venture new to them, but assisted and supplied by local experts, does not really seem so rash.

According to Berton, Franklin, though the expedition's leader, was 'a prisoner of the voyageurs', and goes on to state that when St Germain and Adam wanted to leave everyone else to their fate, he 'in effect made the pair captives'. Houston says Franklin owed his life to the Indian hunters, and that the voyageurs are the unsung heroes of the expedition – with St Germain being singled out as the star.

The logic of the first claim seems to be that if you, for example, go on a wildlife safari in Africa, you are your guide's prisoner. From that point it gets complicated: the officers are prisoners of the voyageurs; those two groups combine to make prisoners of the interpreters: St Germain and Adam. This latter point is true. Their hunting skills were by then a matter of life and death to the whole party and they had entered into a written agreement to stay with them. They could not be released.

The voyageurs were not 'heroes' by any accepted definition of that word. They worked incredibly hard in appalling conditions, St Germain in particular. But other qualities go towards making a hero. The voyageurs lied, pilfered and were easily demoralised. They were suspected of deliberately smashing a canoe, thereby putting lives at jeopardy; St Germain stirred up trouble with Akaitcho and was

---

* Even Berton describes his judgement as 'harsh'.

strongly suspected of persuading the Indians to provide less food in order to sabotage the expedition. If the officers had not maintained discipline the voyageurs would, on more than one occasion, have eaten all remaining food in one binge and paid for it by starving to death soon afterwards. One of these 'heroes' even stole the rapidly declining Hood's precious allowance of meat.

As for the Indians, they ultimately saved Franklin and his men – after nearly killing them. The expedition left Fort Enterprise short of food because they were let down by the Indians, and the survivors who made it back there found that the same thing had happened again. The leaving of food at Fort Enterprise was a promise repeatedly made by Akaitcho, and he failed to keep it.

Franklin and Richardson were in no doubt that Hepburn was the true hero of the story, and a case can also be made out for Back, who slogged for many miles in the same debilitated condition as everyone else in an ultimately successful attempt to get help – it is often overlooked that the Indians, who had left Franklin and the others to their fate without a second thought, only arrived at Fort Enterprise to save the day because of him. But to look for heroes and villains is a wild goose chase. There were failings on all sides. Furthermore, the one element that almost no one seems to mention, yet which I believe contributed more than anything else towards turning the venture into a disaster, was chance.

Winter arrived earlier and was more severe than anyone could have forecast. This was mentioned by Franklin and others, and is confirmed by a tree-ring study quoted by Professor Houston.[19] If this one factor alone were removed from the equation, the easier travelling and just a marginal increase in the availability of food might have made enough difference to prevent any loss of life. Added to this were the damaging feud between the Hudson's Bay Company and the North-West Company, which fate decreed should be settled only when it was too late to be of any use to the expedition; the characters of people like Weeks, who deliberately soured Franklin's relations with the Indians, and Wentzel, who failed to leave a note at Fort Enterprise telling them where to find the Indians; and all the other minor quirks of fate that dogged the expedition. It is not making excuses to say that these factors together played a major role in bringing about the suffering and deaths that blighted the enterprise.

✻

Franklin in the end possessed the physical and mental strength to survive, and he now knew what it would take to operate successfully in this environment. At a time when a twenty-first-century man might have been undergoing counselling for post-traumatic stress symptoms, Franklin was planning to go back and finish the job off.

~ 7 ~

I Am Far From Well...

COMMANDER John Franklin set foot on English soil once more in early October 1822. Eleanor Anne Porden had been writing to him while he was in the Arctic; they were chatty, whimsical letters, with news from England including several references to *Coeur de Lion*, or 'Dicky', as she referred to the lengthy poem she was writing about Richard I. He probably received most of these in the bundle handed to him at Fort Providence at the end of his ordeal. One of them said, 'The last letter, which we saw from you, you said was written on your last sheet of paper. Is that the reason we have since had no intelligence?'[1] which must have raised a wry smile.

He wrote to her while the same *Prince of Wales* that had taken him out three long years ago carried him on the return journey across the Atlantic. He was, he said, looking forward to coming home, but felt himself to be under an 'injunction of silence' regarding the expedition until handing his reports to his superiors in London. He told her about the 'Porden Islands', but overall the letter is typically restrained and decidedly free from the any hint of the romance or passion one might have expected in the circumstances, and perhaps she felt a little deflated to hear that even this honour was a 'tribute of my regard for your family'. Sadly, Eleanor's father never experienced the pleasure of seeing the family name on the map; he had been taken ill in Paris the previous month, and died three days after being brought back to England. Franklin, meanwhile, was already fretting about his next great challenge: 'I do not look with much complacency on having to execute so disagreeable a task as preparing for publication'.[2]

It seems that on finding Lord Bathurst, the Secretary of State for Colonial Affairs, away from London, Franklin made a flying visit to Lincolnshire before returning to make his official report. On his return to the capital, which would now always be 'home' when he was not travelling, he wrote to Eleanor from the Osbourne Hotel, London, during November to say that he would be calling on her the following day (though in a letter to his sister he announced his intention to 'seclude himself from all society' until his book was well underway – 'resisting all invitation of my most intimate friends'[3]). Eleanor sent him a copy of *Coeur de Lion*[*] with the apology that she knew he must be 'much more interestingly occupied'.[4]

After a number of meetings, Franklin proposed to Eleanor. It seems to have been a somewhat tense occasion, and he did not get a definite answer one way or the other. On 5 December she wrote to him before visiting her sister in Hastings, and referred to the awkward encounter between them the previous day. This letter set the tone for much of their future correspondence, and it was not auspicious:[†]

A little more reflexion on what passed yesterday has decided me however not to leave town without addressing a few words to you. Our meeting I could see was painful to you – it was exquisitely so to me. I believe we were both under the influence of strong feelings so jealously suppressed that I think it probable they might give to my manner the same unnatural coldness which they certainly did to yours. I looked several times at your countenance for a gleam which might encourage me to return to our former style of pleasant and familiar conversation, but in vain. I even fancied you parted from me with something like displeasure. I beseech you when I come back, let us if possible get into a more natural and cheerful vein, or what is to become of our 'better acquaintance'?

It has since struck me from some things you said that you seemed to fancy I had some distrust of you in some way or other. What should have given rise to this I know not. It is utterly without foundation. Did I not, as I think, properly estimate the worth of your character, did I not believe that your feelings are likely to be as

---

[*] The copy still exists and is inscribed 'Captain Franklin from his obliged friend the Author'. DPRO – DD3311/142-3.

[†] The letter was addressed to *Captain* Franklin, RN – he had received his commission as Post Captain on 21 November – 'I have arrived at the top of the tree!'

lasting as they are sincere I should perhaps not feel so strong an hesitation lest I should utter one syllable that I was not certain I should be prepared sacredly and solemnly to confirm. All I can say is, that there is no one else in all my acquaintance, who, if I am any judge of my own feelings, could have spoken to me on the subject you have done, without meeting an instant and positive denial. But I am not prepared to say more – I sometimes fear you have a little mistaken my character – or that you may find it changed – I can feel I am not quite the same in feelings or dispositions that I was four years ago.[5]

The 'subject' that Franklin had raised was clearly a proposal of marriage, though the letter reads so much more like the death-throes of a failing relationship than the first steps on the road to marriage that one could be forgiven for not making the connection. Franklin hastily wrote back to try and put the record straight (his letter is in fact marked 'midnight' and bears the same date as her letter):

My dear Miss Porden,
I thank you most sincerely for the relief your letter has given to my anxious mind, by the kind and candid explanation it contains of your sentiments respecting me. I am truly gratified by it and be assured it will be my earnest endeavour when I have the happiness of seeing you again to avoid shewing the appearance of anxiety and uncertainty which threw a shade over our last interview.

I deeply regret that any appearance of coldness on my part should have checked the familiar conversation which I had so much desired – but I trust you will attribute the shade on my countenance to the painful apprehensions I entertained as to the probability of your ultimate determination.

I could not have imagined that any distrust of me occupied your mind, after the kind expressions you used – nor, conveyed any displeasure had you not supposed it, particularly as I felt and expressed myself perfectly satisfied with the reasons you had assigned for the delay in giving an answer to my proposal.

I cannot my dear friend imagine that I have mistaken your character, certainly, I do not perceive any change in your disposition or sentiments since I had the happiness of being first known to you.

The same excellent judgement, amiable disposition and peculiar affability of manner which first [won] my admiration appear to me to mark as decisively as ever your character...

Many thanks for your good wishes respecting my book. It is a sad plague to me, and keeps my mind more on the work than it perhaps would be under other circumstances...[6]

Crossed wires, misunderstandings, feelings inadequately expressed and just as inadequately understood. Traill says that Franklin and Eleanor were 'happy in every respect save one'[7] (her fragile health) but he was being kind, as was the wont of Victorian hagiographers. In fact, later biographers have tended to the other extreme in the assertion that the pair were happy in almost no respects. This is probably also overstating the case, but there were to be more glitches like the one above, particularly on the subject of religion. Superficially, it was not a match made in heaven. He was now thirty-six years old, she twenty-five; on the face of it he was a rather serious, formal man, most comfortable outdoors, on the move, going somewhere, doing something; she was witty, playful, artistic, seemingly happiest exploring the fertile terrain of her own imagination and soul. But these are the obvious things, salient features jumping out at us from correspondence significant enough to have been preserved, or gathered from the few recorded anecdotes of witnesses. It is not at all unusual for people with quite different temperaments to form a lasting union, and we do not know anything about subtler threads of their relationship that may have bound them together. Eleanor certainly was not in danger of being left on the shelf. E M Gell* has calculated that after her father's death she had as many as ten suitors in addition to Franklin.[8] A number of them presumably shared her literary or religious outlook on life, and no doubt several had better financial prospects than a man in a profession that offered danger when in employment and half-pay at all other times. Yet still she saw something in Franklin that made her choose him above all others.

Although he could be grave, Franklin had plenty of charm, compassion, and a wry sense of humour. On social occasions he could be coaxed out of his shell, and once relaxed, happily join in the

* A descendant.

repartee, not being at all averse to dancing and singing. Eleanor's theological outlook was rather more liberal and less conventional than his, but she was nevertheless a committed Christian. In one letter she even complains – surprisingly for one with her interest in the sciences – about the claims of the geologists, who were struggling to gain acceptance of their physical evidence that the world was far older than the Bible appeared to make out.[9]

On top of all of this, there were the factors in their personalities that might be expected to throw up difficulties, no matter how compatible they were. She could express her emotions on paper, but by her own admission not nearly so well in person; Franklin could not even claim one out of the two – and this was almost certainly his very first intimate relationship with a woman. Then there was his recent ordeal, which whilst not appearing to have left any scars may have had mental or emotional consequences that he could not bring himself to admit to – or that he was not even *aware* of.

In any event, his reassuring reply achieved its aim, and her next letter was in a much lighter mode – perhaps she had, after all, made too much of his 'coldness'. She told him about her social life in Hastings, and how she would have liked to have shown him off to the ladies she had become acquainted with – despite his 'horror of new faces'.[10] The subject of her health is raised for the first time when Franklin talks of her cough and the hope that the bracing weather will 'renovate her strength'. He also takes her to task about this supposed 'horror' of his:

> I suspect my dear friend you have a little mistaken my sentiments with respect to mixing in society. Be assured no one enjoys a select circle of friends more than myself...my objection lies against the heterogeneous assemblages where forms and parade abound...
>
> At this time I feel the more averse to entering into such parties because from the circumstances which have recently occurred everyone feels himself at liberty to pay some unnecessary compliment to me...
>
> I presume the day of your return is not yet fixed. I will not however speak of its being distant lest I should again excite your smile or induce you to give me another gentle lecture. I shall only

say it will give me great happiness to see you again in Berners Street* whenever your inclination may lead you thither…[11]

He added the following postscript:

I am happy to say the book feels less irksome, though I yet have a wearying task before me. How often do I wish that I possessed your talent, very different then would be my labour.

In reply, she sent him a poem chiding him about his struggle with the pen. It began:

Heigh-ho! Alack! And well-a-day!
    Was ever wight like me distrest?
What shall I write? What can I say?
    Will this or that way read the best?

And contained the verse:

A field of snow's but one blank page,
    Bears, icebergs, buffaloes together
I'd rather all their might engage
    Than touch that one poor goose's feather.[12]

It probably made him laugh, though whether, after all he had been through, he went along with the sentiments may be doubted. One suspects that at this stage neither Eleanor nor anyone else close to him was fully aware of the true horror of his recent experiences. The poem was quickly followed by a letter that was characteristically witty, but also lengthy and revealing, which taken together with the poem probably shows how much he was on her mind:

My dear Sir,
I hope you have by this time received a fine saucy message of mine which I sent you through my sister, and that you have been duly angry in consequence. I had half a mind to have threatened you with endeavouring to pick up a second hand copy of 'the complete letter writer' for your especial use – but to speak seriously, I am aware that you have so much compelled writing on hand that when you have

* The Porden family home, off Oxford Street, London.

101

done your daily task you are glad to fling pens in the fire, and seek amusement in any other form. Nevertheless, I must confess you have a little disappointed me, for I am apt to think that persons frequently arrive at a more intimate knowledge of each other's feelings and sentiments from unrestrained epistolary intercourse, than even from the interchange of an equal number of visits. But perhaps you have not this feeling. To me the use of my pen was coeval with the power to hold it, else perhaps I might not have written such a strange cramped and unlady-like hand. My father wrote many a long, and now most precious letter to me before I was five years old, and none of our family have ever been three days from home without the communication of all that occurred on either side. I have often laughingly told that we are admirable friends to the Revenue, and I dare say that you are laughing now at the world of nothings which the Mail must often have carried to and fro in our service.

I thank you for your enquiries respecting my cough. It has been rather troublesome since I was here, and indeed I did not expect it to be otherwise. I believe it to be partly constitutional, and would have been mine under any circumstances, but it has been much augmented by over-reading aloud, which it was difficult to avoid when two invalids were almost entirely dependant on me for amusement, and by more than twelve years of nursing and anxiety*, of which I believe no one that has not lived with a paralytic person can have an idea – for one's fears or one's cares can never know a moment's respite. The highest medical authorities have continually told me, that it is nervous, and of no consequence to my general health: indeed that I know by experience, but, I am sorry to find that it is a greater annoyance to others than to myself, and that whenever I am, as now, on a visit to those who are not accustomed to the sound of it, it excites an attention which is sure to increase it. It has lately caused me some serious thoughts, and some in connexion with you, for I cannot bear the idea that it should ever become to another a source of the same uneasiness which it had

---

* She is referring to her mother and father. An unknown hand, probably a descendant, has added a footnote that her father was the invalid she had nursed for twelve years, but it is much more likely to have been her mother, who was 'paralytic' at a time when her father was still entertaining guests.

caused to my poor father. You have unsettled all my plans, and put my head in the most amiable confusion; otherwise it was my intention to have planted myself in the Spring either at Brighton or on top of any good high hill with a keen bracing air, to have turned all care resolutely out of doors, and to have tried whether I could not by a few months of amusement and relaxation have recovered the 'vulgar health and strength' with which I was once reproached...

Indeed I did not misunderstand you about society – but I wanted good naturedly to plague you a little*, and think besides that you have been a <u>little bit</u> out of humour on the subject since you came home...[13]

Her cough would be put down to nerves, the weather and a variety of other things – but the truth lay elsewhere. There would be talk of imminent recoveries, of being over the worst and other optimistic flights of fancy long after they both must have known what was wrong with her. It is possible that the doctors knew, or at least guessed, even at this early stage. Medical science may have been in its infancy, but the practitioners were not fools and her condition was depressingly common. She had consumption, now better known as TB or tuberculosis. Today she would be put on a course of antibiotics; then, the only straw to grasp for was a search for 'better air'.

She soon returned to smoggy London, where they had the chance to iron out their differences face to face. Referring to his visits to Berners Street, she says, 'I feel no objection to them and it is really the only time when we get a little quiet chat together'.[14] It appears Eleanor's sister was staying with her at this time – and certainly it would have been frowned upon for them to meet alone in her house.

On St Valentine's Day 1823, Franklin received a poem in a peculiar hand purportedly from 'The Coppermine River' – apparently Miss Greenstockings was declaring her undying love for the intrepid explorer:†

---

* But she did subsequently repeat the charge to a friend, stating that his 'extreme shyness makes him appear to his disadvantage'.
† In fact, Hepburn was, years later, to claim that Greenstockings had a child by Hood, and even that he had to prevent Back and Hood fighting a duel over her.

Spread thy canvass once more, keep the Pole Star before thee
'Tis Constancy's type and thy beacon of Glory,
By the lakes, by the mountain, the Forest, the River,
In the wilds of the North, I am thine, and forever.[15]

This is the last verse of Eleanor's poem. They were destined to be
apart from each other a great deal, and it is a poignant thought that
with the exception of this banter, neither of them ever felt able,
apparently, to commit anything approaching 'Miss Greenstockings's' ardour to paper. Franklin, after completing his term of
literary hard labour, went to Lincolnshire to spend some time with
family and friends. Eleanor's thoughts drifted back to the early days
of their courtship, and in one letter to him she reflected:

> You once asked me if I had never suspected your attachment to me
> before you sailed. I said no, and felt the next moment that I had
> answered untruly, but I was much too agitated at that moment to
> attempt an explanation. I did not suspect you till you were within a
> few days of embarkation, and then I blamed myself for not having
> withdrawn from your society, which I think I might easily have
> done. I flattered myself however that your feelings would not
> survive half your voyage to Hudson's Bay. I believe you carried a
> large share of my heart with you, for you were certainly in my head
> more than I could account for...[16]

Within a few days they were both back in London, and stumbling
upon a new threat to their harmony. Eleanor wrote:

> Our rambling chat on Friday last, strayed two or three times to
> subjects to which I knew must be felt by both in a manner that ill
> accorded with the light in which we were handling them...
> When I requested my sister to mention to you that I was
> expecting the full indulgence of my literary pursuits...I certainly
> considered that I was asking no favour, claiming no concession. My
> tastes and habits have been fully known to you from the first
> moment of our acquaintance...
> Imagine then (but I believe you will not imagine) the pain which
> your answer gave me. That you had an objection almost amounting
> to horror to anything like publication in anyone connected with
> you, that it was possible your feelings might alter but you could

pledge yourself to nothing. I have seldom received so severe a shock...[17]

Her reaction was understandable. The very reason for his getting to meet her in the first place was due to her writing; one of the first things he must have learned was that she was a published writer, and he had known for months about *Coeur de Lion*. Little is subsequently heard of this particular matter, and Franklin probably made a tactical retreat.

They were temporarily distracted from their differences by ill health on both their parts, and also the publication in early April of his book, *A Narrative of a Journey to the Shores of the Polar Sea in the years 1819, 20, 21, and 22.*[18] A review in the *Literary Gazette* said, 'This is indeed a powerfully interesting production; the personal narrative most affecting, the scientific details equally valuable and amusing...'[19] And this is a fair appraisal. Despite his own dread of being chained to the writing desk, and the reputation he has acquired for being a somewhat dull and overly formal writer (a charge perhaps deriving from, and more applicable to, his personal letters), his *Narrative*, a mammoth tome roughly twice the size of a modern 'coffee table' book, is on the whole a good read. Not everyone would be interested in the scientific observations and data, though obviously this had to be included, but much of the rest of it is fascinating both from an anthropological point of view, and simply in terms of a good old ripping yarn. He was lucky (if you could call it that) in that there was so much drama and incident on the expedition, and also that he was able to draw upon a great deal of Richardson's vivid account to make up for his own lost records. But Franklin's own personality shines through: his code of morality, his frustrations, his dry humour, his compassion.

Publication of the *Narrative* fairly soon brought him fame both at home and abroad. It rapidly went through several reprints and was still selling out a couple of years later, in 1825, when Jane Griffin was kicking herself for not buying a copy sooner. Franklin came to a dinner party at her home and told her that a new edition had sold so well that it was 'hardly to be had'.[20]

Eleanor said, 'Your book was exactly what I expected from my knowledge of you', and she spoke of her 'pride and pleasure at the esteem and admiration expressed by public voices of my country'.[21] In the same letter she mentions sending him some raspberry vinegar for a cough of his own (which seems to have been something of a recurring problem with him), and a later letter refers to her own 'recovering health'. This was the spring of 1823. She had let the family house in Berners Street and was living in nearby Upper Portland Place* with Miss Appleton, a widow who had once been Eleanor's governess and was lately the author of a number of educational books. Eleanor was also seeing Jane Griffin, the woman who would become the second Mrs Franklin, frequently at this time: 'Miss Griffin seems to have undertaken the charge of driving me out in such good earnest...she was kindness itself during our ride yesterday and I really feel so well and strong that I want nothing but a week's mild weather...'[22]

Jane herself found Eleanor in good spirits but 'much altered'.[23] While Franklin was once more in Lincolnshire, she and Miss Appleton were searching for a suitable house for after the marriage, but with little success; they did find one they fancied might be turned into a convent – but irreconcilable differences over which of them was to be Lady Abbess brought the project to a premature end. (They must have made quite a sight, as Eleanor was very short and Miss Appleton was said to be almost six feet tall.) One of her letters from this period gives just about the only brief hint that his experiences in North America had had a more lasting effect than he would like to admit: 'You have been thinking a great deal too much all the winter, and I often saw its effects when I said nothing, and I do not believe you were aware of it'.[24] He reassured her that his own physical health was restored, and also mentioned that he had told his friends of their 'intimacy' – something she had doubted to be the case.

On 16 April she wrote, 'I have often felt I do not behave towards you as I ought, and I thought you felt it too. I am not apt to form

---

* Possibly the house in Devonshire Street off Upper Portland Place, where she and Franklin lived after they were married, and which was the house where she had been born.

sudden attachments or show any warm expression of regard, but I believe my feelings are deep and lasting...'[25] She told how her father had been anxious that her determination to stay single and look after him might mean she would be left 'unprotected' after his death. He had urged her to seriously consider two or three suitors the previous summer but, said Eleanor, 'I was determined to wait your return'.

But trouble never seemed to be far below the surface in this mostly long-distance relationship. The latest, and potentially most serious, storm on the horizon was over religion: particularly their differing views on the Sabbath. He had quite strong views on what it meant to observe the Sabbath – regarding which Eleanor had gently chided him. But Franklin was an expert at riding out storms, and decided to take in his topsails: yes, there might be some difference of opinion, 'though probably not essentially'. (He was even bending his own rule by writing a letter on a Sunday.) Only later did he realise that this was not a squall but a full-blown tropical hurricane.

> If you expect a perfect conformity in our religious opinions you expect what education and habit have alike forbidden in our case, and what I consider fundamentally impossible...

Her religion, she said, was of a 'gayer nature' than his:

> I certainly do not quarrel with you for not writing on Sunday, though I should not scruple to do it in case of urgency... The more earnestly I have joined in the worship of my God, the more do I desire to shew my sense of His goodness by letting my heart expand in love and kindness towards His creatures...
>
> Pardon me if I say that I almost consider the wish of seclusion on that day as partaking of the same aberration of religious zeal which drove many of the early Christians to the deserts of Syria and Egypt. Did you pick it up in North America?[26]

Franklin wisely decided it was time to take shelter in port. He hoped, he said, that he could 'find with her a union of sentiment with respect to the practical part of our duties. We certainly differ at present on these points but I hope a more full expression of each other's opinions will produce an accordance of settlement'. No politician could have put it better. He tells her that he does not expect 'perfect conformity' of religious opinion – but qualifies that with a remark that is perhaps more revealing than it was intended to be: '…however desirable that would have been to me'.[27]

It has to be said that much of their correspondence is quite businesslike, and anyone reading it without knowing the background would be hard pressed to discern that these were two young betrothed people who due to various circumstances had spent precious little time together. She generally commences, 'Dear Sir', and he 'My dear Miss Porden'. Finally she exclaims, 'Why can't you call me by my name…? To my friends I am always Eleanor…'[28] (This had the desired effect, though ironically she continued to address her letters 'My dear Sir'!)

Franklin was in no apparent hurry to return to his fiancee. The above exchanges took place in April and May; in June we find Eleanor packing her belongings in the Berners Street house while he was staying with the Burnsides in Nottingham (brother James had married a Burnside daughter). He tells, without going into detail, of future travel plans the pair have been discussing – but not of a return to London. After hearing of recent deaths in the Burnside family, Eleanor wrote what was, in parts, probably the most intimate letter that was ever to pass between them:

> I wish I were with you now…your sorrows it is my particular privilege to share, and I feel almost defrauded of my right if you are in scenes of affliction without me. Do not scold me for saying so.[29]

She was missing him more than ever now. She had fallen out with Miss Appleton (who, being in a bad mood because of a severe bilious attack, was spoiling for a fight with anyone and everyone – she took it upon herself to banish Eleanor's maid from the house), and she was ill herself once more – which she put down to a cold. She was looking forward to seeing him but, 'I am not sure whether we have not often been more at ease in our letters than in our meetings'.[30]

By no means did all of their correspondence revolve around anguished debate about differences of opinion. Many letters are full of friendly banter and gossip about who has been where and done what. But not much more than a month before they were due to be married, Franklin for some reason passed on to Eleanor some papers and correspondence from Lady Lucy Barry who, as we have seen, appeared to have made a powerful impression on Franklin's religious outlook. Her views also made a strong impact on Eleanor:

> I am conscious that most persons would think me very imprudent in addressing this letter to you, but the simple fact is, that my conscience will not let me be at peace if I do not write it... It appears that there unhappily exists some difference in our religious opinions, and though on points, which I consider of little moment, I perceive the circumstance has given you uneasiness. You proposed that all farther discussion of the subject should wait till your return to London, and having as you know entered on the subject most unwillingly from the beginning, I should be well content to let it rest till we had more leisure for reflexion and quiet conversation, or even till after our union, when I might consider it a matter almost of absolute certainty that our opinions and habits would become in a great degree assimilated, but the remembrance of one occasion when the want of clearer explanation had nearly led to a serious misunderstanding between us, makes me feel it a duty to write this, lest you should mistake my silence for agreement in your opinions...
>
> I presume the writer [of the 'papers' he had given her] to be one whose long habits of intimacy with you, and almost maternal character may have authorized her interference on such a subject, but I feel that the fear of wounding any feelings of respect you may entertain towards her, must not prevent the expression of mine. I perceive that she is a strong Methodist, and very anxious for your conversion. Except some expressions which you occasionally let fall, and which I own startled me at the time, this circumstance would have excited no alarm, but now I conjure you in the name of all which you hold scared to answer me truly. Has she succeeded? Are you become her disciple; or does your heart revolt like mine at the prostitution of Scripture on unnecessary occasions and do you not even feel that there is one passage which approaches blasphemy...?
>
> If you are her convert, and expect me to become so, it is my duty to tell you frankly that you are mistaken. In the name of that God through whom alone I also hope for salvation, I dare to tell you that you would never succeed and that the greatest act of kindness you can perform towards me in such a case would be to bid me farewell.

In other years I might have had the hope of preserving you from that gulf on the brink of which you appear to me to be at this moment, but I feel that my health and spirits are not now equal to the contest...[31]

This is pretty strong stuff – virtually an ultimatum – and an unfortunate situation to be in on the eve of marriage. At the risk of being unfair to Eleanor, there is just a suspicion that 'the lady doth protest too much'. Did she *really* think even for a moment that there would come a time when Franklin would have to choose between Methodism and Eleanor Anne Porden? Her concerns about the extremism of his views are no doubt sincere, and some of his off-the-cuff remarks clearly seem to have taken her aback. But one wonders to what extent she is simply seeking reassurance – or even, in her sick and lonely situation, emotional attention. A more cynical and radical view would be that she was actually trying to provoke a crisis that would result in an end to their engagement, having finally realised that they were not after all compatible.

In this era divorce was almost impossible and socially disastrous. Even to break off an engagement was considered almost equally shameful; once the promise had been made it had to be kept. In a passionate exchange of letters between two young people in this situation one might expect phrases like 'I simply couldn't live without you', yet Eleanor's fear is not of a broken heart: news of their engagement, having become 'unluckily so publicly known', its termination would expose her to much 'painful and perhaps ungenerous remark'. Later in the same lengthy letter she returns to their old sparring subject, the Sabbath:

Our original difference was with regard to the observance of Sunday, respecting which you made an attack upon me which I must say was utterly unexpected after you had the opportunity of seeing so constantly what was my usual mode of passing that day, and had done so without any remark. I had intended to inform you that with your ideas on that point I do not and cannot agree...[32]

She was ready to share with him 'the lot of pleasure or of pain', and in fact she informs him of her general inclination of sacrificing her own wishes to those of others – 'but I own that I tremble at the idea of any future contest with you on either of the subjects which have become a source of doubt between us'.

Franklin quickly replied to reassure her that he was not a Methodist, and that he was 'willing to permit everyone to cherish their own sentiments';[33] he asked to call on her so that they could discuss it. They did meet the following day – and, almost unbelievably, *the subject was never raised!* After he had gone, she fired off another letter to ascertain whether he had received hers of the previous day – which he must have done, since his reply was marked 'nine o'clock' on the day in question. He did not 'enter on the subject' and she 'would not ask you as to whether you had received it, lest I should have been pressing you into the premature discussion of a question which you might wish more time to consider'. Regarding Lady Lucy Barry, Eleanor again begged Franklin to 'fly from her acquaintance':

> Do not...I beseech you, turn the Mercies of Heaven into a curse, by letting the present state of your mind induce you to adopt that dark and unsocial view of human nature – that <u>questionable</u> spirit (to use the word in Shakespeare's sense) to which I feel you are <u>somewhat</u> inclined.[34]

The following day Franklin wrote a conciliatory reply (the wording of all of these letters indicates that this crucial discussion was, incredibly, conducted solely by letter over a period of several days even though Franklin was certainly back in London by this time and residing virtually round the corner from her). He even managed to make a blessing out of a curse, speaking of his 'sincere esteem of the feelings which actuated you on the painful task of writing it'. What is more, her assessment had produced 'such a change of mind...that I have no doubt we shall be able to make some satisfactory arrangements after conversing on the subject at our next interview'.[35] Her reply winged its way across the streets of London the very same day. His note was 'perfectly satisfactory' and she hoped he did not think she was lecturing him. In case he had not guessed, she added that at present she preferred to tackle this subject by correspondence: 'I cannot talk with you on this subject yet...when you begin to question me with your keen fixed eye upon me, I feel that I am still very, very nervous…' As to the question of marriage, 'I have mused upon that subject also till I have absolutely terrified myself into stupidity'.[36]

Back came Franklin with further calming words: he is sure they agree on the essential points, and yes, he admires the zeal and goodness of Lady Barry's circle – but he does not 'assent to their doctrines'.[37]

She seemed at least *somewhat* put at ease by this, and in trying to buck his spirits she gives us another insight into what may well have been lingering repercussions of the expedition, since she refers to him complaining of no longer being interested in 'what surrounded him' – even the company of friends. He should think of it, she declared, like the corresponding exhaustion 'after the excitement of opium'. But in a letter written to an old friend on the same day she sounds less convinced about their prospects for future happiness:

> I believe I am fulfilling what would be my father's most earnest wish with regard to me… I sometimes feel as if I had made an <u>odd</u> choice and at this moment I have naturally all the dangers and perils of such a change arrayed in all their force before me, but on the other hand, I have the strongest reliance on the worth of his character, and his regard for me. I have at least proved that the latter only derived strength from time, distance and suffering…
>
> After writing so long about Coeur de Lion, I have contrived to catch a Lion's heart, have I not?[38]

Asking for an opinion on her future husband's book (the recipient was impressed), she mentions tersely, 'not that I saw a line of it till it was published'.

The storm seemed to blow over during the next couple of weeks. They began seeing more of each other, and taking 'agreeable evening walks', and Franklin thought that they were 'conversing more confidentially and unreservedly than ever'.[39]

On 22 August 1823, *The Times* announced:

> **Married:** On the 19th inst., at Marylebone Church, Capt Franklin, RN, to Eleanor Anne, youngest daughter of the late Wm. Porden Esq., of Berners-street.

Franklin in full uniform at the height of his fame, by Alfred Bock after L Haghe.

The *Bellerophon*, surrounded but undaunted at Trafalgar, with Franklin on her quarterdeck, depicted at the moment of the death of her commander Captain Cooke.

Left: Matthew Flinders, whose family had close ties with the Franklins. He may well have been a major inspiration for Franklin's naval career, and his untimely death robbed Britain of a brilliant navigator.

Right: Eleanor Anne Porden: an early, previously unpublished sketch by her sister.

John Richardson: surgeon, naturalist and lifelong friend of Franklin. A courageous and capable man.

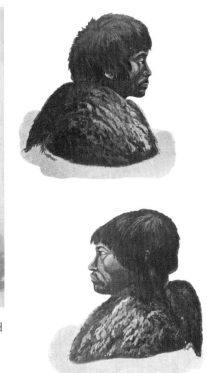

Above: Akaitcho, chief of the Coppermine Indians, and his son, as depicted by Hood. *Above right*: Eskimo interpreters Junius (top) and Augustus (below). The former went missing on Franklin's first overland expedition and was never seen again; the latter survived and played a sterling role on the second overland expedition. *Below*: The hazardous coastal canoe voyage: doubling Cape Barrow.

Top: Fort Franklin, winter base for the second overland expedition, as sketched by Back.
Middle: Richardson's *Dolphin* in danger of being crushed by ice.
Bottom: Eskimo encampment sighted on the second overland expedition.

Hobart, capital of Van Dieman's Land, as it was
when Franklin was Lieutenant-Governor. By E
Duncan/W J Huggins.

Government House, where the Franklins lived
from 1837 until their return to England in 1843.

The Arctic Council pondering over the search for Franklin, by James Scott after Stephen Pearce. The portraits are of Franklin, Fitzjames & Barrow (Snr). Standing: (L–R) Back, Parry, Bird, James Ross, Barrow (Jnr), Sabine, Hamilton, Richardson. Seated: Beafort, Beechey.

Opposite top left: A daguerreotype taken shortly before the 1845 expedition sailed and the only photographic image of Franklin. He was suffering from 'flu at the time, and is said to have hated the picture. *Opposite top right*: Franklin's memorial in Westminster Abbey, with the epitaph by Tennyson. *Opposite bottom*: The Breaking Up of the Ice. How the *Illustrated London News* envisaged the struggle to free the *Erebus* and *Terror*.

Jane Griffin at the age of twenty-two. She became Franklin's second wife fourteen years later.

H. M. S.hips *Erebus and Terror*
{Wintered in the Ice in

28 of May 1847 } Lat. 70°5' N Long. 98°.23' W

Having wintered in 1846—7 at Beechey Island
in Lat 74° 43' 28" N. Long 91°.39'.15" W After having
ascended Wellington Channel to Lat 77° and returned
by the West side of Cornwallis Island

Commander.

Sir John Franklin commanding the Expedition.
All well

WHOEVER finds this paper is requested to forward it to the Secretary of
the Admiralty, London, *with a note of the time and place at which it was
found*: or, if more convenient, to deliver it for that purpose to the British
Consul at the nearest Port.

QUINCONQUE trouvera ce papier est prié d'y marquer le tems et lieu ou
il l'aura trouvé, et de le faire parvenir au phitot au Secretaire de l'Amirauté
Britannique à Londres.

CUALQUIERA que hallare este Papel, se le suplica de enviarlo al Secretario
del Almirantazgo, en Londrés, con una nota del tiempo y del lugar en
donde se halló.

EEN ieder die dit Papier mogt vinden, wordt hiermede verzogt, om het
zelve, ten spoedigste, te willen zenden aan den Heer Minister van de
Marine der Nederlanden in 's Gravenhage, of wel aan den Secretaris der
Britsche Admiraliteit, te London, en daar by te voegen eene Nota,
inhoudende de tyd en de plaats alwaar dit Papier is gevonden geworden.

FINDEREN af dette Papiir ombedes, naar Leilighed gives, at sende
samme til Admiralitets Secretairen i London, eller noermeste Embedsmand
i Danmark, Norge, eller Sverrig. Tiden og Stoedit hvor dette er fundet
önskes venskabeligt paategnet.

WER diesen Zettel findet, wird hier-durch ersucht denselben an den
Secretair des Admiralitets in London einzusenden, mit gefälliger angabe
an welchen ort und zu welcher zeit er gefindet worden ist.

Party consisting of 2 Officers and 6 Men
left the Ships on Monday 24th May 1847

Gore Lieut
Chas. F. Des Voeux Mate

London. John Murray, Albemarl Street. 1869
F. G. Netherclift Facsim lith. 39 An Street Golden Square

The message found at Victory Point which is the only written record of
Franklin's North West Passage expedition ever found. A standard naval form
signed by Gore and Des Voeux, it is annotated around the margins at a later
date by Crozier and Fitzjames.

Eleanor's dress was embroidered at the bottom with three newly discovered (courtesy of Franklin's expedition) flowers: *Eutoca Franklin,* in the centre, was flanked by *Richardsonii* and *Hoodii** . If arrangements Eleanor referred to before their marriage went to plan, they travelled in a 'glass coach', and went on from the ceremony to spend the day in the country cottage of a friend – accompanied by Franklin's brother-in-law and three elder children.

Not even the fairytale coach could ensure that Franklin and Eleanor would live happily ever after. There are some indications that they became better friends, and the birth of a daughter was soon to bring some joy into their lives; but their religious differences did not vanish at the altar, Eleanor's health was declining.[†] The absence of a *Backii* perhaps goes some way towards confirming rumours that he did not endear himself to his fellow officers – supposedly one of the reasons why Franklin chose him for so much 'solo' work during the expedition. and the restless Franklin was to see little more of his new wife after their marriage than he had before it.

Eleanor reported to her sister a couple of months after the wedding that Franklin's kindness towards her 'increases every day'.[40] On a first trip to meet his family in Lincolnshire she was taken ill ('one of my fits of short breathing'), frightening the life out of Franklin's sister, but (contrary to some accounts) she soon recovered, and in fact enjoyed herself at the Horncastle Ball a few days later ('I almost knocked myself up with a Country Dance').[41]

Once back in London, Franklin began planning a return to North America. Parry was being sent on another sea voyage in search of the North West Passage and Franklin, who had discussed it at length with him, wanted to go by land to the mouth of the Mackenzie River – much further west than his previous expedition up the Copper-mine – and trace the coast to its north-western extremity. By now

* The absence of a *Backii* perhaps goes some way towards confirming rumours that he did not endear himself to his fellow officers – supposedly one of the reasons why Franklin chose him for so much 'solo' work during the expedition.
† It has been said that childbirth brought on Eleanor's final decline, but it is clear from her own letters that the event merely exacerbated an already worsening condition.

Franklin was under no illusions as to the size of the task, and when an article appeared in the *Quarterly Review* which implied that he thought the North West Passage could be accomplished with relative ease, he quickly wrote to Parry to set the record straight: 'I never ever fancied the undertaking would be any other than one of great labour and difficulty...'[42]

In November 1823 he wrote to Barrow with his proposal, and in December Barrow passed it on to Lord Bathurst. Approval was granted early in the New Year. Previous to this, brother Willingham had given Franklin some advice regarding Barrow at the Admiralty. It was offered in relation to promotion, while Franklin was still battling to attain the rank of Commander – but Willingham almost certainly intended it to be applied to all dealings with the Second Secretary to the Admiralty. Warning him not to rely on the man, and apparently based on 'inside information', the letter advised:

> His vanity and desire for distinction and importance will carry his patronage far beyond humble merit. He may serve a friend occasionally, but his first cares will always be himself and the Great. He is not however to be neglected as the next best thing to making a friend is not making an enemy. I believe both Lord Melville and W. Croker are liberal minded men...but as for that pretended Patron of Science, W. Barrow, again I say, beware of him. He has already sacrificed you to W. Parry and that is not the last kick he will give you if it is within his power to do it... Still be cautious and do nothing to give him offence, for his bustling speculating spirit has got him into great reputation at the Admiralty.[43]

After Christmas the Franklins moved into their new home in Devonshire Street; it was the stage on which Eleanor came into the world and from which she would depart it in a tragically short space of time. Franklin described her as 'somewhat of an invalid' at this time, and Eleanor, writing to her new sister-in-law Betsy, revealed that although she could potter about the house, she was not well enough to go out, and her cough was 'extremely troublesome' – which, considering the stoical way in which she usually referred to her symptoms, was a more significant admission than it might at first appear. In another letter[44] she revealed that she had been suffering from sickness, faintness and coughing; she rarely managed to make it downstairs before mid-day, and sometimes had to be carried back up in the evening. Her husband was working so hard ('overworking', she thought[45]) on the preparations for his forthcoming expedition that she wryly observed that she was seeing as little of him as if he were on one of his visits to his home county. Every morning saw him making the trip down to the Red Bull Wharf at Deptford to oversee the preparations.

Franklin did take off for Lincolnshire in April after receiving news of the death of his father. In one of her letters to him, Eleanor (now about seven months pregnant) joked, 'No letter to-day, you naughty boy! You don't deserve this from me', and told him gamely that she had 'two or three times been able to keep off that violent pulsation which I complained of...'[46]

But soon it was a different story:

> My cough is so troublesome I scarcely know what to say, and I have taken up my old trade of sickness again in full vigour... I am sure you must be tired of hearing of my complaints, yet if I tell the truth, I can tell no other tale...
>
> I am glad you were able to see your father...it was necessary to close up both my parents so much sooner...the countenances of both were so lovely in death...[47]

She wondered whether he would be wearing black for 'the whole old fashioned twelve months' which he had taken her to task for adhering to on the death of her own father, or the shorter term of six months which was becoming the norm.

Jane Griffin was a regular visitor to Devonshire Street, where she learned that Richardson, currently in Edinburgh, was to go with Franklin on his next expedition, and that Hepburn had written a 'curious' letter offering his thoughts on Franklin's marriage and saying that he was ready to join the new venture if called upon. Jane could not help noticing that Captain Franklin was 'a little deaf' – the result of close proximity to a broadside or two too many. She attended numerous dinner parties at the Franklins' house during the spring, and met many of the players in the Franklin story: Parry was 'tall, large, fine-looking...of commanding appearance'; Barrow of the

Admiralty, said to be humorous and obstinate, 'exhibited both propensities'; Captain Beechey was little and 'never very silent'; Richardson, who had come down in May, was a 'middle-sized' man about the same age as Franklin, 'not well dressed' (nor was his wife, apparently), 'and looks like a Scotchman as he is – he has broad and high cheek bone and wide mouth, grey eyes, and brown hair, upon the whole rather plain but…thoughtful, mild and pleasing. He has a pretty strong accent'.[48]

In spite of all the hard work, Franklin still had time to sit for a portrait by Jackson; and at a ball given by Parry he proved to be so popular with the ladies that Eleanor joked to his sister, 'I wonder they left a bit of him for me…'[49]

Baby Eleanor arrived on 3 June 1824. Franklin informed his sister that the infant was said to strongly resemble him (Franklin's friend Captain Lyon noted that it was like looking at Franklin 'through the wrong end of a telescope'), but he also bore the tidings that Eleanor the mother had been taken ill. She soon rallied, however, and on returning from another trip to Lincolnshire Franklin was joined by Richardson, who stayed at Devonshire Street while they plotted their forthcoming expedition. Eleanor told how the two explorers, taking meridian observations to test their instruments, 'had to dislodge Miss Baby from her sky parlour because the sun would not wait for them'.[50] The boats being built at Woolwich were given blue and gold trimming, she reported, and adorned with such mythological characters as Romulus and Remus.

Becoming a father seemed to suit Franklin. 'Goosey', as they often referred to the baby, took great delight in being tossed in the air and riding on his shoulders, and not only did she look like him ('strikingly' according to mother), there were other resemblances too. 'In three things she especially takes after her father', noted Eleanor, 'for she has great capabilities both of feeding and sleeping, and a great dislike to stay in the house'.[51] Eleanor herself was doing well, having almost lost her cough. The only thing that had not gone away was their impasse concerning Sundays – which was brought into sharper focus now that they were faced with setting an example to their new arrival. Writing to him from Tonbridge Wells, Eleanor said:

I feel that there is not between us on religious subjects that openness and confidence which there ought to be. You seem to think me unworthy of it, and I feel you are unjust... I cannot agree with you respecting Sunday. Last year you would have spent it like an Anchorite. If I have read my Bible right, God blessed the seventh day. What else could you do if he had cursed it? I cannot agree with you, and I could not teach a child to do...

Mild as you usually are, your looks and voice [when discussing this subject] have actually terrified me, and the first time left an impression [from] which I cannot recover...[52]

We do not really know what, if any, understanding they reached over this thorny issue and, anyhow, the problem was rapidly being taken over by other events. Arrangements for the second overland expedition, which would depart early in 1825, were well advanced – and Eleanor was now relapsing into what would prove to be the final stage of her illness.

While Franklin was engaging in a pre-Christmas round of visits in his home county, Eleanor was receiving her own visitors. One was her doctor: 'He comes and looks at me almost every day, but gives me no medicine, says I am going on very well and will not let me go out'.[53] The other visitors were the numerous applicants to join her husband's expedition. 'I wish you would come home and do your own business', she teased, 'for I feel it is very ridiculous to have all these gentlemen coming to me to try the effect of petticoat influence... I am far from well today'.[54] Leeches were tried, and Eleanor seemed to think this treatment beneficial – but a friend later remembered calling on her at this time, and Eleanor proudly showing her the silk Union flag she was making for Franklin to take on his journey. 'But I saw, what at that time her own sister had not suspected, *that she was dying*'.[55]

While they may have been putting on a brave face to the outside world, it is hard to believe they did not have at least a strong suspicion as to the cause of her illness. 'You ask me what I think', Eleanor wrote to her husband. 'The truth is, all these things are very symptomatic but it is impossible to tell yet.'[56] Over the next couple of months, Eleanor declined steadily, and in early February it seemed that the end was in sight.

Jane Griffin and a friend had called at the Franklins' house to leave some presents for Franklin to take on his expedition (a silver pencil, fur-lined gloves, a miniature edition of Shakespeare's plays, and an 'instantaneous light box').[57] But they were unable to see Eleanor, since 'Mrs Franklin was dangerously ill, having grown rapidly worse since the last day we saw her...'[58] On the eleventh of that month, her condition seemed grave enough for Franklin to sit up with her through the night, and they took the sacrament together. She asked him to read her the chapter from Corinthians used in the funeral service, and he later spoke of her collectedness: 'God's will be done', she calmly told him.[59] But then she began to show signs of improvement, and Franklin and the little group of relatives that had gathered around her harboured hopes of a recovery.

We shall never know what emotions whirled in Franklin's mind at that time. He set sail five days after the fraught scene described above. Knowing how much the trip meant to him, Eleanor expressly encouraged him to go – but nobody can have doubted that despite drawing back from the brink there could be very little time left for her. Franklin's sister noted, 'She is alive to the separation from her valued husband and consequently in her nervous state she cannot disguise it...'[60]

~ 8 ~

Fort Franklin

THE underlying principle of this latest venture was the same as for the previous one – an overland party attempting to meet up with a seaborne one in order to establish the viability of a North West Passage. Captain Frederick Beechey, who was with Franklin in the *Trent*, was despatched in HMS *Blossom* and ordered to make an eastern approach to the Passage by way of Bering Strait and, with luck, meet up with Franklin's expedition making its way along the coastline. Many painful lessons had been learned on the 1819–22 expedition, and Franklin was not going to get caught out again:

> I was well aware of the sympathy excited in the British public by the sufferings of those engaged in the former overland Expedition to the mouth of the Coppermine River, and of the humane repugnance of His Majesty's Government to expose others to that fate; but I was enabled to show satisfactorily that, in the proposed course, similar dangers were not to be apprehended…[1]

The Hudson's Bay Company had taken a 'most lively interest' in the new plan and had promised to do everything they could to help. (They had made similar noises before; the difference this time was that the HBC was one unified organisation embracing the old North-Western Company. Perhaps also they felt that to a certain extent their honour was at stake, having not exactly come out of previous disaster covered in glory.) The HBC would ensure that the necessary supplies would be deposited at places specified by Franklin, and provide any other assistance they could. (Someone else taking an interest in the expedition was one Michael Faraday, who wrote from the Royal Institution hoping that Franklin would be able to carry out some 'little experiments' on his behalf while in the Arctic.[2])

One innovation by Franklin on this occasion was the appointment of a manager to oversee, among other things, supplies of fish – a vital dietary source when other means of procuring meat became difficult. Franklin chose Peter Warren Dease of the HBC for this task.

Stores were sent out from England in advance of the main party. The fact that pemmican supplies prepared at home could not be transported to their designated locations on Franklin's route until the spring of 1825 was probably the main reason why the expedition did not set off in 1824 as originally envisaged. (The previous spring Eleanor had written to her sister, 'I am better off, however, than I expected to be, for I always looked forward to his leaving me this spring, and now I shall have his society nearly a twelve-month longer...'[3])

Another change from the last expedition was to send ahead three light boats and some of the baggage, to be looked after by Robert McVicar, and so enable the expedition to make quicker progress to its winter quarters at Great Bear Lake – a place chosen for its proximity to the Mackenzie River, their route to the coast, and its abundant supply of fish. Two larger canoes had also been sent to Penetanguishene on Lake Huron to await Franklin's arrival. One further vessel was the 'Walnut Shell', purpose-built and designed by Franklin's friend Lieutenant-Colonel Pasley of the Royal Engineers. This seems to have been a coracle-type boat, with an ash frame and covered in canvas – making it only 85lb in weight. Easy to disassemble into several portable packages, it was built with a view to overcoming some of the hold-ups caused by tricky river crossings encountered on the previous expedition:

> So secure was the little vessel, that several ladies, who had honoured the trial of the boat with their presence, fearlessly embarked in it, and were paddled across the Thames in a fresh breeze.[4]

One of these intrepid ladies may well have been Jane Griffin, who certainly joined Franklin at Woolwich for trials of the three more conventional craft, which she noted were gaily painted in order that the 'Indians may be induced to take greater care of them'.[5]

As protection against the weather, a new type of waterproof clothing was specially provided by Mr Mackintosh of Glasgow.[6]

Richardson, as we have seen, had been in on the venture from an early stage, and would again be going along in his dual capacity of doctor and naturalist. The other senior members of the party were as follows: E N Kendall, who had sailed to Arctic waters as Assistant Surveyor with Lyon the previous year and was engaged in that capacity again; Thomas Drummond went as Assistant Naturalist; Lieutenant Bushnan, who had sailed with both Ross and Parry, was the final piece of the jigsaw – but his premature death created a vacancy that 'many naval officers were desirous of fulfilling', and left Franklin with a headache.

The Admiralty wanted George Back to go, whereas Franklin's experiences on the last overland expedition had dampened his enthusiasm for a further lengthy spell in his company. Franklin felt that once it became known his former companion was the Admiralty's choice, Back would be publicly humiliated if excluded and, characteristically, put this consideration first. This is probably the only occasion where we can try and convict Franklin of being economical with the truth. He picked up a rumour from Barrow that Back believed he was not wanted, and a brief exchange of correspondence took place: Franklin could not *imagine* where Back had got this notion; he may have dragged his heels over contacting him about the vacancy – but this was because he was worried that it might get in the way of his prospects of promotion. The appointment could have been filled 'over and over again by well qualified men' but for Franklin's desire to have Back with him...

Franklin left Eleanor for the last time on 14 February 1825 and made his way to Liverpool. He later spoke of the 'awful scenes' he and other family members had to endure as they sat with Eleanor in the final stages of her illness – but 'the morning of my departure was brightened by the hope of my dear wife's recovery'.[7]

On the 16th, Franklin, Back (now a lieutenant, despite Franklin's qualms), Richardson, Kendall and Drummond, accompanied by four marines, sailed out of Liverpool on the American packet-ship *Columbia*. One can well imagine that, for Franklin, the Union flag his dying wife had completed packed among his belongings, his thoughts were elsewhere as the other explorers basked in the cheers from the watching crowd.

They were warmly welcomed in New York, where they stayed some days enjoying the hospitality and checking their instruments. Franklin found, as others have since, that despite the common language the ways of some New Yorkers differed in certain respects from those to which he was accustomed at home: 'Some of the gentlemen sat with their hats on in the boxes by the side of the ladies', he noted on a visit to the theatre. 'So much for a young country, and for liberty and independence!'[8]

Moving north, and paying a visit to Niagara Falls along the way, which Franklin thought was the 'grandest feature in nature', the group arrived at Penetanguishene on Lake Huron. Franklin had been writing to Eleanor ever since he had been on board the *Columbia*, and continued to do so from this outpost on Lake Huron. She was never to receive any of these affectionate letters.

On 22 April he started to write:

I daily remember you and our little one in our prayers, and I have no doubt that yours are offered up on our behalf… With what heartfelt pleasure I shall embrace you both on my return! Your flag is yet snug in the box, and will not be displayed till we get to a more northerly region. Mr Back and the men have arrived –

And here Franklin is interrupted from his thoughts of home when an item in a newly arrived English newspaper is brought to his attention. He makes a brief, final addition to the letter he now knows Eleanor will never see:

7.00pm the distressing intelligence of my dearest wife's death has just reached me.[9]

✳

'Poor Mrs Franklin died this evening before 12 o'clock…' her friend Jane Griffin noted in her journal. 'She expired without a struggle or a groan after having been lifted from the bed to the sofa…'[10]

Eleanor had died just over a week after Franklin had left her bedside, shortly before midnight on 22 February. His sister, Hannah, who had been with Eleanor till the end, wrote Franklin a candid and moving letter a couple of days later:

122

God in his greatest mercy has seen fit to take your dear, and suffering wife to himself yet the consolation you receive is the hope that though divided in this world you may meet in endless bliss in that which is to come...

Her sufferings were very great till within a short time of her decease, the violent restlessness and shortness of breath continued without interruption, but certainly she had not such horrifying feelings as when you saw her, nor had she ever so violent a struggle as that night we witnessed on the sofa...

When I went to see her in the morning I found a visible change in her appearance...but still her mental powers remained...

I read to her out of St Matthew's Gospel. I began it the day before, intending to go on with the New Testament, and I am sure it will afford you unspeakable pleasure to know that she approved of my doing it, begged I would read every chapter as it came.

When she was laid on the bed she felt quite drowsy and said she wished to be quiet and sleep... Her sister and I finding her so composed, went to bed. I had just got into it when we were <u>all</u> summoned to the bed <u>not</u> to catch the last breath but to see the eye close upon this world forever. After the painful struggles we had witnessed we were thankful our feelings were spared from seeing a <u>violent</u> struggle at last. Her end was <u>calmer</u>, and <u>composed</u>, the mouth and eyes closed in peace just as we got to the bed side.

I know you will rejoice to hear that the last words she heard read were those of our Blessed Redeemer, and most thankful do I feel that my voice was the last which passed his cheering words upon her ear and gave consolation to her expiring frame.[11]

A Doctor Guthrie performed a post-mortem the following day and found the left lung and part of the right in a state of advanced tuberculosis, though her heart was sound.[12]

On the 24th her death was announced in *The Times*, which also ran an article culled from a local paper. This obituary was full of praise for Eleanor both as a poet and a person, but in also mentioning Franklin and his own achievements, including his latest expedition, it made the following observation:

The separation which took place on the 14th inst., when the Captain left town on the Northern Expedition, was of so affecting a nature as to threaten the melancholic event which has unfortunately occurred.

The following day *The Times* letters column carried a riposte from a sharp-eyed reader:

Sir, – As the account given in your paper of this day makes it appear that the death of Mrs Franklin was caused by the painful separation from her husband, I beg to inform you that this is not the case.[13]

Her illness had been a long-standing one, this insider pointed out. The writer went on to give a brief sketch demonstrating that this was the culmination of a particularly painful period in Franklin's life: news of the death his brother Sir Willingham, a judge of the Supreme Court at Madras, had recently reached England; this was soon followed by the death in childbirth of Willingham's wife; two of Willingham's children and his wife's mother had also died; Franklin himself had lost his father and a brother-in-law. Thus stated the writer, who signed him- or herself 'A.M.', presumably a friend or relative of Franklin.*

This was reinforced in April by an obituary in *The Monthly Magazine*, which stated:

In the circumstances of Mrs Franklin's death there was something unusually distressing. Constitutionally delicate, it had been generally, though erroneously, understood, that the fatal event was occasioned by grief at her husband's departure, acting upon a previously debilitated frame. This, however, was not the case…[14]

Four black horses pulled Eleanor's hearse, and her pall was borne by four naval captains (though not in uniform): Buchan, Beaufort, Lyon and Beechey. Franklin's nephew acted as chief mourner and walked alone behind the hearse. She was buried at St John's Wood Chapel, Paddington. Jane Griffin took Mrs Kay, Eleanor's sister, out for an 'airing' in Regent's Park two days later, and the latter seemed glad of

---

* Captain Alexander Maconochie – who will play a role in the Franklin story later on – is a long-shot, but is said by Jane Griffin's biographer not to have met Franklin until some years later.

someone to talk to, telling Jane how appreciative Eleanor had been of her kindness. Jane Griffin's journal also notes:

> In speaking of her sister, though her tears flowed almost simultaneously, she did not scruple to allude to her faults, or at least those of her manner. She spoke of it as being harsh or hasty. I said I thought her manners had softened either by her illness or her marriage or probably by both. Mrs Kay thought so too, and observed that Captain Franklin's manners were very gentle but that sometimes she had maintained her own opinions too stoutly against him when it would have been more gainful to have yielded.[15]

We will never know how hard this hit Franklin. Fergus Fleming makes the poorly considered observation regarding Eleanor's death that 'Oddly, it was a relief to both of them'.[16] (In his account Franklin is a 'genial giant' and is furnished with an 'oxlike temperament', which would certainly have been news to every single person who has left us with a record of what this stout but below-average-height man was really like.)

That there were rumours about the health of their relationship there can be little doubt. A year earlier, when Eleanor had learned that Franklin's departure was to be delayed, she wrote to Sophia Cracroft, Franklin's niece, that it meant there would be 'time enough for us to get tired of each other according to some people's opinions but I see no sign of such an event at present...'[17] Having read all of the surviving letters that passed between them, I have no doubt that despite their differences, and the inescapable fact that on one level they do seem to have been incompatible, they nevertheless loved each other in their own ways. Perhaps their past conflicts made Eleanor's passing even harder for Franklin than it might otherwise have been – guilt over things said, remorse over things left unsaid, and his absence in her final hour. But *not* relief.

⁕

Franklin arrived at Cumberland House on 15 June 1825, having with his companions drunk to the health of baby Eleanor on her birthday three days earlier. ('Your little darling calls for you often...', his sister Hannah had added in a postscript to the above letter describing

Eleanor Ann's last hours.)[18] From there they moved on to the Methye River, where they had what was no doubt an emotional reunion with Augustus, their Eskimo interpreter the last time they had been out here. They had already covered 2800 miles, and the expedition proper was still to begin!

On 29 July they reached Fort Resolution on the Great Slave Lake, where more old friends awaited them. Keskarrah, and Humpy, Akaitcho's brother, pressed Franklin's hand to their hearts: 'How much we regret that we cannot tell you what we feel for you here!'[19] Akaitcho himself was out hunting for food for the expedition.

Before moving on to their proposed winter quarters on Great Bear Lake, Franklin took Kendall on an excursion to the sea, a journey that 'I had cherished ever since leaving England, without imparting it to my companions...'[20] Ostensibly, this was a reconnaissance mission to learn about the state of the ice, availability of provisions and so on. But Franklin also had a private, ulterior motive, for when he arrived at the coast he raised Eleanor's flag, given to him 'under the express injunction that it was not to be unfurled before the Expedition reached the sea':

> I will not attempt to describe my emotions as it expanded in the breeze – however natural, and, for the moment, irresistible, I felt that it was my duty to suppress them, and that I had no right, by an indulgence of my own sorrows, to cloud the countenances of my companions.[21]

So, while the others were animatedly celebrating their first sight of the sea, Franklin, his heart elsewhere, endeavoured to join in 'with the best grace that I could'.

✳

Winter quarters were established at an abandoned North-West Company fort on a dry sandy bank about eighty yards from the Great Bear Lake. Franklin had intended to name it Fort Reliance, but his companions outflanked him and it was at *Fort Franklin* that an establishment of thirty people began to settle into a routine of lectures, dances, scientific observations and the like – except on Sunday, which of course was a day of rest! There were five officers including Dease, their fisheries manager. Among the others were nineteen British seamen and marines, nine Canadians, and assorted Eskimos and Indian men, women and children. Some of the British seamen were raised out of illiteracy by the popular evening classes.

An insight into how hard the loss of his wife hit Franklin comes in a letter to his brother-in-law, the Reverend Wright, where he confides that even a year on from Eleanor's death:

> I have found the benefit of forcing myself to join the society of my good friends here, and even the merry making parties…at times without this effort, I should probably have indulged in sorrow to excess, and have been with difficulty aroused to fulfil other duties when they required my attention.[22]

Coming from a master of understatement, this revelation can perhaps be seen as pointing to quite a significant and long-term depression. Yet, ironically, what is also revealing about this and other letters to Wright from this period is an air of vitality and enthusiasm lacking in his letters to Eleanor. Much of his correspondence with Wright is taken up with religious matters, and one detects an almost palpable sense of his sheer delight in being able to communicate with someone on his own wavelength. He never wrote to Eleanor, as he did to Wright, 'I long to be edified by you again and to renew the discussions we were wont to have much to the entertainment of Henrietta…'[23]

Food became scarce at one point during the winter and, although things were not half as bad as in 1821/2, Franklin took some pleasure – not to mention pride – in recalling the sentiments of a self-appointed spokesman for the British tars at this juncture:

> Why, sir, we never minded about the short allowance, but were fearful of having to use the pemmican intended for next summer; we only care about the next voyage, and shall be glad when the spring comes, that we may set off…[24]

They greeted the sight of swans in early May as a welcomed harbinger of spring, and the first swallows were soon followed by the ubiquitous mosquito, 'vigorous and tormenting'. By mid-June they were ready to stretch their own wings, and when all was finally ready for the off, they marked the occasion in true sailors' fashion:

> This interesting day was closed by the consumption of a small quantity of rum, reserved for the occasion, followed by a merry dance, in which all joined in with glee…[25]

This was where Richardson and Franklin parted company. The 'Western' party was led by Franklin in the *Lion*, with a crew that included a coxswain, carpenter, bowman, marine, soldier, voyageur and Augustus the Eskimo. Back was in the *Reliance* with a similar crew, including one Robert Spinks, the same impetuous fellow who had shredded his trousers – and more besides – during a hair-raising slide down the side of a mountain on Franklin's North Pole expedition. Richardson and Kendall headed the 'Eastern' party in the *Dolphin* and *Union*. Their mission was to trace the coast between the Mackenzie and Coppermine Rivers and return by way of Great Bear Lake.

Franklin was turning in the opposite direction from the Mackenzie River delta, heading towards the Bering Strait. At the commencement of his journey he could not help thinking of the contrast between this expedition, where everything was in place and things had pretty well gone to plan, and the catalogue of calamities that had befallen him the last time he had visited this region. Franklin's sister, Hannah, had given him a Bible to take with him on this expedition and, no doubt mindful of his previous experiences, he left this in the charge of Dease in the event of his not returning – with a request that it should be sent back to England. Inside, he wrote: 'John Franklin – for his daughter Eleanor Franklin, 19th June 1826. Fort Franklin, Great Bear Lake'. (The Bible did make it back to England, and survives to this day.[26])

They reached the mouth of the river on 7 July, and it was not long before Franklin encountered a large party of Eskimos on an island. Franklin took the *Lion* into a shallow bay and approached them, gesturing that they wished to make contact. Augustus made the reasons for their visit known, pointing out the trading opportunities that would open up to them should a viable North West Passage be found. This news was received with great enthusiasm, and everything seemed to be going well. Franklin gave some gifts to the chiefs who had approached him, but the number of Eskimos in their one-man kayaks and larger oomiaks was growing by the second and, fearing the reaction when it was discovered that there were not enough gifts for all, he decided to withdraw.

Two pieces of misfortune then befell him. The *Lion* was in shallow water and became stuck in mud as they tried to manoeuvre, and then one of the *Lion*'s oars struck and overturned a kayak, and its pilot was rescued by being hauled on board. He showed his gratitude, on seeing the treasure chest that was the *Lion*'s stores, by demanding everything in sight, and communicating his discovery loudly to his companions. Soon, the boat was surrounded by eager, grabbing hands, and attempts were made to board. Back's pistol and Augustus's greatcoat soon vanished. Franklin ordered his men to prevent any Eskimos from coming alongside, and told Augustus to inform the chiefs that if they allowed the expedition to proceed and make its intended rendezvous with the *Blossom*, they would be returning with a much greater supply of gifts.

The Eskimos withdrew, but it turned out to be merely a re-grouping, and they soon returned in an even more aggressive mood. They tried to manhandle the *Lion* and *Reliance* onto the beach; two Eskimos boarded the former and grabbed Franklin's wrists while they tried to snatch a dagger and a gun. During this time, many of the Eskimos were shouting *Temya!* meaning 'peace' – but the mood was becoming rapidly uglier. The Eskimos succeeded in hauling the *Reliance* ashore. Back and his men did their best to resist, but were greatly outnumbered; one of the Canadians had his knife stolen and it was promptly used to cut the buttons from his coat. Three more Eskimos with knives surrounded Back, after his golden anchor buttons. Fortunately a young chief came to Back's rescue, driving his own men away and even trying to retrieve some of the stolen goods.

The *Lion* was at first attacked by smaller numbers and the crew succeeded in keeping the assault at bay with the butt-ends of their muskets:

> Augustus our bold and active little interpreter rushed among the crowd and harangued them on their treacherous conduct, until he was actually hoarse.[27]

But it was to no avail, and soon the *Lion*'s men found themselves in the same precarious position as those in the *Reliance*. Unable to successfully fend off such large numbers, Franklin made a tactical decision to concentrate primarily on defending their own weapons and anything essential for the future voyage. Duncan the Coxswain tied a box of astronomical instruments to his leg, 'determined they should drag him away also if they took it'. Franklin observed:

> In the whole of this unequal contest the self-possession of our men was not more conspicuous than the coolness with which the Esquimaux received the heavy blows dealt to them with the butts of the muskets.[28]

But before long weight of numbers told, and a number of Eskimos scrambled on board the *Lion*. They were after weapons and the men's shot-belts. Franklin was wrestling with three men trying to steal his weapons until Back sent his friendly young chief along to shoo away the invaders. This allowed Franklin to lend his support to the struggle at the front of the boat, which was fortunate since he was just in time to prevent marine George Wilson from discharging his musket. (What Franklin did not know then was that the Eskimo had attempted to stab Wilson, though the blade had only penetrated his clothing. The same thing happened to three other men.)

Soon another fierce battle broke out in the rear and things were looking bleak for Franklin's men; then, suddenly, the Eskimos fled en masse, taking cover behind their canoes and any other hiding place they could find on the beach.

The reason for this soon became apparent. The *Reliance* had been re-floated, and Back, 'wisely judging that this was the proper moment for active interference', had ordered his men to take aim with their muskets. The effect this had on the Eskimos gave Franklin the chance to get the *Lion* re-floated, and both boats got underway with the kayaks in pursuit. He told Augustus to announce to the Eskimos that the first man to come within range would be shot, and this put an end to the chase.

The whole episode had dragged on for several hours and it was now early evening. Many of the stolen goods would have been handed out as presents anyway, but some important items were missing, such as canteens and kettles, tents, blankets and some sails. Franklin named the place Pillage Point. It was not an auspicious beginning to the coastal voyage, but he was heartened by the professionalism of his men. He felt certain that their restraint in the face of the severest provocation had saved all their lives, since superior weaponry would have been of limited value in a close-quarters melee against such overwhelming numbers.

They were still in shallow water, however, and the boats soon became stuck once more. With great reluctance, Franklin allowed Augustus to visit the multitudinous Eskimos on shore – where he proceeded to give them a piece of his mind. The white people had come in friendship, he told them, and they had been rewarded by having their boats pillaged – even Augustus himself had been robbed. It was only because of the whites' humanity that many Eskimo lives had not been lost to their powerful guns. His own tribe had profited greatly from friendly trading with white people – but now they had jeopardised their own chances by their greed and violence. This little interpreter, surrounded by hundreds of recently hostile country-men, told them that had one white man fallen, he would have been the first to have avenged his death with his own gun. 'Such a speech delivered in a circle of armed men', Franklin said, 'was a remarkable instance of his personal courage.' Franklin tested their reported remorse by asking for the return of a large kettle, a tent and some shoes – and this was duly effected.

They managed to get the boats underway again at 1.30am, but a gale soon had them making for shore. In the morning Eskimos approached by canoe, and the boats were hurriedly launched – Franklin, still suspicious, believed he could repulse any attack as long as they were afloat. He was right to be cautious. It was later discovered that the Eskimos had intended to kill them all except Augustus during the first encounter, and this latest 'friendly' overture was a ploy to lure them into a massacre – this time not even Augustus, whom they considered too much under the thrall of the white man, was to be spared.

Happily, not all of their encounters followed this sinister pattern. Further along the coast they encountered ice in sufficient quantity to drive them back on shore, and here they met a different group of native people who were welcoming and friendly. In fact this tribe knew the group further east only too well, having had their own difficulties with them. If Franklin were to come back this way they promised that some of their young men would escort them through the danger zone if necessary. There were numerous other sightings and meetings with friendly Eskimos further on – exactly what Franklin had hoped for in vain during his hour of need some years previously.

Ice continued to be a hindrance from this point on, and progress was tediously faltering. Franklin was very familiar with the phenomenon of the sun never setting at this mid-year season in such northerly latitudes, but many of his men were not and he was amused by the effect it had on the British sailors, who, 'when not employed, a question as to the time of day never failed to puzzle them'. But as July ended the sun fell below the horizon for the first time, and with it their mood grew darker, for it was the first unmistakable sign that approaching winter would soon put a stop to their frustratingly stop-start journey. In early August things got a little better. The sight of seals and a 'black whale' was a good sign, but by now the *Lion* was taking in more water than could be baled, and there was a further delay while repairs were effected. Franklin bestowed one landmark with the name 'Point Griffin', the surname of Eleanor's friend and his future wife, during this time.

The weather steadily deteriorated, with gales, rain, fog and the wilting flowers sending them a clear message:

> These symptoms of decay could not fail painfully to remind us that the termination of our operations was fast approaching; and often, at the time, did everyone express a wish that we had some decked vessel, in which the provisions could be secured from the injury of salt water, and the crew sheltered when they required rest...[29]

Thick fog now trapped them on what became known as 'Foggy Island'. Up until now they had been confident of attaining their goal of Icy Cape, but after two weeks stuck on Foggy Island Franklin had some serious thinking to do:

> ...it was with no ordinary pain that I could now bring myself even to think about relinquishing the object of my ambition, and of

disappointing the flattering confidence that had been reposed in my exertions. But I had higher duties to perform than the gratification of my own feelings; and a mature consideration of all the above matters forced me to the conclusion, that we had reached that point beyond which perseverance would be foolishness, and our best efforts must be fruitless...[30]

He noted that the freezing water was causing the legs to swell among many of the men who had to launch the boats. It was almost five years to the day since Franklin had reached Point Turnagain on the previous expedition, and not until later did he learn that only about 160 miles away, impeded by ice, was a barge from Beechey's HMS *Blossom*. His loyal men made it clear they were behind him whatever he decided, and Franklin afterwards ruefully reflected that, had he known of the proximity of the boat, 'no difficulties, dangers, or discouraging circumstances, should have prevailed me to return...'[31]

Atrocious weather kept them at Foggy Island some days further, a place they had become heartily sick of. It was on the return journey that they met Eskimos from the group that had attacked them, and from whom they received confirmation about the murderous intent of their fellows. Other Eskimos gave them disconcerting information about Richardson's party – which had apparently also been attacked by rapacious natives. They had not long to worry about this before they were once more placed in fear for their own safety. Two young Eskimos scurried to their camp telling of a large party of Indians closing rapidly on them from the mountains, intent on annihilating them. They had European guns as well as bows and arrows. Somehow, their saviours had discovered that the Indians were prepared to hound them all the way back to the Mackenzie River – but thought that if Franklin's people set off in their boats immediately they could outpace them. Saving Augustus was the young men's main preoccupation, and they gave him instructions on the best route to take. The matter-of-fact way in which they accepted their reward for this intelligence proved to Franklin that they were acting out of a desire to save life rather than for material gain.

They embarked as quickly as they could, and reached Pillage Point near the entrance to the Mackenzie, and scene of their last close encounter, without mishap on 30 August. Three weeks later they were relieved to be re-united with Richardson at Fort Franklin – he having arrived back some two weeks earlier. Franklin had journeyed just over 2000 miles in three months – 610 of them through uncharted territory.

Richardson related a story from his trip eastwards towards the Coppermine River that must have sounded very familiar to Franklin. They had encountered a large group of Eskimos, there was some friendly trading, and then the Eskimos became bolder and more aggressive, until they were attempting to drag the boats ashore. But this group was neither as hostile nor as determined as those encountered by Franklin. They took heed of Richardson's protests and backed off, although they pursued the *Dolphin* and *Union* in their canoes for quite some distance, pilfering and pestering, even optimistically inviting Richardson to camp with them ashore.

After a time the *Union* grounded, and the Eskimos swarmed around her and tried to pull her ashore. As the situation deteriorated, Richardson gave Kendall permission to open fire if necessary. The sight of raised muskets from the crews of both boats was enough to scatter the Eskimos; not a shot was fired, and Richardson, like Franklin, praised his men for their discipline and restraint. They were not hampered by fog like the western party, but saw enough ice to persuade them that it was unlikely a ship would be able to force a passage along the stretch of coast they had explored.

On 7 August Richardson had entered 'George the Fourth's Coronation Gulf', making the physical connection between the parts of the coast charted on the last expedition and this present one. They had, Richardson pointed out, 'the honour of completing a portion of the north-west passage, for which the reward of five thousand pounds was established by his Majesty's Order in Council…'[32] But he went on to point out that as the discovery had been made from west to east, and in small boats rather than ships, there was no question of them laying claim to the money. Richardson's men were in the best of health, and for this he praised Franklin's planning of the overall operation.

Along the way, Richardson named a bay after Franklin, adding this testimony to his commander:

In bestowing the name of Franklin on this remarkable bay, I paid an appropriate compliment to the officer, under whose orders and by whose arrangements the delineation of all that is known of the northern coast of the American continent has been effected; with the exception of the parts in the vicinity of Icy Cape discovered by Captain Beechey. It would not be proper, nor is it my intention, to descant on the professional merits of my superior officer; but after having served under Captain Franklin for nearly seven years, in two successful voyages of discovery, I trust I may be allowed to say, that however high his brother officers may rate his courage and talents, either in the ordinary line of his professional duty, or in the field of discovery, the hold he acquires upon the affections of those under his command, by a continued series of the most conciliating attentions to their feelings, and an uniform [sic] and unremitting regard to their best interests, is not less conspicuous. I feel that the sentiments of my friends and companions, Captain Back and Lieutenant Kendall, are in unison with my own, when I affirm, that gratitude and attachment to our late commanding officer will animate our breasts to the latest period of our lives.[33]

*

Food supplies ran low again during the winter stay at Fort Franklin (the Dog-rib Indians who had been hired to hunt had brought in only three deer during the whole time the expedition had been away) but not dangerously so. Christmas 1826 was brightened by Back and Kendall, who put on a comic show featuring cardboard figures behind an illuminated screen, script courtesy of Back. This entertainment was repeated over three nights by popular demand. The New Year was seen in with a dance, and on 4 January Kendall provided a distraction of a slightly more scientific nature. The temperature that day was recorded at −52°, and Kendall fashioned a pistol bullet from frozen mercury and fired it at a door from six paces. Franklin reported that a small portion penetrated to a depth of an eighth of an inch.

They left Fort Franklin for the last time on the morning of 19 February – all except Back, that is, whose lot seems always to have been sent on a lone mission whenever possible. He was to take a number of men to York Factory, and from there board an HBC ship for England. Franklin and the rest of the men headed south, and at Fort Resolution they met up with McVicar, who had cared for Franklin and Richardson during their period of convalescence some years earlier. On 24 June they bid the admirable little Augustus a tearful farewell, knowing there was little likelihood of them meeting again.

The only fatalities on this expedition occurred on the journey to York Factory, where one man succumbed to consumption and another drowned trying to save a boat at a waterfall.

※

Franklin and Richardson arrived in London on 29 September 1827 and went directly to place their charts and drawings before the Lord High Admiral, where Franklin received orders to write up and publish his narrative of the journey.

The expedition had bolstered Franklin's opinion that the North West Passage could be achieved by ship, and he recommended that a further attempt be made to connect Point Turnagain with Parry's progress in the region of Prince Regent Inlet and the Fury and Hecla Strait. A quick glance at a modern map soon robs the modern observer of Franklin's optimism in this respect – and it was to be many years before he got a chance to put his theories to the test. Captain Alexander Maconochie – who will play a role in the Franklin story later on – is a long-shot, but is said by Jane Griffin's biographer not to have met Franklin until some years later.

~ 9 ~

A Woman of Most Excellent Sense

JANE Griffin was born in 1792. Genealogical records indicate that the birth occurred in Bedford Place, London;[1] she was one of four children, and her parents – of Huguenot stock according to her biographer – had married the year Franklin was born. She was still living in the same house with her father – quite close to Franklin – when she first met him, and had moved in similar circles to the Franklins.

We have already seen that she and Franklin knew each other through her friendship with Eleanor, and one or two writers have made the unkind and fanciful insinuation that there was something 'going on' between them before the latter's death, and with the state of the Franklins' marriage in general. After Eleanor's death the D'Israelis passed on to Jane some 'idle and contradictory gossip' they had heard about Franklin's parting from his wife. 'My voice trembled with agitation not unmixed with anger while I replied to all this unfeeling nonsense.'[2] There is absolutely no evidence for any impropriety between Franklin and Jane Griffin and, although stranger things have happened, it would have been as much out of character for Franklin as anything could possibly be. They were certainly friends; when Eleanor was too ill to attend social functions – even in her own house – Franklin, sometimes uncomfortable among strangers, often seemed to gravitate toward Jane, a known and friendly face: 'As soon as Captain Franklin saw Fanny and me he gave each an arm, and seemed to have us under his protection the greater part of the evening which really must have made us an object of envy'.[3] More than likely *he* considered himself under *their* protection!

Jane was certainly a different kettle of fish to Eleanor. Some years older, she took an almost maternal interest in the welfare of her ailing friend; after the funeral, Eleanor's sister

> took the opportunity she said of telling me that her sister had a day or two before her death spoken of us both, but particularly of me, and of our great and uniform kindness to her... I replied that I had always felt a great regard for her sister and had placed great value on our intimacy... 'Yes' replied Mrs Kay 'You are very kind – it's your manner – you are kind to me.'[4]

Miss Griffin liked to travel and to write, being prolific in both areas and frequently combining the two. She did not write for publication, like Eleanor; she wrote letters, and recorded her experiences at great length in her private journals. Everywhere she went she noted, with travel-guide attention to detail, the topography, culture and architecture of the places she visited, sometimes adding rough ink sketches. Eleanor had travelled abroad too – and may have continued to do so if her health had permitted – but Jane, although by no means Eleanor's intellectual inferior, was more of a 'doer' than a dreamer, and in that sense temperamentally more like Franklin. She took an interest in the world and in some small ways contributed her ideas to it. Undoubtedly she might have made a mark in the world in her own right had she had a mind to, but she had no material ambitions, and was happy to be the woman behind a successful husband. She was highly intelligent and a shrewder judge of human nature than Franklin, and he would come to benefit from her counsel in a way that perhaps would not have been possible with Eleanor.

She, too, was a devout Christian, and there were none of the differences of opinion between them of the kind that had plagued Franklin's previous relationship. In later years she began to compile a 'Commonplace Book'[5] in which she noted down her sincerely pious insights and reflections. She decided, for example, to introduce a 'mid-day devotion', since 'The devotion which is exercised only at the beginning and close of the day will increasingly become weaker and weaker as it struggles against the manifold trials of Domestic life'. There are thoughts on 'How to Deal with Doubts' and epithets like, 'This world was not meant for delay', and '<u>All</u> sin must be subdued'. One phrase that she perhaps derived strength from in the years to come was 'In the higher interests, nothing is worth thinking of that is not difficult'.

Sophia Cracroft, Franklin's niece and Jane's constant companion in later life, penned an assessment of Jane's qualities after her death as an aide-memoire for a future biography. The list included: Clearness of perception; Strong reasoning powers; Tenacity of purpose; Power of sympathy; Intense longing for truth; Desire for Knowledge; She could sit in judgement upon herself, as if she were another being; Love of perfection and seeking after it.[6]

Although still single at the age of thirty-five, this was not down to any lack of interest on the part of the male population of London and further afield. She was said to be dark, blue eyed and very attractive, and the portrait of her made some eleven years earlier seems to bear this latter view out. Franklin biographer G F Lamb[7] quotes an unnamed female as describing Jane, at the age of almost forty, as 'the most beautiful woman I have ever seen'. By the time Franklin became 'available', it is quite possible that Jane was beginning to feel that she was running out of both time and options.

She had received numerous proposals, and almost certainly broke a number of hearts – her own included – during the previous fifteen years or so. At one time she had been particularly keen on Peter Mark Roget, later of *Thesaurus* fame. It sometimes seemed that she encouraged (or at least was slow in *discouraging*) the attentions of men whom she had no real intention of marrying, as if she were unable to deny herself the 'thrill of the chase' and the boost to her conventionally well-suppressed ego. There was no conscious strategy at work – she was not nearly so callous; sometimes she seemed to be looking for excuses as to why she could not finally commit herself, and it is quite possible that in one or two instances it was only her own fear of making the great leap into the unknown that prevented her from accepting. Certainly there were those among her family and friends who began to grow impatient with her prevarication.

There was one period during the summer of 1824 which, through her journals, allow us a peek at – and perhaps represents a microcosm of – the state of her love life. It was beginning to seem to her that either everyone she was interested in was getting married, or she was not interested in *them*. On 5 June she was surprised to receive a letter from a Mr Benson, from whom she had till now 'seen no signs of a heartfelt affection but only an excited imagination, venting itself in this as in a hundred other instances, in ardent but careless language…'[8] Then later the same day she learned that one General Harris was to be wed, the shock of which left her 'turning red and pale by turns':

> It seemed to me as if my destiny was closing in, tho it only rendered that event impossible which was before highly improbable…tho the habit of giving reins to my imagination had sometimes made even this thought find a place in my reveries…[9]

She seemed to think that on hearing this news, 'if I felt emotion or disappointment, no one could notice it' which, considering the earlier admission of her passable imitation of a traffic light, seems optimistic to say the least.

As if that were not enough, only days later Jane was visited by friends, Mr and Mrs Gilbert, who brought her news of another fish that had slipped through the net; the manner in which the news was conveyed indicates that this was someone for whom she must at one time have had high hopes. Mrs Gilbert could barely bring herself to look at Jane, and hesitated before uttering the name 'Dr Keane':

> She revealed that 'that he was going to – to – (looking down all the time very seriously) going to – to bring home a lady'… 'Indeed!' I said, and tho I felt a little pale I believe I behaved well.[10]

Henry Keane was a Cambridge don whom Jane had known for several years and regarding whose financial prospects her father harboured grave reservations. Later, as they were leaving, Mr Gilbert summed up Jane's current lot in life succinctly, if perhaps rather cruelly: 'Ah Jane! When we won't have when we will, when we will have we shall have nay!'[11] for which impertinence he received a slap on the cheek, 'and we parted laughing – but I felt no inclination for laughing when they had gone – on the contrary, I felt a little sick, the shock was so unprepared and unlooked for'. Dr Keane, it appears, had proposed to her more than once in the past, and she had harboured hopes of him trying one more time. Now it was too late, and she was left only with the unwanted attentions of Mr Benson, who, after contriving to snatch a minute alone with her, pleaded to know: 'was what he had at heart impossible – quite impossible? "Yes indeed – impossible",' came the response.

Little wonder that Jane reflected, 'How quickly in a few short days have subjects of emotion crowded upon me'.

Unlike Franklin's courtship of Eleanor, there is very little record of what led up to his proposal of marriage to Jane. He called at the Griffin residence in Bedford Place the day after arriving in London – but Jane and her father were in Scandinavia at the time. Franklin's card awaited them on their return. They threw a party for him a couple of months after his homecoming from the successful expedition, where he sat at Jane's side and argued with her brother-in-law about the viability of the North West Passage.

One assumes that they were able to see enough of each other to obviate the necessity of copious letter writing*. It is not hard to envisage a scenario of Franklin and Jane confiding in each other over the death of his wife and her friend, and growing closer in the process; and of Jane helping to ease him back into their social circle by providing her arm and her moral support.

In any event, at the beginning of July 1828, less than a year after his return from the Arctic, and in his own forty-second year, Franklin sent to Mr Griffin what was possibly his most long-winded and convoluted letter of all, which begins:

> From the very kind manner in which you received the first intimation of my desire to address your daughter Miss Jane...I feel convinced that it will be a source of true gratification for you to learn as it has been to me to feel, that the various interchanges of ideas and sentiments which have recently taken place between Miss Jane and myself have assured us not only of our entertaining the warmest affection for each other but likewise that there exists between us the closest congeniality of mind, thought, and feeling, and I have further an extreme pleasure in communicating to you

* Though it is worth bearing in mind that Sophia Cracroft, Franklin's niece and soon to become Jane's companion, is widely believed to have destroyed certain 'sensitive' documents after Jane's death.

that if it would meet with your approbation, we propose to cement these affections by uniting in matrimony…'[12]

It was an age in which a formal letter to the prospective bride's father was the way things were done. Later that month, Franklin was able to inform Richardson that the wedding plans were finally being drawn up.

Jane and her father had planned a trip to Europe, and Franklin's original scheme, outlined in the letter, was for him to go out and meet up with them in St Petersburg, which 'seems to be the only city where we can with certainty meet and where there is likewise a certainty of finding a minister of our Established Church…'[13] But for some reason this plan never came to fruition. They did meet up in St Petersburg in September, travelling there separately on Jane's insistence: among other reasons, she felt a 'strong sense of impropriety in the arrangement' of going together.

Once there, Franklin let it be known that he would like to meet the Empress Mother. She had both heard of and taken an interest in Franklin's exploits, and informed him that she would depart from the usual etiquette attendant to such matters and invite Franklin to dine with her. They conversed in French, and Franklin noted in his journal that she had 'followed every step of my proceedings while employed on my recent discoveries with the greatest interest'.[14] She was particularly moved by the account of his first overland expedition, and found it hard to believe he had been prepared to expose himself to the risks a second time. It also transpired that she was an admirer of Richardson, and had no qualms about his shooting of Michel: 'Had he not done so, all your lives would have been sacrificed', was the authoritative royal view.

Soon after their return to England, the wedding took place on 5 November in Stanmore, Middlesex: now part of the urban sprawl of Greater London, then what Franklin called a 'most picturesque' village.

Just prior to the marriage, Jane had written to Franklin:

Whenever I think I am imposed upon my spirit rises, and I struggle harder to resist than is perhaps consistent with the meek and resigned spirit which men endeavour to teach us is not only becoming but obligatory, and which we poor women, endowed with acute sensibilities though with less energy and much less power than men, often find to be our surest and safest way to happiness…

She felt it was his duty:

as my beloved and most honoured husband, to control even this disposition when you think it improperly excited…

If you are a prudent man you will put this letter by and turn it to account on some future occasion when I am in a rebellious mood; and upon consideration I think you ought to feel infinitely obliged to me for furnishing you with so valuable document.[15]

It is doubtful whether Franklin ever felt a need to brandish the letter before her in the way that she perhaps only half jokingly recommended. In fact, it was for her indomitable spirit that Jane would perhaps be best remembered – particularly during the final episode of her husband's life.

The newlyweds emerged from the old church onto a path strewn with flowers by well-wishers, and made their way to the wedding breakfast (weddings were commonly quite early morning affairs then) at the home of Jane's sister and brother-in-law. They sent little Eleanor all the ornaments from the wedding cake. She was staying with Franklin's sister Isabella Cracroft, and in the accompanying letter he pointed out that Jane should henceforth be referred to as Eleanor's 'mamma' [sic] and should be made fully aware of the 'change which has transformed her dear friend Miss Jane Griffin into the more interesting relationship of a Parent'. Jane herself added to her new husband's letter the worry that she must appear to Eleanor 'rather a supernumary and obtrusive mama' and did not expect that 'she can feel reconciled to admit me all at once to so high a honor [sic]'.[16] Two weeks after the ceremony, the newlyweds, accompanied by two cousins and a travelling servant,* set out from Bedford Place at 4pm on the first leg of their honeymoon, arriving 'by moonlight at the Mitre Inn at Chatham', where they planned to meet

---

* Even now they were married it was not the done thing to honeymoon alone.

up with Richardson, who was by now Surveyor at the naval hospital there. They were entertained by Richardson and his wife the following day. Shortly afterwards they crossed the Channel and made their way to Paris, where Franklin was again feted by the rich and the royal. They visited Amiens, and then at Boulogne there was a poignant meeting with old Captain (now Admiral) Walker, under whom Franklin served for eight years in the *Bedford*. 'He is not in affluent circumstances', Jane noted in her journal, 'and is probably living in Boulogne on this account…'[17]

✳

Returning to England, Franklin's mind turned to the future. He had had a plan for another Arctic venture – to chart the last remaining unknown stretches of the North American coastline – peremptorily rejected by the Admiralty, and he himself had turned down a quite lucrative offer of employment in Australia. He was beginning to reap the accolades and rewards of his services to his country and to exploration: during this period he was presented with a gold medal by the Geographical Society of Paris, awarded (with Parry) an honorary degree by Oxford University, and became 'Sir' John in the spring of 1829. But he was still a sailor at heart, and the main reason why he had turned down other employment was a fear that such a move would jeopardise his chances of pacing the quarterdeck of one of His Majesty's ships once more.

The opportunity to return to his favourite domain was not long in coming. For some time, Greek Christians had been revolting against Moslem Turkish rule. Although Britain supported the Greek cause, it went to great lengths to avoid armed intervention and also to try to restrain the Russians, who for strategic reasons were keen to gain a foothold in the region. For several years the Greeks fought on with the moral but not the military support of a number of European countries. When Egypt joined forces with Turkey, Russia could be held back no longer, and France and Britain agreed to use force if political pressure on the Turks were ineffective. In 1827, after Turkey had broken the terms of a truce, ships from the British, French and Russian navies annihilated the Turkish and Egyptian naval forces at the battle of Navarino. Russia declared war on Turkey, and the French sent troops to the region. Turkey was forced to back down, and ultimately, in 1830, accede to Greek independence. Sadly, this in no way heralded an outbreak of peace in the country. Different Greek factions which had already been at each other's throats now had the opportunity to settle their differences, and it was for this reason as much as any further threat from Turkey that the three European powers would remain on hand to endeavour to police the arrangement. In August 1830 Franklin was given command of a 28-gun frigate*, HMS *Rainbow*, bound for the Mediterranean. The timing, at least, of this appointment was something of a surprise to him – he told his sister he had thought he might be sent to the Mediterranean in the spring of the following year. All of his friends were congratulating him: the station to which he was bound was an 'object of ambition with the men of most rank and influence'.

Despite being back in his natural element, the parting from Jane and five year-old Eleanor, who travelled to Portsmouth to see him off, was not an easy one:

> I took leave of my dearest wife and child...before daylight, having first taken dear Ella to supply my place in her Mama's bed. They were both much affected at the separation and so indeed was I...[18]

Jane would have liked to have sailed with him, an idea 'which', she commented, 'is indeed contrary to the rules of the service, tho' it might have been winked at...'[19] This was not possible, and she planned instead to go out to meet her husband within a few months, but little Eleanor would not be able to make the trip, and perhaps knew it. When Franklin tore himself away to join his ship she was 'in a flood of tears'.

He had not been gone long before Jane was writing to him with some career advice. She rightly pointed out that once his Mediterranean duties came to an end it might be two or three years before he got another ship, so: 'why not strive to resume your chieftanship in your own particular department?'[20] She was, of

---

* The *Rainbow* is usually referred to as 26 guns, but in a letter to his sister (29 Aug 1830) Franklin says 28, and I believe this a more customary configuration for a frigate.

course, referring to Arctic exploration. Franklin did indeed write to Barrow reiterating his belief that the North West Passage – 'the last geographical problem that remains to be solved, for we Northern folks'[21] – could be achieved. Nothing, he said, would make him happier than to be given a crack at completing the survey of the coast on his return from his present station. But that would have to wait for now.

'I never witnessed a prospect more striking or imposing than Malta represents',[22] Franklin declared on his arrival after a rough twenty-one day passage. By March 1831 Jane was hankering to come out to him. Despite the disturbed state of the continent and the probability of war, 'I had much rather be in the midst of it…Malta must be a safe place for me… I shall not be in your way…and I am sure you will never find me any hindrance…'[23] It was several months before she got her way, and even when she arrived she was able to get within shouting distance of him only because of strict quarantine regulations in force at the time: the legacy of a devastating visitation of the plague upon Malta some years earlier. They were finally able to spend some time together in Corfu, after which Jane embarked upon an extensive tour of the Mediterranean, which included visits to Egypt (she sailed to Alexandria on the American warship *Concord*, under the command of, and befriended by, the same Captain Perry who would go on to make his name by 'persuading' Japan to open her ports to the West) and Turkey. Franklin, writing to sister Betsey, talked of Jane's 'favourite pursuit of travelling', but stressed that it was a genuine urge to learn more about the world, rather than an 'empty desire' to boast of the places she had been to. He also gave a brief pen-picture of his second wife:

> She possesses simplicity and frankness of mind, a very benevolent heart…she is timid and often reserved which is frequently mistaken for pride – of which in its worst sense she has none, though she highly respects the advantage of birth…[24]

There was much more in this vein; one would have to search hard to find evidence of Franklin eulogising in such terms about his first wife.

Franklin's duties took him to Malta, Corfu, Nauplia, and finally

Patras. By this time the euphoria of independence had given way to internecine squabbling deteriorating into virtual anarchy. In 1832 a British, French and Russian naval presence was at Patras because of fears of an attack by a disaffected group from the north of the country, and when he got there Franklin also found himself dealing with various simmering disputes. The most serious of these was the threat by renegade General Zavellas (with a sizeable force at his disposal) who wrote to Franklin threatening to totally destroy the town if the new governor was not sent away immediately. Franklin's diplomatic reply pointed out that 'the departure of the governor does not depend on us...'[25] But the small contingent of British and French sailors was in no position to take on Zavellas's soldiers, and in order to avoid bloodshed he was allowed to take over the reins in Patras.

While the English and French were enjoying a rare outbreak of harmony in their approach to the succession of politically tricky situations, the attitude of the Russians was driving Franklin to distraction. He rarely had a bad word to say about anyone, but after enduring nocturnal spying activities against the *Rainbow* and a French ship, followed by a disingenuously inadequate explanation and subsequent fabricated counter-accusations against the *Rainbow*, his patience was wearing thin. In a letter to Admiral Hotham, in overall command of the British naval presence, Franklin wrote of the Russian admiral Ricord, 'I shall really rejoice if the means be afforded of exposing his conduct to the world...'[26]

Franklin's activities were not confined to the Greek troubles, as an account that did not surface until after his death demonstrates. Towards the end of his Mediterranean service, the United States consul in 'Beyroot' was involved in a dispute with the Syrian authorities over the treatment of a missionary, Reverend Bird. He had been arrested and 'most cruelly used by the rough soldiery' after being accused of throwing a stone at a Syrian soldier caught robbing his orchard. (It had actually been Bird's servant who threw the stone.) Hardly an incident of international diplomatic proportions, but Chasseaud, the consul, found himself getting nowhere with the Syrian authorities. Then one day a British frigate hove into sight, and ashore came Captain Sir John Franklin, RN, declaring: 'Mr

Chasseaud, I have heard that an American citizen has been insulted, and I have come here to see that proper satisfaction be given'. They proceeded to the Governor's palace, where Franklin let it be known that if the guilty soldiers were not brought to book, 'he would take such measures as would bring the matter to immediate settlement'. This had the desired effect.[27]

In February 1833, a Bavarian prince, Otho, arrived in Greece as its new king, and before long the *Rainbow*'s Mediterranean duties came to an end. The British Consul at Patras wrote to Franklin congratulating him on his release from 'this anxious and wearisome duty' and regretting the loss of his company. 'The humane object of your mission is now fulfilled', he congratulated the *Rainbow*'s commander.[28] King Otho saw fit to award him the Golden Cross of the Order of the Redeemer. Franklin's nephew, Frank Simpkinson, sailed on the *Rainbow* and later recalled a happy and contented ship, and regarding her captain: 'I never saw him the least out of temper or heard him speak harshly to any of his officers'.[29] *

There was an interesting visit to Constantinople on the return journey, where the fleet anchored off the 'fields of Troy', then a stay in Naples. Naval officers, particularly ones of Franklin's standing, were never short of invitations to this ball or that party when in port, and the Neapolitan social scene eventually had Franklin reflecting, 'I never was fond of the bustle of what is called Society or large parties though it has been my lot to be forced among them...'[30]

He arrived home late in 1833 (while Jane was still on her travels) and was finally paid off from the *Rainbow* in January 1834 with Admiral Hotham's praise ringing in his ears for his handling of what had always been a delicate and potentially explosive situation. Before travelling to Brighton to be re-united with little Eleanor, Franklin also succeeded in making a good impression on his new sovereign, William IV – whom he had previously known as Lord High Admiral – during what would now perhaps be called a 'debriefing'.

Another personage interested in Franklin's opinions on the

---

* We have Frank Simpkinson to thank for the revelation that Franklin detested floggings so much that to witness them had him 'trembling from head to foot' – evidence enough for some modern writers that he was 'weak'.

situation in the Balkans was the new Lord High Admiral, and at the conclusion of this interview Franklin did not waste the opportunity of declaring his keenness to get another ship. Competition, as he well knew, was great, and patronage a not insignificant factor. The Lord High Admiral advised Franklin, in so many words – but very politely – not to hold his breath.

He travelled to Cornwall in October 1834 and met Jane's ship when it docked at Falmouth. As was so often the case, she was not in the best of health and their return to London had to be put off while she recovered from a fever. There was a visit to Lincolnshire, then the following year saw them both exploring Ireland. Eleanor was staying in Guernsey with the Cracrofts. According to family friend Caroline Fox, while they were trekking in Ireland they had to make their way along a difficult pass – presumably with something of a drop beneath it, for Jane apparently kept saying to her husband, 'John, you had better go back – you are certainly giddy'. This was news to Franklin, who carried on happily. In the end Jane had to concede that it was she who could not continue, and Franklin enlisted Colonel Sabine to help him carry Jane back. When Sabine hesitated, Franklin remarked, 'Don't be afraid, Sabine; she never kicks when she's faint!'[31]

Jane had heard rumours of new plans for northern exploration, and was keen for her husband to be involved – not because she wanted to be rid of him, but because she knew how much it would mean to him; and of all the places in the world the navy could send him, 'a freezing climate seems to have a wonderful power in bracing your nerves and making you stronger'.[32]

There had been some mixed signals about the possibility of a new Arctic expedition, but when the latest venture was announced, its commander was to be George Back, now a captain. He had recently been in the region in search of an overdue expedition under the Rosses: James and his nephew Sir John. Franklin must have been deeply disappointed not to have been given the chance to fulfil his long-awaited ambition of completing the survey of the coast between Prince Regent Inlet and the infamous Point Turnagain, but it was in keeping with his character that he betrayed no feeling of bitterness or resentment.

When an offer of new employment finally did arrive, it was for an opening that could hardly have been further from the 'bracing' Arctic. On 21 March 1836 Franklin wrote to Jane from the Admiralty, telling her she would be surprised to hear why he had not yet joined her in Dover. He had received a note from Lord Glenelg, Secretary of State for the Colonies, telling him that the governorship of the tiny Caribbean island of Antigua was vacant, and that if Franklin was interested his name would be put before His Majesty. The offer, Franklin informed Jane, was made in the 'most flattering and satisfying manner'.[33]

But Franklin wisely avoided making the mistake of letting the flattery go straight to his head. He consulted his friend Captain Beaufort, whose advice was to give him some thinking time by requesting the chance to discuss the matter with Jane. The shrewd Beaufort counselled him to take the climate into account (a far more important point then now – in some cases a matter of life or death for northern Europeans). He also advised Franklin to look into the stability of the political situation on the island.

The expediency of Beaufort's advice, and Franklin's instinct to follow it, became clear over the next few days, and he brought Jane up to date with the outcome of his investigations. He had consulted several people, including the London agent for Antigua. He wanted to know not only about Antigua itself, but how such an appointment would affect his future naval prospects. At the age of almost fifty Franklin still cherished hopes of active employment – and while he remained a fit and healthy man there was no reason why he should not. Adams had informed him that accepting the appointment would have no adverse effect on his career prospects, but Beaufort's advice was clear: do not take the post. This was echoed by a Mr Meyer at the Colonial Office, who told him that any reports he sent home would go through Sir Evan McGregor, who had overruled the previous governor on more than one occasion. And someone who had resided on the island told him that it would be impossible to 'keep up any appearance' on less than £2000 a year – his salary would be £1200.

Jane was also against it, but left it for him to decide; when Franklin revealed to Beaufort the contents of a letter giving her reasons, he described it as 'the letter of a woman of most excellent sense, judgement and feeling…'[34] Beaufort advised Franklin to see Glenelg and decline the post on the grounds that he would not be able to communicate directly with the Colonial Office, thereby diluting his authority, plus health considerations. (Jane was particularly worried about this. Despite being a seasoned traveller she was prone to vague illnesses and fainting fits; some commentators have, not unreasonably, put these episodes down more to her temperament than to her physical constitution.)

And so Franklin went to inform Glenelg of his decision. 'His Lordship said at once that my reasons were most powerful and satisfactory', he reported to Jane. Glenelg had told him, 'I admit your case to be different from that which is merely due to rank, you have a high station in public regard and in private society…'[35] Franklin's decision was accepted with regret, and the two men parted amicably. Beaufort reassured Franklin: 'Depend upon it you have now taken a step that will increase Lord Glenelg's regard and respect for you…'[36]

Within days a more interesting proposition was dangled before Franklin's nose: the post of Lieutenant-Governor of Van Dieman's Land (now Tasmania). Although to an Englishman this was perhaps just another distant island, Van Dieman's Land had a thriving economy and played a central role in the system of transporting convicts to the southern hemisphere. It presented a far different challenge to Antigua – in more ways than one, as will be seen.

Beaufort said, 'Well, Franklin, I suppose you will accept this. I cannot see one reason why you should not. As for the idea…that the Admiralty might consider you as put on the shelf by accepting that appointment, depend on it that is "all my eye".'[37]

But a comment by Sir William Parker, on the board of the Admiralty, was perhaps the most significant – though not in the way he intended it to be. He urged Franklin to accept. 'Colonel Arthur and this Board have had some unpleasant letters passing between us, and on this account we shall be glad to have a man of our own, and especially you, there.'[38]

Colonel Arthur was the outgoing governor. But Arthur had not operated in isolation, and although he was returning to England, his loyal cohorts were not. Franklin little realised that he was going into the lions' den.

~ 10 ~

Hearts of Stone

BEFORE leaving for Van Dieman's Land, Franklin made a farewell tour of his friends and relatives in Lincolnshire, where he was now more of a celebrity than ever. From Friskney, he informed Jane (who had not accompanied him) that the leading citizens of the area had all chipped in to put on a dinner in his honour. The event was announced in the local press 'with some flattering observations as to the propriety of such a distinction being conferred on me'.[1] It is sometimes reported that a firework display was also arranged to celebrate Franklin's prestigious appointment, but this is not entirely accurate. A fireworks display did take place on the same evening of the dinner but – as Franklin revealed to Jane – this was no more than the happy coincidence of a travelling pyrotechnist happening to be in the area at the time.

Nevertheless, Spilsby presented him with a silver plate and Horncastle gave its children a day off school and rang its church bells. More kudos came Franklin's way when William IV conferred upon him the honour of Knight Commander of the Guelphic Order, something that Franklin hoped would give him a little extra credibility in his new post.

The Franklins arrived at the Fountain Inn, Portsmouth, late on the evening of 24 August shortly before they were due to set sail for their new life. They were not travelling alone. Franklin's Private Secretary, Captain Alexander Maconochie, accompanied by his wife and six children, was a navy man with whom it seems Franklin had become acquainted after his return from Mediterranean duties; he was to play one of the starring roles in the soap opera that was Van Dieman's Land during the coming years.

Nieces Mary Franklin and Sophia Cracroft were in the party, as was Henry Elliot, as Franklin's aide-de-camp, and good old John

Hepburn, who would eventually become the superintendent of the Point Puer convict establishment for boys.

Eleanor, now twelve years old, would have the opportunity to be with her father and stepmother on a daily basis probably for the first time in her life. Franklin got on well with her, and once in their new home they would enjoy early morning strolls together. But Eleanor and Jane were never to see eye-to-eye. As in all the best fairytales, the wicked stepmother has been blamed. Known examples of her strictness regarding Eleanor's upbringing, and especially her education, seem harsh to modern sensibilities, but probably reflected attitudes and practices that were commonplace in nineteenth-century England. Descendant E M Gell, author of a biography of Eleanor's mother, stated that Jane 'never understood' her stepdaughter, and speaks of the child's 'embittered years of adolescence'.[2] Sophia Cracroft was later to observe: 'Eleanor absolutely hates my aunt', and most writers have put the lion's share of the blame at Eleanor's door, pointing to her squabbles with Jane over Franklin's estate after his death as being indicative of her shrewish nature.

A governess, Miss Williams, was accompanying Eleanor. Among the rest were Archdeacon Hutchins, Lieutenant Thomas Burnett of the Royal Navy, and Jane's French maid.

They sailed on the *Fairlie* on 26 August 1836. The ship was packed. Once it became know that Franklin was to sail in her the passenger list rapidly filled up with 'hopeful place-hunters and social climbers', according to Kathleen Fitzpatrick in her authoritative account of Franklin's time in Van Dieman's Land.[3] Like most of Franklin's voyages, it was eventful: one man fell over the side and was rescued; they were almost rammed by a whaler, which bore down on them, Franklin thought, like a pirate ship intent on boarding; several people died and were buried at sea; there was a violent storm lasting three days. Jane whiled away the time taking lessons from an artist, and herself organised drawing classes for children. Captain Maconochie gave lectures expounding his own fanciful theories in the fields of anthropology, metaphysics and phrenology. He was perhaps ahead of his time when he mooted the idea that the distant ancestors of Europeans may have been black, but on less certain ground when surmising that 'the secretion which in the savage blackens the skin, flies off in proportion as he becomes a more intellectual being to his brain…'[4] After his talk on phrenology Sophia Cracroft told Jane dryly that 'the hearers thought somewhat the worse of the science than they did before'.[5]

The *Fairlie* arrived at Hobart Town, capital of Van Dieman's Land, in January 1837, and was greeted on a cold morning by members of the Executive Council and the Commandant of the Troops. Franklin received a 'wildly enthusiastic' welcome. People were excited at the prospect of having a genial hero as their new leader – but that was only half the story. Many of them were also glad to see the back of Franklin's predecessor, Colonel Arthur.

⁎

Abel Tasman had discovered and named Van Dieman's Land almost 200 years earlier; it is an island roughly the size of Ireland which looks on a map as though it has dropped off the south-eastern corner of Australia (and presumably did in some far-off aeon). By the time Franklin arrived, the island had been inhabited by Europeans for a little over thirty years,⁎ yet by the time of his departure the indigenous population had fallen to an alarming fifty-four, compared to the over 40,000 immigrants and their offspring. The natives had been gradually wiped out by sickness – surely imported by the Europeans – and, ostensibly at least, broken hearts – a malaise that would have been instantly recognisable by their Native American counterparts on reservations.

It was an island of mountains, lakes, rivers and forest and a climate not dissimilar to that of Britain; the daunting terrain meant that large areas remained unexplored. The two towns of any size were the capital Hobart in the south, and Launceston in the north.

Almost half the population were transported convicts, though the 'free' community also included the families of convicts, and convicts who had completed their sentences. The rest of the inhabitants were settlers – such as farmers and merchants, military

---

⁎ When Franklin had accompanied Flinders during his charting of the Australian coast in 1801 it had yet to be settled.

personnel, and officials of one kind or another. It was an isolated, close-knit community: a situation which tends to generate either warmth and hospitality or aloofness and paranoia. Franklin was soon to discover which category Van Dieman's Land fell into. G T W B Boyes, who was to be one of Franklin's officials, observed:

> The people of this colony very much resemble the Americans in their presumption, arrogance, impudence and conceit. They believe they are the most remarkable men on the Globe and that their little island 'whips all creation'… Their views are of the narrowest and most selfish kind. They are incapable of any generous sentiments and ever ready to impute the basest motives to their fellow Colonists. Lying, slandering, envy, hatred and malice are their daily ailment and the consumption is incredible.[6]

And then there were the newspapers. Van Dieman's Land seems to have had a surfeit of newspapers, considering the size of the population, and most of them seemed to have pandered to the traits described above by Boyes. If anyone thinks that the excesses of today's tabloids are a modern phenomenon, a glance at the sniping, malice, exaggeration and often pure spiteful fantasy that passed for journalism in *The Colonial Times*, the *Courier*, *Murray's Review* and others would quickly put the lie to that misconception.

The previous – and Van Dieman's Land's first – Lieutenant-Governor, Colonel Arthur, was an extremely unpopular figure during his reign and for many years afterwards. The convicts hated him for the strictness of his regime. The rest of the populace took exception to the fact that, in the words of Kathleen Fitzpatrick, 'He and the group of friends and relations he had gathered about him [the 'Arthur Faction'] as administrative officers regarded Van Dieman's Land as a legitimate field for plunder'.[7] When his term ended it is said that people all over the island celebrated by lighting bonfires.

Franklin was to all intents and purposes the Governor of Van Dieman's Land. His title of Lieutenant-Governor was a throwback to earlier times when the island had come under the jurisdiction of New South Wales. The Governor ran the colony in conjunction with the Executive Council and the Legislative Council. It all sounds very democratic and civilised – but Van Dieman's Land was not as simple as that. Franklin later recorded that he was aware of the 'strong party feeling' on the island,[8] but even so he had joined a game whose rules he did not fully understand, and for which none of his previous life experience could have possibly prepared him.

The expectations of him were such that he could hardly win no matter what he did. The Arthur Faction seemed to think that in Franklin they were getting a docile simpleton who would do as they, the professionals, told him. He had already done just about everything and made himself a hero: why should he not simply let them get on with the work – in their own way – while he sat back and made himself lots of money? But though Franklin was so good-natured as to find it hard to recognise bad in others, they were to discover that he was also strongly principled and totally incorruptible.

Then there was the school of thought that hoped Franklin was coming to liberate them, to clear away the old ways; even, maybe, to fight for their independence from the British Government. Here again, Franklin, although fair-minded and humane and having his own ideas of changes that were needed, was conservative and dutiful. An early tactical error (he realised with hindsight) was, out of a sense of duty, to praise the work of his predecessor and publicly support Arthur's henchmen, Montagu and Forster – thus denting the optimism of those looking for a new broom to sweep the place clean.

To counter this impression he opened up sessions of the Legislative Council, till now closed-door affairs, to the public; and he quickly introduced onto that body 'a gentleman of great wealth and of superior talents…but whose politics were conscientiously opposed to the late Lieutenant-governor'.[9] Furthermore, in subsequent appointments he tried to represent the diversity of opinion in the colony and 'counteract the too prevailing influence of one family and its partisans'. He wanted, he said in an address soon after his arrival, to restore 'social unity and harmony'. In his own cautious and scrupulously fair way he did what he felt he could, but he was not one of life's reformers or crusaders. However, the man whom he had brought with him as his Private Secretary was, and there would soon come a time when Franklin perhaps wished he had never heard the name Alexander Maconochie.

Life in Van Dieman's Land was never going to be some kind of leisurely retirement for Franklin. There was a great deal of administrative work, decision making, ruffled feathers to be smoothed, endless visits to make and visitors to be received. It is said that he visited every convict ship arriving from England and listened to any grievances from the prisoners. (It is something of a myth that most transported convicts were desperately poor people who had merely stolen a loaf of bread. The majority, including females, already had a criminal record before being sentenced to transportation.*) The Franklins and many of their retinue set up home in Government House in the centre of Hobart, overlooking the port and the river and standing in its own tree-lined grounds. It had been added to over the years, but the main structure was a long, two-storied building fronted by a veranda.

One of the first crises arose because of the actions of the man who could and should have been Franklin's main ally during the trials and tribulations that were to come. Alexander Maconochie had lost no time in immersing himself in the preparation of a report for the Society for the Improvement of Prison Discipline in London. He was acting in a private, not official, capacity, though with Franklin's prior approval. This was a time when Britain was doing a great deal of navel gazing regarding its social responsibilities. Slavery had already been abolished, and these years saw the passing of the Great Reform Act, the Poor Law Amendment Act, and acts providing some protection for children working in factories and mines. The Molesworth Parliamentary Committee was looking into the transportation of convicts, and its findings would be heavily influenced by Maconochie's recommendations. It is widely believed that Maconochie had already made up his mind about the general thrust of his report before he ever set foot in Van Dieman's Land. It is also generally accepted that he was an honest and well-meaning man who saw himself as prosecuting a mission that would benefit at least one small section of humanity.

Where it all began to go wrong was that even the people who wanted to improve the lot of the convicts (those who actually *knew*

* For detailed statistics see *The Fatal Shore* by Robert Hughes.

the situation in Van Dieman's Land, that is – including Franklin) felt that Maconochie's main remedy actually made things worse for them. This was compounded by the way in which Franklin's Private Secretary released his politically sensitive conclusions.

The majority of transported convicts were set to work for free settlers, an arrangement known as 'Assignment', which Maconochie thought morally and practically wrong. Although this was a reasonable point of view, and must have seemed particularly so to the well-meaning reformers back in Britain, the reality of the situation was not so simple. Maconochie wanted all convicts to be kept separate from the rest of the population and put into work teams, where they could earn – or lose – points according to their behaviour. But it was clear in Van Dieman's Land that the convicts currently in work gangs were actually worse off than their 'assigned' counterparts, and that the assignment system, if not ideal, was in fact more humane and suited almost everyone. (Maconochie's solution contained some outlandish elements, and when he did eventually get a chance to put it into operation elsewhere it failed miserably.)

Worse than this, though, was the manner in which the report, which described the system in Van Dieman's Land as 'cruel, uncertain, prodigal; ineffectual either for reform or example; can only be maintained in some degree of vigour by extreme severity…',[10] became public knowledge. He committed a major breach of protocol by forwarding a summary of the report directly to Britain instead of through Franklin, and without his superior being fully aware of the explosive nature of its contents. The first Franklin came to hear of 'the incorrect and even reckless assertions',[11] as he described them, was when he read about them in a newspaper from home – the Molesworth Committee had thoughtfully provided the press with Maconochie's aspersions against the system over which his chief presided.

Magnanimous though he was, this was a situation Franklin could not and did not gloss over, and in fact it was not the first time Maconochie had displayed a 'want of openness' with his Governor. This was merely the straw that broke the camel's back, and Franklin had no choice but to immediately dismiss his Private Secretary. The *True Colonist* took this as a sign that the Arthur Faction, which infamously brooked no opposition, already had Franklin doing their bidding, adding that Maconochie and his family, who had been staying with the Franklins in Government House, Hobart, were ejected on the same day as the official dismissal.

Neither assertion was true, though it was a journalistic trend that Franklin would soon learn to get used to. Franklin was taking the only course open to him, which had nothing to do with any influence or pressure by the Arthur Faction. And in fact neither he nor Jane disliked the Maconochies,* and they all continued to live under the same roof until suitable accommodation could be found. Henry Elliot, who had come out on the *Fairlie* with Franklin, took over as his Private Secretary. Elliot was talented, but very young and inexperienced, which left Franklin naturally relying more and more on the insights and opinions of his intelligent and astute wife. This, as we shall see, left Jane open to accusations of interfering in matters which were none of her business, and Franklin of being a weak leader who could not make a decision without his wife's say-so.

At around this time, early 1838, another incident occurred that at first glance seemed trivial by comparison with the Maconochie affair, yet ultimately proved, like the proverbial 'want of a nail', to have a far more damaging outcome for Franklin. He was asked to intervene in a case that involved two of Van Dieman's Land's senior figures.

Alfred Stephen was Attorney-General, and although nominally an Arthur man, he knew his own mind and was not intimidated by the Faction when their views and his did not coincide. Captain John Montagu, just over forty years old, had fought at Waterloo and was now Van Dieman's Land's Colonial Secretary – only Franklin himself held higher office. He had come over with Arthur after marrying his niece, acquired land and money, but was heavily in debt to his mentor. He was an able, extremely clever and cunning man, yet seems to have been so wrapped up in his own ambitions and machinations that he was unable to distinguish truth from fiction where such considerations came into conflict with his plans and

---

* Interestingly, in Lady Franklin's journal covering the problems with Maconochie, sizeable sections have been neatly and deliberately excised – presumably by Sophia Cracroft (SPRI – MS 248/85).

schemes. His own biographer speaks of Montagu's youthful 'disregard for truthfulness' giving way to 'honesty of purpose and a decided straightforwardness of action...'[12] Perhaps this is couched in deliberately ambiguous language, since one could argue that even a bank robber could have honesty of purpose (that is, the purpose of robbing a bank) and certainly straightforwardness of action... Franklin noted from the outset that he was supported far more enthusiastically by Montagu in implementing 'Arthurian' plans than when trying to introduce measures to heal the rifts between the warring parties.

An emancipated convict called Clapperton had embezzled money from Alfred Stephen over a period of several months while acting as his servant. It was a gross breach of trust, and until discovered had shown Stephen in a bad light among various tradesmen, whose bills were not being paid. Clapperton was found guilty and sentenced to fourteen years' hard labour. But Montagu knew that Clapperton had something of a reputation as a cook – and happened to need just such a person. He applied to Forster, the Chief Police Magistrate, to let him come and work in the Montagu household. One only needs to be aware that Forster was a fellow army man, who had come out with Arthur, and married another of his seemingly limitless supply of nieces, to guess the outcome. Stephen was, not unreasonably, outraged by this apparent trivialisation of the wrong that had been done to him, and there followed something of a public outcry when the details of the case became widely known.

This was the point at which Franklin was called upon to act as umpire. Montagu's particularly lame justification was that it was Stephen's fault for putting Clapperton in a position where he could be so easily tempted, a line which Forster also took. Franklin looked into the details of the case and had little difficulty in deciding that Clapperton must leave his position with Montagu and serve his hard labour. In doing this, Franklin made an implacable enemy of his humiliated Colonial Secretary. For his part, it was convenient for Montagu to allow himself to believe that Franklin had been cowed into his decision, and that this demonstrated his weakness as Governor.

One of the ways in which Montagu was far more deviously astute than Franklin was his ability to quietly manipulate the views of others to his own ends, a trait he began to demonstrate now by promulgating, through his former chief Arthur, a completely misleading account of what had happened. 'I am most anxious you should know all the facts to be able to defend Forster and myself at the Colonial Office',[13] he said. He spoke of the 'deplorable state of weakness' of the government of Van Dieman's Land (standing up to the more experienced, second and third most powerful men on the island hardly smacks of weakness to the outside observer), and for the first time raised the issue of Jane's role behind the scenes: 'It is painful beyond description to act under a Governor who has no firmness of character, and the tool of any rogue who will flatter his wife, for she in fact governs'.[14] It is widely agreed that if Franklin did show any weakness it was in not going the whole hog and dismissing Montagu (and possibly Forster), as had happened to others in similar circumstances of which Montagu would have been well aware. In fact, Franklin sent Montagu a magnanimous letter (it may well be that Franklin had no idea of what Montagu was up to behind the scenes) but to no avail. This marked the beginning of an anti-Franklin propaganda campaign by Montagu.

Montagu returned to England in February 1839, having been granted eighteen months' leave of absence, ostensibly to arrange his son's education. It was widely believed that he had no intention of returning. The fact that he sold his house and furniture helped fuel this belief; and Franklin later discovered that Montagu wrote two letters on the same day: one to his chief saying he would be back, and the other to Forster revealing that there was 'little or no probability' of this happening.

Nevertheless, the Franklins put the Montagus up at Government House while they were waiting to depart, and Franklin provided Montagu with letters of introduction that would help him when he arrived in London. Jane told her sister what to expect: 'I am not sure that you will like them, but you will find them gentlemanly and ladylike, and you will find Mr Montagu clever'.[15]

Montagu told Arthur how well Franklin had treated him – but typically put this down to Franklin's 'guilt' over the way he had treated his Colonial Secretary. An example of the way in which

Montagu's mind worked was to come in the near future. When the balloon finally went up, Montagu would ascribe his reason for leaving to health problems: Franklin's inadequacies meant that he was having to work too hard. The fact that Franklin's administration did not collapse (quite the opposite) without Montagu to prop it up during his two-year absence seemed to escape him.

This left the colony needing a new Colonial Secretary. Montagu had recommended Forster, the Chief Police Magistrate, and Franklin, after a great deal of thought, endorsed his choice. This went down badly with John Gregory, the Colonial Treasurer, and one of the few non-Arthur Faction men in senior positions. He reacted very petulantly, taking the decision as a personal slight and applying, like the man whose position he thought he deserved, for eighteen months' leave of absence. But worse for Franklin was when Gregory jumped on the anti-Jane bandwagon. Franklin had innocently (Jane used the mild rebuke 'incautiously') told Montagu that he was going to make his final decision after talking to his wife – but he had virtually made up his mind about Forster already by then. What spin Montagu put on this we can only guess, but it was certainly the kind of scenario he was capable of exploiting to the full.

The role played by Jane in supporting her husband was to hold great significance for his enemies. Franklin was a man who knew his own mind, but never made any secret of the fact that he consulted and conversed with her regularly regarding the running of the colony (he had few others to turn to). It suited those who sought to portray him as weak and foolish to cast Jane as the true power behind the throne. Her role as confidante – and as one who had her own independent schemes for the improvement of the Colony – was far more daring and against the grain then than we can appreciate today. Ladies were supposed to sit at home writing letters or go out paying visits to other ladies; they might engage in intellectual discussion about the state of the world – but they were not supposed to actually *do* anything about it.

One day Jane had been chatting to Forster about life in Van Dieman's Land in general, and they got onto the subject of female convicts. She told him that this was a subject of particular interest to her, and that she had been commissioned by the famous Quaker and prison reformer Elizabeth Fry to investigate the conditions of female convicts in the Colony. Thinking that he shared her enthusiasm, she suggested he write down his thoughts on the subject and show them to her, and she would do likewise. 'He looked at me intently, (just as if he was able to see me which I knew his near-sightedness prevented) but said nothing, which I thought odd and did not feel encouraging.'[16]

By now, into only his second year in Van Dieman's Land, the constant sniping, innuendo and political in-fighting was beginning to get to Franklin, who had spent most of his life in the disciplined and comradely atmosphere of naval ships. 'Sir John has not the power and the cunning to deal with persons such as Mr Gregory...', Jane wrote to her sister:

> All this has hurt Sir John more than you can imagine – one thing comes upon another – he takes little exercise, loses in some respects even his appetite, creates imaginary evils, asks me if I can bear if he is recalled in disgrace, and in fact is more agitated and depressed than I have ever seen him... I am sure he is far from well. Sir John's sensitiveness is beyond conception and it is in a country where people should have hearts of stone and frames of iron...[17]

Thankfully, some things in Van Dieman's Land went less awry for Franklin than others. He instituted a regatta to mark the discovery of the island by Abel Tasman. The *True Colonist* snootily declared that, 'neither theatrical amusements, nor horse-racing, are conducive to the morals and interests of society in a young Colony...'[18] but the young Colony thought otherwise, and the event was a great success. So enthusiastically did the islanders throw themselves into the spirit of the occasion that in future years alcohol-fuelled disturbances began to cause concern; Franklin's attempts to impose an element of restraint only led to the populace staging their own regatta without his patronage.

Franklin also took a close interest in the future of the young of Van Dieman's Land, realising early on that apart from a few private schools for those who could afford it there was no formal tutelage available for the majority of the children. Kathleen Fitzpatrick says, 'Sir John Franklin's unique contribution to Tasmanian history is his work in the furtherance of education…'[19] (To what extent the previously free-roaming children themselves appreciated Franklin's efforts is not recorded…) He set up a Board of Education charged with putting schooling onto a more organised and formal footing, and after ironing out disputes between the different church factions as to the religious content in the curriculum, a number of Day Schools were up and running within a couple of years.

These schools were for the younger children, but he was also keen to follow the idea to its logical conclusion and establish a college to provide secondary education. Franklin turned to his friend the famous Dr Arnold of Rugby for advice on this project. It was an idea Arthur had toyed with but was never able to put into effect, and was predictably rubbished by the *True Colonist* when Franklin decided to revive it.

There were the usual headaches along the way, including more inter-denominational bickering over the religious fare to be provided by Christ College; one of the main reasons Arthur never got anywhere was this religious 'diversity of opinions' as Franklin euphemistically described it.[20] Montagu was also strangely obstructive. His main grouse seemed to be over the siting of the college, leading Franklin to suspect that the man who was to become his arch-enemy stood, because of some unknown land deal, to lose or gain financially depending on where the college was built. Bureaucratic and other delays meant that the college was not to open until after Franklin's period of governorship had ended.

*

Maconochie's report, and the findings of the Molesworth Committee, finally came home to roost in the middle of 1840, when the assignment system was formally ended. It seems certain that the decision was a purely political one with little regard to the adverse effects it would have on both the islanders and the convicts themselves. In Franklin's opinion they were replacing a cruel system with a crueller one. Life in Van Dieman's Land had evolved on the basis of convicts providing the labour force for the settlers, and however unfair this might seem it actually suited both parties. The settlers got their cheap labour and the convicts got some kind of meaningful employment instead of being confined to a prison gang and possibly consigned to a lengthy period of 'hard labour'. To change the system virtually overnight threw the island into a state of panic, with some (including, naturally, the *New Colonist*) laying the blame at Franklin's door. He had, of course, no choice but to implement the home government's decision, while attempting to phase in the changes as gradually as possible and informing the Secretary of State of the problems the changes were causing. He was also extremely hurt and annoyed, on behalf of the islanders, by the negative picture of Van Dieman's Land conjured up by the Molesworth Report, which, he said, had been 'ignorantly and so unjustly heaped upon you in the mother country'.[21]

Life for Franklin in Van Dieman's Land did have its few precious bright spots, and probably the brightest was the arrival in August 1840 of two ships which would, sooner than he could possibly have imagined, play a major part in the Franklin story: the *Erebus* and the *Terror*. On board were Franklin's old friend James Clark Ross, who had ventured into the Arctic with Parry on numerous occasions, and Francis Crozier, another old Arctic hand, who would sail with Franklin on his last expedition. They were on an expedition to study magnetic variations in southern latitudes and Antarctica in particular. Franklin personally supervised the building of an observatory on Van Dieman's Land for them, and their presence seems to have boosted his morale greatly. Not only did he have the companionship for several months of true and trusted friends who spoke his language; they also embodied the way of life he would surely have given anything at that time to have gone back to – they were explorers.

Jane wrote, 'They all feel towards one another as friends and brothers, and it is the remark of people here that Sir John appears to them quite in a new light, so bustling and frisky and merry with his new companions'.[22] They stayed at Government House, and when they came back from Antarctica he proudly displayed in his drawing room two rock specimens they had brought with them. They in turn had named an island on the fringes of the southern continent after him. The farewell ball for Ross and Crozier was the biggest social event in the young Colony's history. Three hundred and fifty people attended; there was dancing on the *Erebus* and food on the *Terror*, a regimental band playing, and all in all no effort spared in making it an occasion to remember.

Another diversion for Franklin was an expedition of his own into the little-known interior of the island, through a region between Lake St Clair and Macquarie Harbour on the west coast, known as Transylvania. It would be no Sunday jaunt. It was such an inhospitable environment that few convicts escaping from the prison at Macquarie made it out alive. Nevertheless, the intrepid Jane was going along. She, like her husband, had been badly demoralised by the unremitting obstreperousness of the Van Dieman's Land's 'Mafia', and despite not being in robust health this was an opportunity to get away from it all for a time. Franklin's official reasons for the venture were to assess the viability of the region from the perspective of the ever-increasing demand for land, and also to identify possible locations suitable for the growing number of convict work gangs. But one cannot help thinking that, more than this, he simply wanted to go off exploring.

Franklin's party was supported by twenty hardy convicts, and set out on 24 March 1842 on what the *Colonial Times* called 'a foolish expedition, at an unpropitious time of the year'.[23] Franklin must have thought that if he had any hair left he would probably have been criticised for the side he parted it on.

Before long the weather turned against them, and the numerous rivers became difficult to cross. They became bogged down for a time at what Franklin christened 'Detention Corner' (a typical Franklinism). One convict later recalled how Franklin rallied the sinking spirits of some of the less stoical adventurers: 'Come, come, my boys, this is nothing at all, you should laugh at this!'[24] And when food supplies began to dwindle, he gave short shrift to the suggestion that the rations of the 'men', but not the gentry, be cut. On 16 April Jane, like a stage magician, produced a plum cake which she had smuggled along so they could celebrate her husband's birthday.

They finally reached Macquarie Harbour, and a schooner called the *Breeze* which was waiting for them, on 22 April; but bad weather prevented their departure for a further three weeks. This caused some consternation back in Hobart, where they were overdue, and searches by land and sea were organised – the famous *Beagle* broke off from its mission to lend a hand. The *Launceston Advertiser*, unaware whether all were dead or alive, callously declared, 'Unexpected deprivations and difficulties are the penalties justly due to so wild and senseless a freak... Pity is out of the question. The natural consequences of an indulgence in folly...merit no commiseration'.[25]

Wild rumours about the fate of his little expedition were beginning to circulate. One had Franklin falling from a horse and breaking a limb, which story amused Franklin, who had deliberately thrown himself from his stumbling mare since she 'must come down if my weight remained on her', and his tumble caused him to 'feel not the least inconvenience'. In a separate incident Lady Franklin had also fallen and was unhurt.

As ever, Franklin did not neglect the Sunday service. One of his travelling companions, David Burn, recorded in his diary:

> His excellency, with the earnest and impressive piety – the distinguished feature of this truly good man and exemplary Christian, performed service... As usual, the auditory proved a most attentive one; indeed, it has never been my lot to listen to any reader who so completely enchains his hearers; the devout and forcible manner of Sir John's delivery exciting the most marked attention.[26]

Before reaching Hobart, Franklin was much gratified to put to the test a difference in the accounts of Matthew Flinders and another explorer as to the latitude and longitude of Van Dieman's Land's South West Cape – and find in his hero's favour.

~ 11 ~

The Basest of Actions

JOHN Montagu arrived back from England in March 1841. He never informed Franklin (though Forster was kept apprised and fed Franklin snippets) of meetings he had had with Lord Stanley at the Colonial Office, or that he had effectively been lobbying against his chief. Montagu had a swagger about him on his return; Franklin observed that it 'could scarcely be doubted that Mr Montagu's return to the subordinate office of Colonial Secretary was in his estimation an act of condescension'.[1] Now, whenever there was a difference of opinion between them Montagu stuck to his guns with the hubris of a poker player who knew he had the winning hand. Within five months of resuming his post he became the protagonist in a chain of events that would lead to Franklin's downfall. It started fairly innocuously, with what has become known as the Coverdale Case.

In August 1841 the young District Surgeon in Richmond, Dr Coverdale, was rebuked by the Principal Medical Officer for not attending a patient who had fallen from a cart and subsequently died from his injuries. A message had been delivered to the Doctor's servant about an accident at a local farm but, on the flimsy grounds that no name had been mentioned and there were several tenants on the farm, he decided the matter could not be that important and failed to respond; when he heard nothing further about it during the course of the morning he proceeded on his afternoon rounds. Another doctor was eventually found to attend the patient, but too late to save his life. Montagu decided Coverdale's negligence was worthy of dismissal – a verdict with which Franklin initially concurred. But Coverdale appealed on several grounds: no one had ever had cause to complain about his judgement or actions before; he was (as doctors are to this day) continually called out on 'frivolous' matters; strictly speaking, he was a doctor to the convict population and the patient was a free man; the deceased was already a sick man and was drunk when he fell from the cart.

Franklin, who subsequently discovered he had not been given the full facts of the case, was petitioned by the people of Richmond to show clemency, and eventually came to the conclusion that a reprimand was punishment enough. Unfortunately for Franklin, the district of Richmond was an area that had never succumbed to the charms of Arthur or his cohorts, and was therefore a constant thorn in Montagu's side. Montagu was not giving up without a fight, and persuaded Franklin to hold fire while he prepared a memorandum on the case. But this report, which contained what amounted to a veiled threat – that 'the honour and character of your Government require that the effect upon the community should be further considered'[2] – did nothing to make the Governor change his mind. Montagu let it be known that this decision would lead to 'evil consequences', and in this at least Franklin would later have cause to concur with his contumacious subordinate.

It so happened that Jane had discussed the case with Forster. She knew from friends in Richmond that it was felt the dismissal was unwarranted and was apparently of this view herself. Montagu, naturally, got to hear about this on the Arthurite grapevine and told Franklin to his face that he believed her ladyship was guilty of both interfering in official matters and in sullying his own good name. He knew who had 'got up' the petition. Although Franklin and his wife had been in Richmond at around this time, and Jane had stayed on a day longer than her husband, the accusations were totally without foundation. The Reverend Aislabie had in fact 'got up' the Richmond petition and said so publicly – it had nothing to do with Lady Franklin whatsoever and he resented the use of her name in connection with it. Even this cut no ice with Montagu. Jane recorded:

> Sir John came in to me afterwards much excited and disgusted with Mr Montagu, and asked me a question as to whether I had or had not said the particular thing attributed to me… I perceived it as well as Sir John had that Mr Montagu's real errand was to strike a blow at me – blow of revenge for the past, and one which should paralyse

me for the future… I gave Sir John the simple denial he expected from me.[3]

Even though Jane was in many ways the stronger of the couple, behind her façade she was very much prone to stress and its effects, and the affair brought her down physically and mentally to the point where she considered returning to England; it was mainly her reluctance to leave her husband alone in the lion's den that stopped her. She wrote forceful letters to both Montagu and Forster, and Montagu afterwards reported that from this time on Franklin was 'formal and reserved with him' – as if it came as some kind of surprise.

In fact it was Montagu who became formal and reserved. He told Franklin that he 'must not in future expect the same assistance he had hitherto rendered'[4] him. In effect, he began what would now be called a 'work-to-rule'. Many of the duties he performed, and the way in which he carried them out, were not formally prescribed – as in many jobs, they had evolved over time. This meant, cunning man that he was, that he could get away with doing as little as possible as inefficiently as possible – while swamping Franklin with queries, incomplete paperwork, and generally being as pedantic as he could – without breaking his terms of employment:

> The subtle character of Mr Montagu's conduct was such as to make it extremely difficult to embody as specific charges, that thorough disaffection, and those minute but incessant reticences of duty which were productive of more serious impediments in the administration of affairs than a more open opposition would have been.[5]

Franklin heard that Montagu had boasted 'he would speedily bring me to terms'.

The next – and final – stage in the fracture between Franklin and Montagu revolved around one of the more recent journals to appear on the already overcrowded news-stands of Van Dieman's Land: the *Van Dieman's Land Chronicle*. The difference between this and all the others was that this was established with the intention of being sympathetic to Franklin's government and giving accurate accounts of government business; Franklin's administration provided full co-operation by giving the paper access to verbatim government despatches for publication. Yet strangely, as soon as Montagu fell out with Franklin, the *Van Dieman's Land Chronicle*, most of whose writers belonged to Montagu's coterie, began taking pot shots at Franklin, his administration and his wife. The attacks were of a vicious and personal nature (though no worse than some of the other newspapers). The Colonial Secretary pleaded ignorance, but there was little doubt that he was the one behind it.

Eventually, Franklin demanded to know what Montagu was up to. He reminded him that when the newspaper had started they had had a discussion in which it had been decided that his government would give the newspaper its full support. Montagu brazenly denied that any such interview had taken place, and said that they had merely decided to lend the editor the odd journal obtained from home. Franklin, knowing this to be untrue, tactfully queried Montagu's recollection of events. Montagu's written reply was grossly insulting to his superior:

> While Your Excellency and all the members of your government have had such frequent opportunities of testing my memory as to have acquired for it the reputation of a remarkably accurate one, your Officers have not been without the opportunity of learning that Your Excellency could not always place implicit confidence upon your own.[6]

Montagu, cool and calculating though he normally was, had gone too far. Franklin had little alternative but to suspend him, which was implemented on 25 January 1842 – three months after the start of his 'work-to-rule'.

If there was one person whom Montagu despised more than Franklin, it was Jane – yet once he realised how serious things had become he took the extraordinary step of appealing to her to intervene on his behalf! He was now playing the role of the broken and totally contrite, but essentially honest, man. Surely – like Coverdale – he deserved a second chance? Two days after being told of his suspension, and through an intermediary – Dr Andrew Turnbull – he promised to apologise unreservedly and carry out his duties in the future with the 'utmost zeal'. He persuaded Jane to peruse the draft of a letter he intended sending to her husband. Jane told him candidly that she did not think it would get him anywhere – but was good enough to advise him on the kind of letter he *ought* to write if he were to stand any chance at all. And it should contain no 'mystification' and have 'some little warmth and feeling in it'.[7]

This Montagu duly did, and there was a feeling that, Franklin being Franklin and Montagu being Montagu, the former would be moved enough to go against his better judgement and the latter would wriggle off the hook once more. But not this time. Franklin *was* moved by Montagu's repentance, but not enough to make him change his mind, and anyway it was too late. The apology came six days after the announcement of the suspension and only a day before the new incumbent was due to take up the reins. However, 'It enabled me to put more warmth into the terms by which I sought to avert from Mr Montagu any permanently serious consequences either to his reputation or his pecuniary interests from steps I had taken'.[8] Even in this, Franklin could not do right for doing wrong. It was later used against him along the lines of, 'If the Colonial Secretary wasn't so bad after all, weren't you wrong to dismiss him?'

In any event, all this was wasted on a man like Montagu; it would ultimately be Franklin who suffered the 'serious consequences' to his reputation. 'Be it so', Franklin declared much later when Van Dieman's Land was but a speck on the horizon. 'I may stand convicted of a political blunder, but I retain the blessed consciousness of having done no man, not even Mr Montagu, more injury than the stern demands of duty forced upon me'.[9]

And as for Jane and her generous efforts in acting as an intermediary, Montagu had his own way of rewarding her. Their go-between, Dr Turnbull, told Jane that if Montagu ever spoke of her with anything less than respect and gratitude after what she had done on his behalf, 'I say it will be the basest of actions'. There are no prizes for guessing what came next.

Once back in England, Montagu took his grudge to Lord Stanley, Secretary of State for the Colonies, where it all became Lady Franklin's fault. It was because of her interference in official matters, and his bringing it to Franklin's attention, that he had *really* been suspended. What is more, the idea of putting a word in on his behalf had been *her* idea, and because he had not agreed to some of the preconditions she had laid down for having his suspension lifted, an accusation tantamount to blackmail (and which Turnbull, who passed all the messages to and fro, categorically denied), she had personally seen to it that the suspension stood.

Franklin came through the drama very well considering how badly he had been affected by previous bouts of chicanery. Jane reported to their friend James Ross that the business actually seemed to have toughened him up. He himself must have heaved a sigh of relief at the departure of Montagu, and certainly noticed an improvement both in the efficiency and the morale of his administration: 'If tranquillity were not at once restored, yet the heaving of the waters was only the remains of the storm that was passing away'.[10] But to her sister, Jane also recorded one of Montagu's parting shots regarding Franklin: 'I'll *sweat* him. I'll persecute him as long as I live'.[11]

※

Franklin sent word of Montagu's suspension to Lord Stanley on 8 February 1842. It was almost a year before he heard anything, and that came in the form of gossip that he found hard to credit. By January 1843 stories began to circulate that Lord Stanley had informed *Montagu* of his decision regarding the suspension in September of the *previous year*.

What had happened was that Montagu had been busy in London pulling strings and selling his almost surreal version of the truth, and Lord Stanley, for whatever reason, had bought it completely. Stanley's subsequent treatment of Franklin went beyond mere contempt and bordered on the vindictive. He overturned Montagu's suspension, and before even sending off his judgement to Van Dieman's Land he informed Montagu without putting him under any constraints of confidentiality; Montagu in turn gleefully spread the news far and wide, hence the stories reaching Van Dieman's Land well before Stanley's shabbily tardy despatch.

Stanley's lengthy and patronising despatch informing Franklin of his decision, when it finally arrived, took a swipe at the 'voluminous

papers' Franklin had sent in relation to the case. 'I shall not
to enter with any minuteness into the various details and
circumstances of the transactions to which they refer...'[12] Regarding the Coverdale case and Montagu's subsequent obstructive
behaviour, Stanley decided that 'It may be difficult to condemn a
Public Servant who faithfully and ably performs whatever lies within
the strict range of his duty for not advancing further...' though
Stanley added that Montagu was 'not altogether exempted' from
reproach in the matter.[13]

Regarding the manner in which Montagu made use of Lady
Franklin then proceeded to slander her when it did not get him
anywhere, 'I pass as speedily as possible from such a topic, confining
myself to the single remark, that the imputation does not appear to
me to be well founded'.[14] Considering Stanley was basing his
judgement solely on Franklin's documentation (and he had no idea
what accusations Montagu was going to make behind his back so
could hardly defend himself against them in advance) and Montagu's
word, this is a very bold decision, to say the least. Similarly, after
'weighing every part of this case' Stanley was able to 'entirely acquit'
Montagu of having anything to do with the way in which the *Van
Dieman's Land Chronicle* had turned on Franklin.[15]

Then there was Montagu's insulting letter to Franklin that led to
his suspension. Here, Montagu was 'entitled to be entirely acquitted
of blame'. Montagu may have used an 'inadvertent expression' but
no insult was intended and, anyway, he gave a humble apology
(thanks, of course, to Jane's 'coaching').

Stanley summed up thus:

> The result of my consideration of the whole subject is, as you will
> see, to relieve Mr Montagu from every censure which impugns the
> integrity or the propriety of his conduct... It cannot be too
> distinctly understood that Mr Montagu retires from the situation he
> has so long filled with his Public and Personal character unimpaired,
> and with his hold on the respect of Her Majesty's Government
> undiminished...
>
> I am not aware that it could answer any useful purpose to enter
> more fully into the merits of this particular protracted controversy.
> But reluctant as I am to employ a single expression which is likely to

be unwelcome to you, I am compelled to add that your proceedings in the case of Mr Montagu do not appear to me to have been well-judged; and that your suspension of him from office is not in my opinion, sufficiently vindicated.[16]

This was tantamount to saying that he was happy to take Montagu's word over Franklin's, and that he did not really want to be bothered with any more inconvenient questions about it. To rub salt into the wound Stanley reported that it was 'gratifying' to him to be able to appoint Montagu Colonial Secretary at the Cape of Good Hope, a reward which he had 'cheerfully accepted'. This, in keeping with various other aspects of Stanley's handling of the case, appears to be designed as a deliberate slight, an unconcealed attempt to humiliate Franklin, as though the mere act of undermining his authority was not enough. As if to emphasise this, Stanley later communicated to Franklin that he must pay Montagu's salary (in addition to that of his replacement as Colonial Secretary) from the time he was suspended until he took up his new post, and 'It will be necessary that you should acquaint the Legislative Council that the double expenditure has been incurred in consequence of my disallowance of your suspension of Mr Montagu'.[17] This was another despatch whose contents were fully known and gossiped about in Van Dieman's Land months before the arrival of the official document reached the Lieutenant-Governor's hands.

As for the actual reasoning behind the decision itself, Franklin biographer Lamb describes Stanley as 'One of those who have the gift of being able to make up their minds upon a case without the tedious formality of impartial study of the evidence...'[18] while Kathleen Fitzpatrick quotes Rousseau: 'Let us begin by brushing the facts aside'.[19] Franklin himself ruefully reflected that 'Had Mr Montagu been allowed to dictate it [the despatch] himself it could hardly have more tenderly and delicately identified itself with him'.[20]

The Van Dieman's Land newspapers, of course, had a field day, and they were taking bets on how long it would be before their Governor was recalled.

Franklin, as Jane had observed, had been toughened up by the shenanigans of the last few years, and his reply to Stanley was forthright:

As your Lordship has not allowed me the usual privilege of being made acquainted with the counter statements and arguments of the individual with whom I am at issue, and the grounds upon which your Lordship has arrived at a conclusion deeply affecting my interests and character, I am under the necessity of feeling that my own vindication is incomplete, from want of means being afforded me, which might have rendered it otherwise...[21]

And regarding the manner of his being informed of the decision:

This unqualified censure, which is not relieved by a single word or consideration which might have softened its harshness, has been conveyed to me under circumstances and at a crisis when it would be a cowardly dereliction of my duty to abandon the Post from which your Lordship has not thought fit to remove me.[22]

He did, however, ask that Stanley either speedily appoint someone to succeed him or let him know that he could be assured of the continuing confidence of Her Majesty's Government. Unbeknown to Franklin, a new Lieutenant-Governor was already on his way out.

Aware that he desperately needed allies in London – where only Montagu's version of events was circulating – he wrote to Ross asking him to at least try to clear Jane's name:

God knows in whatever she has done or said in the Colony she has been activated by the purest spirit of Christian philanthropy, and, and to promote the interests of the Colony – but Montagu and his party neither wished that Education on the firmest basis be promoted nor science encouraged, nor general intercourse, their leading object being to get money, to keep the people subservient to their wishes and views.[23]

Meantime, Franklin could only listen to the rumours and wait. At the beginning of April 1843 the word was out in Hobart that Stanley had at last recalled him. He had to suffer the humiliation of writing from Launceston to Boyes, one of his few allies and Acting Colonial Secretary in Montagu's absence, asking if he knew of any substance to the stories. Then, later that same month, James Bicheno arrived from England to take over from Boyes, and under pressure from

Jane admitted that Stanley had told him her husband was soon to be relieved of his post.

This was not the only gossip he brought. Montagu had given him a book (without divulging the nature of its contents) and asked him to deliver it to Forster. Forster read part of it then handed it to Captain Swanston of the Derwent Bank and another of the Arthur Faction, who 'extensively circulated it in the community'. The 'Book', as it became known, was a scurrilous and libellous attack on Franklin and Jane. It told how Montagu was a victim of Lady Franklin's hatred of him and how she had got him suspended; it called Franklin a 'perfect imbecile' who could not cope without Montagu to prop him up. Almost like a character from *Alice in Wonderland*, Montagu even accused Jane of stopping his supply of plums and cabbages from the government gardens and adduced a letter from the head gardener to this effect as proof. Franklin had the man interviewed by the Police Magistrate, and he revealed that not only had he never received such an order from Lady Franklin and was not the author of the confirmatory letter, but that whoever had written it had got the initial of his name wrong! There was no doubt as to the true author, but of course it could never be proved.

Franklin was certain that he could have a field day in any court of law he if could get his hands on the Book, and demanded that Swanston surrender it to him. Although it was quickly removed from the public eye, Franklin heard nothing until, after sending Swanston a reminder, the latter replied that there was nothing as terrible in it as Franklin was claiming, and as it was a 'private' communication he refused to hand it over. Franklin later discovered that Swanston had been playing for time in order to have the worst passages excised.

By this time, opinion began to swing for once in the Franklins' favour. Turnbull was persuaded to admit to the Book's lack of veracity, and even Forster condemned Montagu – though he would not make his views public. And not all of the newspapers were against Franklin; the *Launceston Examiner* attacked both Montagu and his Book.

July arrived with still no official news. Then one evening a guest of Jane's, who had been out of the room, returned clearly distressed, telling her that a ship had just arrived with a four month-old newspaper containing an official announcement of her husband's successor. Franklin was told, and Jane recorded his reaction: ' "Well", he said, "is it true?" "Yes" – "Very well", replied Sir John, "So much the better. I wish him joy in what he has in store for him".'[24]

The *Colonial Times* trumpeted the Governor's recall as 'Glorious News!' But still Franklin remained the official incumbent and had to carry on with his work.

Sir Eardley Wilmot, Franklin's successor, arrived unencumbered by any explanation or documentation from Lord Stanley on 17 August 1843, beating the despatch telling Franklin he was to be recalled by three days. The six month-old notice glibly stated that since Franklin had served more than six successive years Stanley assumed he was anticipating the arrival of his successor. (Arthur had served for twelve years.) The letter contained no hint of the appreciation for services rendered, sincerely felt or otherwise, normally expressed in such circumstances.

The Franklins moved out of Government House as soon as they could and awaited their return passage to England. There is no doubt that although he was despised by the Arthur Faction, their minions and most of the press, the same did not apply to the population as a whole. Jane spoke of the good feeling towards him, and how an old Van Dieman's Land hand had told her that 'he had been witness to other Governors leaving their Governments, but such a universal feeling of respect and attachment as is shewn to Sir John, he had never witnessed before'.[25] Franklin himself noted that he was 'greeted in public with more outward demonstrations of respect than even in the days of my government'.[26] When he sailed from Hobart on 3 November 1843 thousands of cheering well-wishers turned out, and on calling in for the last time at Launceston over a thousand people signed a farewell address:

> By your example you have checked vice and encouraged virtue; your personal excellence has been conspicuous in your public career; you have sought no private object in the execution of your important trust; you have had the welfare of the Colony sincerely at heart; it has been your constant aim to promote the social, intellectual, moral and religious welfare of the people...[27]

Between them, Sir John and Lady Franklin had swum against the tide of nepotism, corruption and self-aggrandisement, and suffered for it. They laid the foundations for organised education, founded a museum, the Tasmanian Philosophical Society, the regatta, sponsored the Mechanics Institute, and what was to become the Tasmanian Royal Society; Jane had established the Tasmanian Ladies' Society for the Reformation of Female Prisoners, a botanical garden, sponsored lectures, and even implemented a scheme for the killing of the island's troublesome snakes! (This was based on a reward system for each dead snake; needless to say, her Ladyship was unable to emulate St Patrick, but at least for a time a lot of people were able to earn themselves some pocket money.)

Franklin's assessment of his governorship is given in his *Narrative*:

> I am justified, I think, in believing that they will look back to my government of Van Dieman's Land, as one, the influence of which was for good and not for evil, – one which promoted the moral and religious interests of the colony, and did not neglect its economic welfare...[28]

*

The Franklin of old might have let matters drop once the dust had settled. He still hoped and believed he had something to offer the Royal Navy (he was now fifty-eight years old); rocking the boat rarely aided one's career, and furthermore this was an age when it might be looked upon as 'bad form' to complain about one's treatment – even if one was in the right. But even as he sailed home on the *Rajah* to face a British public that by and large still only knew what Montagu and Stanley had cooked up between them, Franklin was busy fighting his corner.

One of the charges against Montagu that Stanley had brushed away so lightly was that Montagu had authorised the expenditure of government money on a tower and spire for St George's Church, and had deliberately not informed Franklin, whose authority should have been sought. Stanley had 'entirely absolved' Montagu, who claimed to have seen no documents giving the go-ahead to this project. Subsequently, written authorisation in *Montagu's hand and bearing his signature* had been discovered and passed on to Franklin, who wrote from on board the *Rajah* to relay this incriminating evidence together with other similar material that had come to light:

> From the careful perusal of these documents…your Lordship will discover the extreme difficulties the Governor in VD Land has to contend with in his endeavours to extricate the truth, or gain that information which is necessary for the public interests, when the Head of a Department, or his inferior officers conceive it to be their interest to conceal or with-hold them; or as Capt Forth chooses emphatically to term it – have determined 'Not to sell their friends'.[29]

Franklin went to the Colonial Office soon after his arrival back in England in June 1844 – but found a letter waiting for him ignoring any points he had made and stating that his Lordship had no intention of entering into a debate with a 'subordinate officer'. Franklin was not to be fobbed off so easily, and managed to get his interview some days later – for all the good it did. Stanley tried to reassure him that his recall had nothing to do with Montagu's suspension – and in fact the delay in sending the despatch was so the two events were not seen to be connected. Franklin retorted that he was not complaining about being recalled – that was his Lordship's prerogative. His complaint was with all the circumstances surrounding these events – the way Stanley had readily accepted Montagu's version of events over Franklin's; had not informed Franklin of the accusations Montagu had made behind his back; not to mention the way in which Montagu had been informed of the judgement long before his superior, Her Majesty's representative for the Colony, and allowed to make the details public. 'I took the liberty of remarking to Lord Stanley that I believed the act of giving to an inferior officer a transcript of the exact terms in which his superior was censured was without a parallel in the annals of his office.'[30]

Lord Stanley 'answered me nothing, except by an expression of incredulity or surprise at finding his despatch had been published in an English newspaper'.[31] Since this had been the talk of the town in both London and Van Dieman's Land, this remark seems disingenuous to say the least. And when Franklin tried to bring up the way Lady Franklin had been made to suffer in this affair, Stanley interrupted him, getting on his high horse and exclaiming his 'extreme repugnance at bringing the name of a lady into the discussion'.[32] Franklin thought it was a little late for that.

Regarding the Book, Franklin had not expected Stanley to say much, 'but he said less than I expected'. All his Lordship would concede was that this might need to be re-investigated, and so Franklin expressed his wish to be kept informed.

Franklin was banging his head against a brick wall. Even the one area where he had caught Montagu with the smoking gun – the documentary evidence that he had blatantly and unequivocally lied about repairs to St George's Church, accusing Franklin of authorising the expensive work when in fact he had done so himself without his superior's authority, even this was contemptuously waved away by Stanley.

After further infuriating attempts to make some headway, and receiving only condescending and increasingly tetchy replies from the Secretary of State, Franklin realised he was going to get nowhere – but that did not mean the matter was at an end. 'Lord Stanley miscalculated my deference to his judgement when he expected me to be satisfied with such a measure of justice as this.'[33] In a terse letter he informed Stanley that the terms of his response 'are inadequate to afford me the satisfaction I expected from you'.[34] In earlier times this kind of talk might have been the prelude to a duel at dawn; fortunately, Franklin resorted to a less drastic, but still mildly controversial, attempt to repair the damage to his and his wife's reputations. He would publish his own account of the whole saga.

This was a decision that aroused mixed feelings among his friends. Ross was against it, Jane had her doubts; Richardson and even Barrow were in favour. The *Narrative of Some Passages in the History of Van Dieman's Land during the Last Three Years of Sir John Franklin's Administration of its Government* came out in 1845 – but there was a sort of compromise in that it was distributed privately rather than being opened up for general publication. Apparently, each copy bore a hand-written inscription that it had been given to the individually named recipient 'By orders of Sir John Franklin'. In the preface, Franklin wrote that the account was intended mainly for his friends in Van Dieman's Land, 'in order not to leave them in ignorance of the steps which I have taken to vindicate the honour of my late office, and my character as their Governor…' Montagu had had his Book; now it was Franklin's turn. But Franklin's riposte was of a very different nature to Montagu's machiavellian volume; the introduction to a modern facsimile edition notes that it is written with 'surprisingly little rancour or prejudice'. It is a thorough and factual record, mainly Franklin's version of events concerning Montagu's tawdry campaign against him and Stanley's subsequent mishandling of the affair.

Stanley was on the distribution list, but remained unmoved. It is quite possible that having got his side of the story out into the open, Franklin would have let the matter rest there; but before there was any chance for further developments – in fact before he could actually finish working on his *Narrative* (the final touches would be made by Jane) – the course of his life took an unexpected twist which was to put all thoughts of the nightmare of the last seven years into the shade.

~ 12 ~

I Wish You Could See This Ship

THE North West Passage had captivated the imagination of men for centuries; its seekers were the alchemists of exploration. To reach the North or South Pole might bring fame and some scientific benefits, but to turn the North West Passage into a commercially viable route would, for the northern European countries, be like turning base metal into gold.

There is speculation that the Norsemen were the first to probe for what we now call the North West Passage, lured west from Greenland into the icy channels in search of land, trade or conquest. But we have to leap forward to the age of Drake for the first notable voyages to the region. Drake himself, after a set-to with the Spaniards along the coast of Chile, headed north with a view to making an opportunistic attempt from the western side, an approach which Captain James Cook was to emulate two centuries later. But Drake was unprepared for the kind of climate he was to encounter, and got nowhere near far enough north before being forced back by the cold. At around the same time, during the 1570s, Martin Frobisher, another English adventurer, was making a more organised attempt, getting as far as what is now Frobisher Bay, just above Hudson Strait. The following decade John Davis ventured further north into the Strait that now bears his name, landing on Baffin Island.

Early in the following century Henry Hudson passed through a strait to the south of Frobisher Bay and found his way into a vast new bay – strait and bay are both named after him. William Baffin followed this up with several voyages to the region, pushing further north than his predecessors into what became Baffin Bay, and, without realising its significance, locating Lancaster Sound – the door to the North West Passage. There was then very little progress for many decades. Even the admirable Captain Cook, as mentioned above, found his way barred by ice before he could even begin to probe for an opening. It was not until Franklin's time that attempts to solve the puzzle of the North West Passage were resumed in earnest.

Ann Savours, in her definitive *Search for the North West Passage*,[1] says that by Franklin's day 'a commercial route was no longer of great significance'. This certainly seems to be the consensus among modern commentators – as is the notion that the Admiralty had to find something to do for at least part of its powerful navy during peacetime.

However, until the maze of islands, straits, sounds and inlets had been fully explored there was always the slim chance of a way through, and consequent savings in time, costs and possibly human life. Some still believed in this possibility. Barrow, by now turned eighty and close to the end of his reign as Second Secretary of the Admiralty (and unofficial First Patron of Naval Exploration), refused to let go of the idea until completely proven wrong. Franklin still believed a passage could be found, although whether he still envisaged it would be any good for trade is doubtful. Before long he would be asked for his views on the prospects of a new expedition, and he would cite only scientific, not commercial, benefits.[2]

The idea that Arctic exploration gave the navy 'something to do' is a little more suspect. Exploration could be expensive yet had comparatively modest manpower requirements – usually one or two very small ships with a handful of officers. These officers were selected from a tiny pool of men who, although often war veterans, had spent much of their careers evolving into 'specialist' explorers anyway. At a time when hundreds of officers were unemployed and probably thousands of destitute tars haunted the coastal towns, this does not seem a very cost-effective way of solving the problem of naval unemployment. Although Arctic (and Antarctic) exploration provided officers and men with a stiff test and would have been wonderful for character- or team-building, a nebulous phenomenon much beloved to this day by corporate management gurus, the specific lessons they learned and much of the experience they gained in that alien environment would probably be of little use to them anywhere else in the world, and certainly not in wartime.

National pride, a more prevalent and less self-conscious trait then than now, obviously played a significant part in fuelling the wish to complete the North West Passage. But there was also a genuine desire for the geographical and general scientific knowledge that expeditions like this achieved, and Barrow, for all his faults, seems to have been a sincere and enthusiastic seeker in this respect. So was Franklin, and he had the added incentive of wanting to see through to the end a quest he had begun many years ago.

✻

Franklin's immediate concerns on his return from Van Dieman's Land were to do with the injustices he had suffered at the hands of Montagu and Lord Stanley, and the damage to his and Jane's reputations. This sordid affair could have nagged away at him for the rest of his life, and might well have made a depressing anti-climax to his career. But by a sort of heaven-sent coincidence, within a short time of his return to England he received news sufficiently interesting to distract him from his recent tribulations – it was probably the only thing that mattered to him enough to achieve this transformation.

Sir John Barrow is usually quoted as the prime mover in the attempt to get another North West Passage expedition off the ground. It might not have happened without his enthusiasm, but Captain Frederick Beechey claimed the credit for stimulating interest in this latest venture. It was also Beechey, Franklin's second-in-command in the *Trent* in 1818, and commanding the *Blossom* trying to meet up with Franklin's overland party in 1826, who urged the use of screw propellers powered by steam.

Barrow put his case for a new expedition to the First Lord of the Admiralty, Lord Haddington, in December 1844. His *Proposal for an Attempt to Complete the Discovery of a North-West Passage* began:

> There is a feeling generally entertained in the several scientific societies, and individuals attached to scientific pursuits, and also among officers of the Navy, that the discovery, or rather the completion of the discovery, of a passage from the Atlantic to the

185

Pacific, round the Northern coast of North America, ought not to be abandoned, after so much has been done, and so little now remains to be done...[3]

Barrow went on to cite voyages by Parry and Ross through Lancaster Sound, 'one of the open gates' of the Passage. He described how in 1820 Parry, having reached Melville Island, saw 'something like the looming of land to the Southward' which had been given the name Bank's Land (now Banks Island). If one were to set a course between Bank's Land and the North American coast one would be 300 leagues away from the long sought-after goal. What no one knew then was that Bank's Land and Victoria Land were islands of sizeable proportions – the former comparable in size to mainland Britain and the latter much bigger – and only a narrow channel divided them. (The final leg of the Passage actually lay to the north of Bank's Land through what is now McClure Strait.)

Barrow pointed out the importance of adding to Britain's data on terrestrial magnetism in the Arctic – as part of an ongoing worldwide survey – and the benefits to geography and hydrography. He helpfully brought to his Lordship's attention the fact that the *Erebus* and *Terror*, which had proved their worth with Sir James Clark Ross in the Antarctic, would require little time to be made ready.

Barrow was convinced that the North West Passage would be completed one day, and, 'if left to be performed by some other power, England, by her neglect of it, after having opened the East and West doors, would be laughed at by all the world for having hesitated to cross the threshold'.[4]

Lord Haddington sought the opinions of Franklin and others before giving the green light to the expedition. The First Lord of the Admiralty both wrote to and discussed the idea in person with Franklin on 24 January 1845; Franklin replied to the written query by return of post confirming his enthusiasm regarding a new search for the North West Passage. He, too, enthused about the 'advantage of Steam' and suggested a route between Cape Walker and Bank's Land, or failing that north through Wellington Channel; Parry and others echoed these views. But even before these discussions took place, the rumour mill must have been at work, because during the final month of the previous year much of the talk had been about who would be given command of such an expedition.

It is generally agreed that Sir James Clark Ross, a veteran of numerous expeditions taking in both Polar regions, would have been a virtually automatic selection, and there is a certain amount of mystery surrounding his decision not to go. He is purported to have declared himself too old, though at forty-four he was more than ten years younger than Franklin. A more credible explanation is that on his recent marriage* he had promised his wife and her father that his wandering days were over. Although this was not a common trait among explorers of any kind (particularly bearing in mind Franklin's leaving of Eleanor on her deathbed), it is by no means beyond the realms of plausibility, especially considering that Ross had already been through a lot of hardship during his illustrious career. But there is another possible slant to this.

Kathleen Fitzpatrick, in her book about Franklin's time in Van Dieman's Land,[5] slipped in a theory about this particular matter which has been overlooked by later writers but which I think may well contain at least a grain of truth. Franklin and Ross were close; on Van Dieman's Land Jane wrote that they (together with Crozier) 'feel towards one another as friends and brothers',[6] and Franklin confided in and sought the advice of Ross on various matters, including his spat with Stanley. The younger man knew as well as anyone except Jane what Franklin had been through these last few years; he was aware of how much this gentle man had suffered inwardly over the callous and unjust way he had been treated, and his maddening inability to be able to do anything about it. It is tempting to think that Ross was in two minds as to whether to accept the leadership of the expedition, and that his regard for Franklin tipped the balance. One could go even further and wonder whether Ross *did* want to go, yet still was prepared to make this great sacrifice for a friend whom he knew would never get another chance to achieve this lifetime's ambition. He may well have discussed the matter with

* During his stay in Van Dieman's Land, Franklin's niece Sophia Cracroft had fallen for him but she was too late – the woman he was to marry was awaiting his return to England.

187

Parry, who was of the opinion that Franklin would 'die of disappointment' if he were not to go. All of this is, of course, pure conjecture – and could only ever be, for Ross, being a true gentleman of his era, would never have allowed such a truth to be known.

Just after Christmas 1844 Franklin met Ross, and in a letter subsequently told Jane about a curious conversation they had had (probably at the Athenaeum club, from where he was writing). Ross, swearing Franklin to secrecy, said he had grounds for thinking that 'some underhand work was in operation', and that 'he suspects Back to be the cause of it'.[7] By now Sir George Back, a shadow had always hung over the character of the man who was a midshipman on Franklin's first overland expedition over twenty years previously. Fergus Fleming describes him as a 'conceited bounder',[8] and although there can be no doubting the vital and courageous part he played in saving the lives of Franklin and others back then, few seem to have held him in very high regard as a person.

Ross said that Back had come to see him, sent by an unnamed 'friend' at the Admiralty on a mission to persuade Ross to change his mind about not going on the new expedition. When this attempt failed, Back asked Ross if he would be recommending Franklin. 'Of course', Ross answered. But what, Back wanted to know, about Franklin's age, and the way he suffered greatly from the cold? Ross said he did not know what Back was talking about – there had never been any suggestion that Franklin suffered unduly in the cold; and as for his age, Ross pointed out that he 'knew from actual observation' that Franklin was as 'active and rigorous as ever he was, both in body and mind'. Suspecting the motives behind Back's line of questioning, Ross finally refused to continue with the discussion.[9] But that was not the end of the matter.

A couple of days later, Edward Sabine, an army officer and old friend and neighbour of Franklin, came to see Ross saying he had been sent by Captain Beaufort, the navy's Hydrographer and another of Franklin's friends, apparently 'on the same errand as Back'. What struck Ross was that when he reiterated his view that Franklin was the man to lead the expedition, Sabine echoed Back's words in disagreeing with him. Following this episode, Ross wrote to Beaufort underlining his decision not to accept command of the expedition, and describing Franklin as 'the fittest person to have it'.[10]

Franklin went to see Beaufort, who proved reluctant to discuss the matter. Franklin said he believed himself to have 'the prior claim for consideration' for leading the North West Passage expedition, and tried to put the lie to the objections circulating against him. No one, he said, on the expeditions he had commanded had suffered less from the cold than he; and as for his age, 'my reply is that as to bodily health and energy I am as fully competent to undertake the duty as ever I was'. He had taken the precaution of having his old friend Richardson check him over, and had been passed fit. Franklin knew that Richardson, having his best interests at heart, would not have hesitated to say if he felt his friend should not go. He went on to see Barrow about the same matter and was 'received very kindly'; the old man expressed the opinion that Franklin was probably the front runner for the expedition. But yet again, the business of suffering from the cold cropped up in conversation – it was as if someone had been running an effective propaganda campaign against Franklin – and the latter again 'positively contradicted' the story.[11]

He moved on to Parry – another very experienced Arctic officer who might have been considered for the position but apparently had no interest in it. Parry reassured Franklin that he had handled things well – particularly in not approaching Lord Haddington directly to 'compete as it were with the other candidates'. Parry had no qualms about Franklin's condition, saying he could see 'no alteration' in him.[12]

Jane preserved for posterity a record of a conversation Franklin had with Lord Haddington which has gone down in the annals of Franklin folklore. Haddington was naturally concerned about his prospective expedition leader's age, and no doubt the stories in circulation about his physical condition had reached his ears also. During the course of some gentle probing, Franklin quite rightly pointed out that although an *overland* expedition would be out of the question for him now, this was a shipborne venture and well within his capabilities. Haddington admitted to feeling a 'great responsibility' in the matter, something which bears out Franklin's own assertion that Haddington was concerned for his officer's welfare rather than cynically looking for excuses to put him out of the running.

The First Lord, according to Jane, said, 'Your services have been very arduous ones. Latterly you have been on a civil service which must have cost you great care and anxiety'.

'No anxiety on the expedition could equal that', Franklin retorted wryly.

'It is bodily wear and tear I am thinking of. Everyone knows how arduous your land expeditions were, and how you got through them, but you are not so young as you were. You see, I know your age: you are fifty-nine.'

'Oh no, my Lord. I am only fifty-eight.'[13]

*

Several modern writers have glanced at the last picture of Franklin, a daguerreotype showing a heavy-jowled man in his late fifties – who happened to be suffering from a severe bout of 'flu at the time the picture was taken – and pronounced him 'unfit'. He was old; he had spent much of his life on the quarterdeck and the last few years behind a desk on a remote island; he was fat. How could he possibly be fit? But this is too simplistic. Of course he did not go to the gym, an aerobics class, or take off for altitude training – he was not fit in the modern sense of the word. But throughout his life he had proved himself to be fit in the 'hardy' sense, and in Van Dieman's Land he walked and rode. The fact is we do not know exactly how much exercise he took, although it is known that he did like to walk. He had a natural tendency to put on weight, but 'fat' by no means equals 'unfit' (nor does 'old'), and from this distance it would be a risky business to ignore the opinions of Ross, Richardson, Parry and Franklin himself because of what we may perceive as circumstantial evidence to the contrary.

In February, Lord Haddington finally plumped for Franklin as expedition leader, and events began to move quickly. On 6 March 1845 *The Times* made the following announcement:

Naval Intelligence, Woolwich, March 5th. The Erebus and Terror, experimental vessels, were commissioned at Woolwich on Tuesday, and the following officers have been appointed to them:-

To the Erebus – Captain Sir John Franklin, KCH, to have the command of the Arctic expedition; Commander James Fitzjames (1842) FORMERLY Commander of the Clio, 16 gun sloop, on the Indian station; Lt Henry TD Le Vesconte (1841) formerly serving in the Clio; mate, Charles F Des Voeux (1844), from the Excellent, gunnery ship at Portsmouth; second master, HF Collins, from the Shearwater steam vessel, employed by Captain Washington in the surveying service; clerk, GF Pinborn; Gunner JG Robinson; Boatswain, JG Terry; Carpenter, W Weekes.

To the Terror – Capt FRM Crozier (1841); Lt Edward Little (1837); Lt Hodgson, (1842); carpenter, Thomas Honey.

A full list of the officers and crew of the expedition is given in Appendix Two. It is said that Barrow originally wanted Fitzjames as second-in-command to Franklin but, despite having a distinguished naval record, he seems to have had little experience of exploration and had never been to the Arctic.[14] He had seen action (and was wounded) off the coast of Syria four years before he joined the *Erebus* under Franklin, who put him in charge of magnetic observations. Fitzjames was in his early thirties, and from his accounts of the final days before the ships sailed away into the unknown he seems to have been a witty and gregarious officer.

Beneath Franklin and Fitzjames on the *Erebus* was First Lieutenant Graham Gore, whom Fitzjames rated a man of 'great stability of character, a very good officer, and the sweetest of tempers…'[15] He had been promoted to lieutenant while in the Arctic with George Back, and saw action in the Opium War before joining the *Erebus*. Lieutenant Henry Thomas Dundas Le Vesconte had also fought in the war with China, and was recommended for this expedition by Fitzjames, with whom he had served in the *Clio*. Lieutenant James Fairholme was another Fitzjames recommendation, having served and seen action off the coast of Syria with him in the *Ganges*. Also worth mentioning are Harry Goodsir and James Reid. Goodsir was a qualified doctor from the east of Scotland and officially the *Erebus*'s Acting Assistant Surgeon, but his main role was that of naturalist. Ice Master Reid was chosen for his experience as a whaling captain. His humour, knowledge and straightforwardness – not to mention his strong Scottish accent – seem to have kept Fitzjames well entertained.

Captaincy of the *Terror*, and role of second-in-command overall, went to the vastly experienced Captain Francis Rawdon Moira Crozier, known to Franklin from his visit to Van Dieman's Land with James Ross. Ten years Franklin's junior, he was a native of Banbridge, County Down, who had been in the Royal Navy for over thirty-five years, having made three Arctic voyages with Parry between 1821 and 1827, and was second-in-command to James Ross on his 1839 Antarctic expedition. Cyriax says he was an authority on terrestrial magnetism, and Fitzjames mentions using his 'Fox', a dipping needle invented by Crozier.[16] Crozier had told Ross that he hesitated 'not a moment' to be second to Franklin and even confessed to feeling that he was not up to leading the expedition (despite his experience he had never led one).[17] Lieutenant Edward Little had served in the Mediterranean shortly after Franklin's stint there, and had been rescued from eighteen months' enforced idleness on half-pay for this expedition. Lieutenant George Henry Hodgson was another Fitzjames protégé and distinguished veteran of the war with China. Lieutenant John Irving was another Edinburgh man. He was unusual in having left the navy to emigrate to Australia. He returned after six years and resumed his naval career only two years before the expedition sailed.

Cyriax says of the crews in general that they were 'north-country' sailors, perhaps echoing the same observation made by Fitzjames.* This may have been true of the officers, with several Scots and Crozier an Ulsterman. But anyone armed with the personnel details given in Appendix Two and a pencil and paper would soon be able to work out that this was not the case of the crews as a whole. Taking the combined crews of the two ships, and including the marines, it is evident that in fact there were more than *twice as many* southerners as northerners, with the southeast of England alone providing more sailors than all the northern ports put together.

---

* During the research for this book I was told that Richard Cyriax knew more about the final North West Passage expedition than Franklin did himself, which anyone who reads his book will agree is probably no exaggeration.

The average age of the crew was twenty-nine, with those in their twenties forming a larger portion than all other age groups combined. These figures again includes the marines, although it is noticeable that the marines themselves were generally older – mostly in their thirties. Theirs was effectively a policing role perhaps better suited to more mature men. The oldest member of the crew was forty-six (David McDonald from Peterhead in Scotland, the quartermaster of the *Terror*). The youngest were the three eighteen year-old 'boys'* – the other being nineteen – all from Kent. Both ships carried an experienced Ice Master and engineers and stokers for the steam engines, in addition to the usual ranks found on a ship of the Royal Navy.

Many tons of supplies poured into the Woolwich Dockyard: biscuit, pemmican, meat, vegetables, wine ('for the sick'), chocolate, tea, lemon juice, soup, and so on. The expedition was to be supplied with food of a quantity calculated to keep them going for three years, and integral to this plan was a large supply of meat, vegetables and soup in cans supplied by a company called Goldner's. Goldner's had never supplied the navy before, and their part in fulfilling this massive contract remains a controversial one – of which more later. Suffice it to say for now that Goldner's had problems completing the contract on time and, according to one account, actually delayed the expedition's departure.

Canned food was a fairly recent innovation – though by 1845 not quite the novelty depicted by some. The use of steam power also fits into this category. The dockyards at Chatham had turned out their first steam-powered ship over ten years earlier, in 1832,[18] but this, like many of the earliest ships of its kind, was a paddle steamer. The *Erebus* and *Terror* were fitted out with ex-railway steam engines powering a screw propeller which could be hauled out of the water to prevent ice damage; these engines were small and not particularly powerful (a mere sixteen years had passed since the building of Stephenson's *Rocket*) and only intended for use when conditions

---

* Modern forensic tests carried out on skeletal remains of expedition members indicates that at least one of the 'boys' was much younger than his stated age – supposedly 12–15 years old. But were these bones from the Franklin expedition? It is hard to believe that they would have knowingly included one so young in a hand-picked crew.

made traditional sailing impossible. It is interesting to note that within just four years the Admiralty would become so convinced that the future of naval warfare lay with steam that it would bring an end to the building of pure sailing ships (and the end of the wooden warship was only thirteen years away. In 1858 the French would produce *La Gloire* ironclad battleship, followed by the British *Warrior* in 1860 – still to be seen at Portsmouth).[19] The use of steam also enabled the installation of a form of central heating to be conveyed by pipe around the ships, though with coal supplies limited (only enough for twelve days according to Lieutenant Irving) and the proposed judicious use of the propellers, it would presumably have been considered a luxury rather than a routine comfort. There were some diversions to help the crews pass the time when they were not working, including a hand organ on each vessel to provide musical entertainment, and over a thousand books.

The two ships were put through their paces on the Thames. The steam engines did not provide great speed, but would, as Irving commented, 'astound the Esquimaux not a little'.[20]

After inspecting the *Erebus* and *Terror* at Woolwich in February, Franklin made one of his usual farewell tours of his home county, and then on his way south he called on his niece Catharine and her husband the Reverend Drummond Rawnsley at Little Hatton in Hertfordshire. Their son, Willingham Franklin, was to be baptised and Franklin had been given the honour of standing Godfather to him. Franklin gave the boy a prayer book and Bible in one volume, in which he had inscribed:

Willingham Franklin Rawnsley
From his affectionate Uncle and Godfather on the day of his Babtism, 23rd March 1845
John Franklin

Search the Scriptures
Pray with the spirit and pray with the understanding also.

In later years Willingham Franklin Rawnsley recalled: 'Sir John was not a Greek scholar and the spelling of Baptism with a "b" was as he always pronounced it'.[21]

On 8 May there was a reception at the Admiralty for Franklin which was attended by the expedition's officers and all of the big names in British Arctic exploration of the day: Parry, James Clark Ross, Back, and Barrow. Four days later, after an official tour of the *Erebus* and *Terror* by Lord Haddington and other dignitaries, the ships left Woolwich for the last time. They were towed line-astern further down the Thames to Greenhithe, although the *Terror* took the opportunity to try out her engine again for some of the way. Jane and Eleanor went with Franklin thus far on board the *Erebus*. Franklin, and probably Jane and Eleanor, stayed at the White Hart Inn in Greenhithe while the final provisions and a spare propeller found their way to the ships.

On the final Sunday before the ships' departure, Franklin led the Divine Service, creating his usual impression on those who had not heard him before. Commander Fitzjames wrote, 'I defy any man not to feel the force of what he would convey... Every one was struck with his extreme earnestness of manner, evidently proceeding from real conviction'.[22] On this day Franklin wrote his last letter before sailing to a Mr Griffin (presumably Jane's father):

> I wish you could see this ship now – she is almost as clean as she will be at sea, and quite ready for sailing. The officers and the crew all fine young men and in excellent spirits. This day we had the happiness of joining together on board in Divine Worship, to praise God for past mercies and to implore His guiding and protecting Providence. In this spirit we all hope to begin, continue, and end our voyage.[23]

He added the postscript, 'We sail tomorrow'.

The spare propeller arrived early on 19 May; at 10.30 that morning, the *Erebus* and *Terror*, and their supply ship the *Barretto Junior*, were towed out of Greenhithe for the open sea.

According to Cyriax[24] the two vessels had black hulls, white masts, and a broad yellow band running along the length of the hull. It must have been a difficult parting for Jane. 'Poor Lady Franklin was in a sad state before we left', wrote Crozier to his sister, adding, 'You would like her much she is so full of kindness'.[25]

Eleanor told her aunt in a letter that her father was looking much better 'since he left off the snuff' (he had been stricken with influenza, as mentioned above).* The officers, she describes as being in 'sanguine' and 'harmonious' spirits. The crew were not quite so harmonious, having been brought only two months' pay instead of the six-month advance they were due. Franklin sent the clerk scurrying back to the Admiralty for the rest of what his men were owed – and he duly returned on the Sunday interrupting Franklin's reading of the Service. Eleanor's letter also mentioned an incident that occurred upon the departure of the ships:

> Last Monday, just as they were setting sail, a dove settled on one of the masts, and remained there for some time. Everyone was pleased with the good omen, and if it be an omen of peace and harmony, I think that there is every reason of its being true. We were very much pleased with the officers, especially the Commander, Captain Fitzjames, and the 1st Liet [sic] Mr Gore...they seem already attached to him (Papa).
>
> You will be glad to hear that dear Papa left in excellent spirits, he puts his trust in God, his only Refuge and Strength...[26]

From the quarterdeck of his ship as it glided down the Thames, Franklin could make out among the crowd Jane, Eleanor, and Sophia Cracroft, and vigorously waved his handkerchief in their direction. He never knew whether they had seen him, nor that this was the last time he would see their faces.

*

The Admiralty soon heard that Franklin had run into contrary winds in the North Sea, and sent a steamship called the *Blazer* chasing after him with instructions that he should turn back and head for the Channel if there was no change. He reassured them that although the north-east wind had caused them to anchor off Aldeburgh on the Suffolk coast, conditions had improved and they were on their way north towards the Orkneys once more. The *Rattler*, which had towed them out of the Thames, had been assisting both the *Erebus*

---

* William Jerdan, an acquaintance of Franklin's mentioned earlier, stated that his health was 'perfectly restored' by the time he set sail.

and *Terror* ever since,* but this operation had become dangerous in the heavy seas, and fearing a collision Franklin ordered the hawser connecting the ships to be cast off, and sent her to rendezvous with the *Barretto Junior* which had parted company from them. He took the liberty of commandeering the *Blazer* to replace the *Rattler*. By the time he wrote this letter, the ships had reached Aberdeen.

As they made their way northward, Daniel Bryant, Sergeant of Marines on board the *Erebus*, wrote home to Inverness to tell his family about his Captain:

> I am happy to say that Sir John Franklin is a very religious man and has forbidden all drunkenness and swearing and all bad language by any reason. We have Church twice a day...
>
> We had Church this morning and Sir JF read to us a very beautiful sermon... 'And the barrel of meal wasted not, neither did the cruse of oil fail, according to the Word of the Lord...'† Sir John called the ship's company's attention to that part of the sermon and the whole of the ship's company were very much pleased with Sir John's appropriate text, and [?] in the point of view as Sir John, and that is to accomplish our object which we have in view...²⁷

Crozier wrote to James Clark Ross praising Franklin and saying that all was going well, but adding pessimistically, 'We are I fear sadly late...What I fear is that from our being so late we shall have no time to look round and judge for ourselves, but blunder into the ice and make a second 1824 of it'.²⁸ (He was a midshipman on Parry's third voyage, which had got no further than Prince Regent Inlet before being defeated by the ice, suffering the loss of the *Fury* in the process.) Franklin, however, on reaching Stromness in the Orkneys at the beginning of June 1845, wrote to his wife that 'the most experienced Davis-Strait seamen here and at Peterhead declare that we are quite in time...' He spoke of a 'kind note' he had received

---

* The *Rattler* was a steam-sloop that has helped to prove the value of the screw propeller over paddles. In a contest at Chatham she had taken part in a 'tug-of-war' with the paddle-sloop *Alecto*. They were tied stern-to-stern, and the *Rattler* managed to pull the *Alecto* astern.
† From I Kings, Chapter 17, Verse 17.

from James Ross, which made mention of the Admiralty having been so keen to have him as the expedition's leader that they had been prepared to postpone it for a year in the hope that it would change his mind. Franklin expressed his great admiration and affection for Ross, but added candidly:

> I think perhaps that I have the tact of keeping the Officers and men happily together in a greater degree than Ross, and for this reason he is evidently ambitious and wishes to do everything himself. I possess not that feeling, but consider that the Commander of any Service having established his character before, maintains it most by directing the exertions of his officers… I have the satisfaction of perceiving that they all defer to my opinion even on points not immediately connected with our present pursuits. Fitz-James even looks surprised when it comes out that I have been in this or that kind of Service, of which he had not previously been informed.
>
> The more I see of Gore, the more convinced I am that in him I have a treasure and a faithful friend… I like the Ice-Master Reid. As he begins to approach the field of his labours, he opens out and becomes communicative on the subject of Ice and its motions.[29]

Even at this juncture, Franklin could not forget the trauma of Van Dieman's Land. Jane had taken charge of the final stages of the production of the pamphlet putting his side of the story, and he told her that he 'greatly rejoiced' at the progress she was making in that direction.

Commander Fitzjames recorded that the crew of the *Terror* were not given general shore leave at Stromness, but one man from each mess was allowed to leave the ship for provisions; for him to make this observation leads one to infer that the men on the *Erebus were* allowed ashore. In any event, according to one account there was some questionable behaviour at this time. It is possible that, in the tradition of the British sailor on land with new money in his pocket, the tars did not forbear to provide whatever drinking establishments existed on Stromness at that time with a sharp boost in trade, and it may have been the fall-out following this release from Franklin's 'no drinking and no swearing' edict on board ship that left the islanders with less than glowing memories of the visit. The source for this emerged years later, when the explorer Dr John Rae engaged in a war of words with none other than Charles Dickens about the fate of the expedition, and as a side-issue happened to toss in the following observation regarding the crews of the *Erebus* and *Terror*:

> What their state of discipline was I cannot say, but their conduct at the very last British port they entered was not such as to make those who knew it, consider them very deserving of the high eulogium passed upon them in *Household Words*.[30]

It has been pointed out that Rae was no fan of the Royal Navy, but if he is to be believed it was perhaps with a sense of relief that the people of Stromness said farewell to the expedition's ships on the morning of Tuesday 3 June. Franklin makes no mention of any trouble, telling his wife:

> Let me now assure you my dearest Jane, that I am now amply provided with every requisite for my voyage and that I am entering on my voyage comforted with every hope of God's merciful guidance and protection and especially that He will bless and comfort and protect you my dearest love, my very dear Eleanor and dear Sophy – and all my other relatives.
>
> Oh how I wish I could write to each of them to assure them of the happiness I feel in my officers, my crew and my ship.
> Your affectionate husband,
> John Franklin[31]

A series of letters from Commander Fitzjames to his sister were passed on by her for publication in order to let the public know of the expedition's progress. Like others, he talks of the good mood on board the ships: 'Every one is shaking hands with himself'.[32] By 8 June the ships were about eighty miles from Stromness, near the island of Rona, and making good progress in clear, calm weather. They finally parted company with the *Blazer* and the *Rattler*. Fitzjames described how their two escorts came alongside and gave them 'not three, but a prolongation of cheers...and in an hour or two they were out of sight, leaving us with an old gull or two and the rocky Rona to look at; and then was the time to see if anyone flinched from the undertaking. Every one's was, "Now we are off at last!" '[33] They drank Lady Franklin's health 'at the old gentleman's table', and also the health of Eleanor, whose birthday it was.

Franklin discussed with Fitzjames the importance of the scientific side of their journey, emphasising that he should observe 'everything from a flea to a whale',[34] and gave the rest of the officers a similar pep talk, producing and reading out some of the instructions from his very first visit to the region almost thirty years ago on the *Trent*, to illustrate the point. 'He spoke delightfully of the zealous co-operation he expected from all, and his desire to do full justice to the exertions of each.'[35]

Franklin had also been showing a draft of the Van Dieman's Land pamphlet to some of his officers, who all 'expressed their indignation' at the way he had been treated by Stanley and Montagu (they were probably sincere – but we have to remember that these were the same men who 'defer to my opinion even on points not immediately connected with our pursuits'!). Fitzjames remarked somewhat admiringly that in his *Narrative* Franklin 'cuts up Lord Stanley a few' and told them he was 'haughty and imperious'.[36] Franklin invited his officers to dinner most days, and ate with Fitzjames every evening, who noted that they were all very fond of their leader, who 'improves very much as we come to know him. He is anything but nervous or fidgety; in fact I should say remarkable for energetic decision in sudden emergencies...'[37] He regaled them with tales of his earlier travels in the region, and they were amused by his recollections of Akaitcho, the Indian chief.

Franklin passed some of his time preparing a system of signals ready for when the ships might become parted from each other by ice; he perused Barrow's account of earlier voyages to this region; and morning and evening he read a chapter from the Old Testament. Every morning he led prayers on deck, and there was a reprise in the evening in his cabin for those who had not been able to participate earlier.

Franklin told Jane:

I rejoice at being able to tell you that my cough has entirely left me, and that I really am in such robust health as to cause the officers to exclaim 'What a surprising change the coming to sea has produced in your health and appearance. You look quite a different man from what you did at Woolwich.'[38]

In the early hours of 4 July, during the season of perpetual daylight at this latitude, the ships arrived at Disco among the Whalefish Islands off Greenland – inside the Arctic Circle, where Davis Strait meets Baffin Bay – guided to a safe anchorage by two Eskimos in canoes. They had lately made rapid progress ('The only difficulty I had', said Fitzjames, 'was to get Sir John to shorten sail...'[39]) While the crew were busy cramming supplies from the *Barretto Junior* into the already overcrowded ships, Franklin visited a Danish whaling station on shore, where he received news that the ice had broken up almost two months earlier, thus improving their chances of crossing Baffin Bay to Lancaster Sound, the eastern 'door' to the North West Passage. From the Eskimos he obtained a pair of sealskin boots which he sent back to Jane – his 'contribution to your Arctic Stories' – together with sealskin pouches, ideal for keeping a watch in, for Eleanor and Sophia.

By 12 July the transfer of supplies was completed. The *Erebus* and *Terror* were now low in the water, and so tightly packed that Franklin was surrounded by tinned potatoes in his own cabin. As if this were not enough he had allocated Assistant Surgeon Harry Goodsir, a naturalist, a table to work at, and 'his stuffed birds are also spread out to dry'. He cheerfully told his old friend Robert Brown that by the time they got to Bering Strait (at the exit of the Passage) 'we shall be in good sailing trim and have room to stretch our limbs, which we have now hardly room to do, so perfectly full is every hole and corner'.[40]

On that bright and sunny day the *Barretto Junior* left for England carrying Franklin's last letter to Jane. He reassured his wife that they had a full three years' supply of provisions: 'I mention this the more particularly that you may not have the slightest apprehension respecting our welfare though we should have to winter twice...' He spoke of their plans for buying some land where they could live once he returned: 'Our means would necessarily cause the purchase to be small...' It was a dream they were destined never to fulfil. These were his last words for Jane:

I have written to each of my dearest friends to comfort and assist you with their best counsel. To the Almighty care I commit you and dear Eleanor, that He will shield you under His wings and grant the continual aid of His Holy Spirit. Again that God bless and support you both is, and will be the constant prayer of
Your most affectionate husband,
John Franklin[41]

Commander Fitzjames' final assessment of his Captain was thus:

He is full of life and energy, with good judgement, and a capital memory – one of the best I know. His conversation is delightful and most instructive, and of all men he is the most fitted for the command of an enterprise requiring sound sense and great perseverance. I have learnt much from him and consider myself fortunate in being with such a man – he is full of benevolence and kindness withal.[42]

~ 13 ~

The Haven Where They Would Be

THE *Barretto Junior* carried back to England three crewmen and a marine – two were sick and two plain incompetent; they were fated to be the most fortunate men on the whole expedition.

Franklin informed the Admiralty of their progress so far, and concluded, 'It is unnecessary of me to assure their lordships of the energy and zeal of Captain Crozier, Commander Fitzjames, and the officers and men with whom I have the happiness of being employed in this service'.[1]

The officers made a final check of their scientific equipment, then the *Erebus* and *Terror* sailed north into Baffin Bay. The ships were probably sighted about a week later by a Captain Straiton of the *Eagle*, who reported seeing two barques off Upernavik on the west coast of Greenland. Towards the end of July 1845 two whaling ships encountered them moored to an iceberg waiting to cross Baffin Bay for Lancaster Sound. Captain Dannet of the *Prince of Wales* sighted the *Erebus* and *Terror* on 25 July, and the following day a number of officers were rowed over to visit him, the consensus being that one was Fitzjames, but that Franklin remained on the *Erebus*. He found the men well, and received an invitation to dine on the *Erebus* with Franklin on the 26th; a favourable wind arose, however, and he decided to take advantage of it.

Another whaler also met up with the two ships at around this time: the *Enterprise*, Captain Martin. Martin did get to speak to Franklin, as well as other officers, 'all of whom with the crews of both vessels were in excellent health and spirits'.[2] In November, when he arrived home in Peterhead, Scotland, he wrote a brief statement of his encounter and forwarded it to the Admiralty, and it appears to have been filed away and forgotten (though it still exists among the Admiralty papers relating to the expedition).[3] When in later years he was asked to enlarge on his note of the meeting, he told the Admiralty that he drew alongside the *Erebus* and *Terror* for about fifteen minutes, during which time he spoke with Franklin and his Ice Master, Reid. One of the peculiarities of this conversation is Martin's recollection that Franklin said they had enough food for *five* years, as opposed to the official figure of three, and that they could even make it 'spin out' for *seven*. The expedition was categorically provisioned for three years. Cyriax suggests that the officers Martin spoke to a couple of days after his talk with Franklin got a little carried away owing to their enthusiasm. But the estimates are so specific, and the officers so experienced and professional, that this seems an unlikely explanation; more probably, Martin mis-interpreted what Franklin told him. Just possibly, Franklin told him they might not reach *home* for five to seven years. Although the achievement of the North West Passage might have taken the full three years, this would still have left them a long way from home. Assuming they made it through the Bering Strait they were due to call at either Panama or the Sandwich Islands so that an officer could be despatched directly to England with the good news, and it is quite likely there would have been lengthy delays at these or other ports for re-fitting, re-provisioning and recuperation. (It is, however, hard to see how this could have added more than one or two years to the journey.)

Like Dannet, Martin was unable to get over to the *Erebus* to dine with Franklin, and a couple of days later he lost sight of the two ships.

✳

Naturally enough, little or no news was expected from the expedition for quite some time. The meeting with the whaling ships had been a fluke; they were entering what was still largely a little-known, little-understood region where there would be no outposts or passing ships to take their letters and despatches home. The analogy often used is that of sending men to the moon, yet even that is an inadequate comparison. Dangerous though space exploration was and still is, the NASA planners were able to calculate with minute precision the timing, distances, trajectory and so forth of the moon landing. They would be in constant communication with the astronauts. The very course the *Erebus* and *Terror* were expected to take was a physical impossibility: the inviting blank spaces they were supposed to sail through after Cape Walker were in fact crowded with land and ice. And if anything went wrong, no help could be summoned and no one would know about it; perhaps until it was too late.

The first person to air a view about the need for a relief expedition was Sir John Ross, fellow Arctic explorer and uncle of Franklin's good friend Sir James Clark Ross; he claimed to have promised Franklin that he would go in search of him if necessary. But this was in September 1846, when everyone else deemed it far too early to be thinking along such lines. John Ross offered his services to the Admiralty for Franklin 'and his brave companions', but was informed that 'no search is at present contemplated by my Lords'.[4] In fact, not long after this James Ross was in correspondence with Lady Franklin, who had been on her travels once more, reassuring her that there was no need for concern at this stage. 'Your view of their position and prospects is very satisfactory', she replied:

> And I sometimes think it is better that we should thus be happy in ignorance of any disaster that may have happened to them or of any dreadful difficulty they may have got to overcome than to be viewing, as if through a magic mirror in a fairy tale, their daily vicissitudes.
>
> And should it please Providence that we should not see them return when we are led to expect them, will you be the man to go in search of them, as you did so nobly for the missing whalers?[5]

Among the Admiralty papers relating to this expedition, there is a memo from Sir John Barrow, at the end of which is a note marked, 'A few loose thoughts concerning Sir J Franklin and his companions', which says, 'The anxiety that prevails, regarding Sir John Franklin and the brave fellows who compose the crews of the two ships, is very natural, but somewhat premature...'[6]

By the beginning of 1847 even experienced Arctic officers like Parry were still not unduly concerned: 'I entirely agree with your Lordships, that there is not at present any cause for uneasiness respecting the Expedition under the command of Sir John Franklin'.[7] But Sir John Ross continued to sound the alarm. He believed that the ships had been carried by the ice 'into a position from which they cannot be extricated'. He again volunteered to sail north, warning the Admiralty that 'unless an Expedition is sent out to enquire after their fate…few, if any of the officers and crews will ever return to this country…'[8] The following month Ross repeated his call, and added the surprising information that if necessary Franklin had planned to put his ships into the drift ice at the western end of Melville Island, where he hoped that provisions might have been deposited for him. The Admiralty maintained that there was no cause for alarm but conceded that 'steps must be taken' if nothing had been heard by the end of the year. As for the story about provisions on Melville Island, their Lordships consulted Arctic officers such as Parry, James Ross, Sabine and Richardson. If anyone should know of this, they should.

Richardson, from his post at Haslar Hospital in Portsmouth, wrote to say that he had never heard Franklin speak of provisions being left for him at Melville Island or anywhere else, even though they had spoken and written about the expedition at length. He quite rightly added that if Franklin had told anyone about such plans it would have been the Admiralty, and concluded that he believed fears for Franklin to be premature – the time to worry would be if nothing had been heard by the winter.

Parry concurred with these views – with the exception that he thought preparations should commence now for a rescue so that they would be *ready* to go once it was deemed necessary. James Ross had 'not the smallest reason for apprehension or anxiety'.

In the meantime, Captain Beechey had come up with a plan for the relief of the expedition, which comprised a joint land and sea search. Captain Baillie Hamilton, who had by now replaced Sir John Barrow as Second Secretary to the Admiralty, again took counsel, and Richardson opined that Beechey's measures were impracticable and still as yet unnecessary.

Jane herself was beginning to feel a little uneasy, though far from panicking. Before travelling to Italy with Eleanor she wrote to James Ross asking about his discussions with the Admiralty, adding, 'We think we shall be back in August, more than early enough I fear to get any news of the ships…'[9]

But the number of anxious voices was slowly increasing. Lieutenant Griffith, who had commanded the *Barretto Junior*, now joined in. He had read in *The Times* that there was no official concern for the safety of the expedition, and wrote to tell Barrow, 'I cannot divest myself of the fear that some accident may have occurred…' It was true that they could make their rations go further by resorting to short allowances, but – 'Jack can well stow away double his whack after a day's sawing through packed ice'.[10]

Jane and Eleanor arrived home at the end of August to find there was still no news, and so Jane was unable to commence what should have been the satisfying adventure of locating a plot for the modest home she and Franklin had planned to retire to. 'I have very nearly given up the ships', she now confided to Ross.[11] She did, however, discover that the Admiralty had finally decided it was time to act. James Ross was to take the *Enterprise* and the *Investigator* after her husband, and Sir John Richardson would be returning to familiar territory – along the coast between the Mackenzie and Coppermine Rivers. At the beginning of the year he had told the Admiralty that, in his opinion, if there was no confirmation of Franklin's reaching the Pacific by the middle of February, 'it may be concluded that he has not been able to cross Behrings Straits, and the Expedition in search of him will have to proceed without further delay'. He formally requested to be relieved of his duties at Haslar Hospital so that he could make himself ready to go.[12]

Additionally, a Captain Kellet was approaching from the western entrance to the Passage through Bering Strait. Jane assured James Ross that if he found her husband, 'you will have your reward'. In fact, in spite of a general expectation that at least *one* of the search parties must achieve its goal, not a single trace of Franklin's expedition was found, and the only reward Ross got was a feeling in some quarters that he had returned having not given his all. He had sailed along Lancaster Sound as far as Port Leopold on Somerset Island, and from there sent out search parties which failed to turn anything up. After this the *Enterprise* and *Investigator* became trapped in ice and were carried all the way back out into Lancaster

Sound; Ross decided nothing more could be done that season, and set a course back to England.

Jane was devastated by the news of Ross's fruitless voyage. She first heard he was back from an article in *The Times*, which a friend at the Admiralty told her to ignore – yet just an hour later Ross himself turned up at the Admiralty. 'I will only say', she told an American correspondent, 'that it put an almost fatal extinguisher on my hopes which had been centred mainly in Sir James Ross's exertions…'[13] Neither Richardson nor Kellet were any more successful; Richardson returned, but left a party in the region under the leadership of Dr John Rae. In the meantime, whaling ships had been offered a reward of not less than one hundred guineas for any information they could provide as to the whereabouts of the missing ships and men, and Jane had put this in the shade by issuing her own reward of £2000.

With the Admiralty's help she made a trip to both the Orkney and Shetland Isles, attempting along the way to follow the same course and see the same sights that had been her husband's last view of his country. Her hopes were raised somewhat while she was staying in Kirkcaldy on the Firth of Forth, when she heard a tale from a whaling captain about Eskimos seeing ships stuck in the ice at Pond's Bay, Prince Regent Inlet, and that all aboard were safe. It was promising – but 'meagre and confused enough it all is… We may well doubt what amount of fact we have obtained from the whole…' was Jane's judgement.[14] A whaling master had warned her that there were serious doubts about the veracity of the story. He pointed out the extreme difficulty of getting accurate information from the Eskimos; they were often keen to answer a leading question in the affirmative, and if the ships were in Pond's Bay they would have been close to an area of whaling activity and been able to make contact before now. Parry, too, wondered whether the Eskimos had been unwittingly 'led' by an over-enthusiastic interrogator. In his experience you could make them say almost anything, and once they were tired of being questioned they would say 'yes' to any question just to get rid of you, even to the point of contradicting a previous question. He told Jane that they must wait for more information; he was 'full of uncertainty, but not unmixed with lively hope'.[15] The

Historic Times ('A family Journal of Education, Literature, Science, and General Intelligence (6d)') had no doubts about the Eskimo story and urged that ships should be sent to Pond's Bay as soon as the spring arrived.[16]

Franklin and his men had been away for over four years now and there was serious concern for their welfare throughout the country. There was much newspaper speculation, and letters had for some time been appearing both at the Admiralty[17] and in the press with well-meaning but not always practical suggestions for a solution. A Captain West suggested ice-hammers attached to the paddles of a steam ship, while Richardson received a letter which advocated propelling boats over the ice using steam engines. Balloons and explosions seemed to captivate the imaginations of many concerned citizens. A civil engineer, Mr Shepherd, had witnessed an experiment on the Danube where holes had been blown in the ice with explosives and urged the Admiralty to send ships out with the requisite amount of gunpowder immediately – and offered his services 'should the above means be deemed advisable'. Parry commented that Mr Shepherd was 'a good specimen of what an intelligent man may write who knows nothing of the subject. His plan for blowing up the ice is an admirable one – for the Serpentine!'

A Mr Jones of Whitby thoughtfully provided the Admiralty with a sketch of his proposal for a ship engulfed by three enormous hot-air balloons attached to the upper deck ('His complicated scheme is, I think, fairly ridiculous'). Another correspondent planned to send a plucky 'aeronaut' up in a balloon attached to a line of 'some fathoms', and this highlights one of the salient features of the public perception of the problem – many people appeared to have no comprehension of the sheer *scale* of the landscape in which Franklin was lost. The whole region of the Passage is very roughly comparable in area to Western Europe – if anything, probably greater. Mr Smith of Hastings was sure that if kites were sent up every ten minutes they would soon cover the whole Arctic region. (Presumably he was counting not only on the kite manufacturers of the world uniting to facilitate his scheme, but also on there being a fortuitous succession of north, south, east and west winds…)

My personal favourite is Herr Trapp's Heath-Robinson style

'Blowing-Up Machine'. Herr Trapp, of Giessen in Germany, wanted to make it clear that if for some strange reason the Admiralty failed to make use of his wonderful invention 'either a recompense be awarded to me' otherwise, 'no use whatever, either wholly or partially' should be made of the idea. Someone – possibly Beaufort – wrote in the margin, 'There may be far more cleverness in all this…contrivance and machinery than I am able to make out…'

One anonymous writer wondered whether the searchers could administer themselves with 'stimulating substances' to keep them going. Captain Merrel of Bath thought what the Admiralty needed were velocipedes capable of carrying two or more persons. These vehicles could move along the 'common roads' at up to 10mph, and the good captain pointed out that they ought to be able to slither along the ice at a much faster rate. The reader at the Admiralty was finally lost for words, but his underlining of the word 'velocipede' and adding three exclamation marks in the margin spoke volumes.

There were to be many other suggestions appearing in the press that one might kindly call 'imaginative', and around the beginning of 1850 a completely new and radical approach to ending the mystery opened up – for those of an open-minded persuasion. Accounts appeared in the press of the 'Bolton Clairvoyante'.[18] This 'mesmeric patient', when in a trance, 'asserted positively that Sir John Franklin is still alive, and now comparatively well'. He would be located on the north side of Hudson Bay. A Mr Haddock was sent to see the girl in question – supposedly sent by 'an officer of rank in the royal navy, a friend of Sir John Franklin'. Mr Haddock reported back to Captain Maconochie, who may well have been the 'friend' in question. (Despite the problems he had caused them in Van Dieman's Land, the Franklins appear to have resumed their friendship with him upon their return to England – he was certainly in regular and amicable contact with Jane at this time.[19]) Haddock told Maconochie that he was not unimpressed – Emma, the Bolton Clairvoyante herself, had been 'strikingly correct' in her description of Franklin. This report was later annotated by an unsigned hand: 'Strikingly correct certainly – a perfect transcription of the descriptions I wrote'; the document was forwarded to Hamilton to see what he thought of it all, and it could well be his exasperated note in the margin declaring, 'I know what *I* think'.

The concept of mesmerism had been around a long time, but spiritualism was a brand new American import (a country with which Jane had strong contacts), having taken off in New York only two years previously. It is not known whether Jane became involved in the 'Bolton Clairvoyante' story, but she certainly took a personal interest in the strange case of 'Little Weesy'. Little Weesy was Louisa Coppin of Londonderry who had died in 1849 at the age of four, only to reappear as a 'ball of bluish light' and provide a written report on the position of the lost expedition, complete with illustrations, on a wall of the family home. When Little Weesy's father came to London he decided to visit Lady Franklin and tell his story. It is said that Jane gave a great deal of credence to the tale, something which has surprised many and dismayed some – her biographer bemoaned the fact that there was 'reason only to grieve that a fine mind should be thus prostrated'.[20] But it must be remembered that spiritualism was an exciting new development that was capturing the imaginations of a broad spectrum of the population; additionally, each day that passed lessened the chances of Franklin being found alive, and Jane's desperation was beginning to take a toll on her health by now.

Quite how accurate Little Weesy's revelations were is shrouded in mystery and always will be. There did exist documents of dubious provenance but, according to Franklin authority Ralph Lloyd-Jones, Sophia Cracroft – Jane's niece and by now constant companion – destroyed, upon her aunt's death, any documentary evidence that existed to allow us to form an unequivocal judgement – presumably either to avoid embarrassment or because of her own more uncompromising Christian views on the matter.[21]

*

The hunt was now really on. The Admiralty rewards were increased – £10,000 for finding the ships, £20,000 for rescuing them. Jane, who had been in constant contact with the Admiralty, even suggested some very sensible changes to the wording of the reward notice.[22] Many writers have portrayed her as 'bombarding' the Admiralty with letters, and they as regarding her as something of a nuisance. Like much modern Franklin commentary this is little more than a parody of the true situation. It is clear from the correspondence – most of which has been painstakingly preserved – that although the Admiralty did not or could not always go along with her views, they heeded her as the highly intelligent and well-informed, yet naturally anxious, woman that she was. Her editorial changes for the reward notices – which related solely to syntax and clarity and not her opinions regarding the strategy itself, were perfectly reasonable and duly adopted by the Admiralty before going to print. It was only in later years, as the old guard who knew her gradually gave way to new faces, and with seemingly little more to be achieved, that her indomitable spirit began to cause them some embarrassment.

During 1850, the *Enterprise* and *Investigator* were sent back out, this time to approach from Bering Strait whence the *Erebus* and *Terror* had been expected to emerge and at which end of the Passage it was thought the ships must be stranded. Captain Collinson took the former search ship and Commander McClure the latter. Four ships under the command of Captain Horatio Austin were despatched, and whaler William Penny took the *Lady Franklin* and the *Sophia*. The American Government and the Hudson's Bay Company also sent ships. Even Jane got in on the act, putting Commander Charles Forsyth (who, according to the *Herald* had served under Franklin and also met him in Van Dieman's Land) in charge of the *Prince Albert*, towards which she had committed £1000 of her own money. Rae was still in the region, and Jane had not neglected him, writing regular kind and encouraging letters. It was in a letter to him in May 1850 that she sounds her first defeatist note: 'If you find traces or the melancholy remains of the lost ones…a mourning country and mourning relatives will thank you for closing their melancholy and heart-rending suspense'.[23]

With the whole region swarming with searchers, it seemed that *some* trace of Franklin's expedition must be discovered. And this time, it was.

Captain Erasmus Ommanney, second-in-command to Austin, took HMS *Assistance* through Lancaster Sound to Cape Riley, Devon Island. There he came across the very first tangible evidence of

Franklin's expedition: scraps of clothing, pieces of English elm identified as belonging to a ship's boat, Goldner's meat cans, a clay pipe with tobacco still in it, and other sad debris. More finds were made as the searchers began to converge on the area, but no written record. Then, on the shore of nearby Beechey Island, a row of three headstones was spotted, and on closer inspection the following epitaphs were revealed:

Sacred
to the
memory
of
William Braine, R.M.
H.M.S. Erebus
Died April 3d, 1846
Aged 32 years
'Choose ye this day whom ye will serve'
Joshua, ch.xxiv., 15.

Sacred to the memory of
John Hartnell, A.B. of H.M.S.
Erebus
Died January 4th, 1846
aged 25 years.
'Thus saith the Lord of Hosts, consider your ways.'
Haggai, i., 7.

Sacred
to the memory of
John Torrington
who departed
this
life January 1st,
A.D. 1846,
On board of H.M. ship Terror
aged 20 years

The discovery of the graves was poignant, but the first two inscriptions were – and remain – an intriguing hint at possible trouble among the crews. Royal Marine Braine's epitaph from the

Old Testament alludes to Joshua's warning the elders of the tribes of Israel to abandon their old gods and serve the Lord. The obvious conclusion seems to be that poor Braine was guilty of either some extreme form of blasphemy – but enough to warrant such a final, lasting indictment? Even if he had been delirious and cursing in his death throes, surely allowances would have been made? The other way of looking at it is as an allusion to mutinous behaviour, which would be much more likely to incur this kind of unforgiving wrath on the part of the officers.

Hartnell's quotation from Haggai is part of an admonishment concerning reluctance to rebuild a temple: 'You have sown much and harvested little; you eat but you never have enough; you drink, but you never have your fill; you clothe yourselves, but no one is warm...' Possibly the sailor affected morale with protests about the size of the rations or the climate, or the physical hardships they were expected to endure; but again, the resulting condemnation would seem harsh. Perhaps this is taking the passage more literally than was intended; could the quotation again point to some kind of mutinous behaviour? We shall never know, but we do know that none of the men died the violent death that might have added fuel to this theory.

John Torrington's body was exhumed and autopsied in 1984 by a team led by Canadian forensic anthropologist Dr Owen Beattie.[24] Although no definite cause of death could be established, pneumonia was considered the most likely culprit. Hartnell and Braine were exhumed in 1986; the former was discovered to have been autopsied soon after death – probably by the *Erebus*'s surgeon Harry Goodsir – and probably died from tuberculosis.

When Captain Penny brought the news of the discoveries back to England there was naturally a great deal of comment in the newspapers. Penny himself was criticised in the *Morning Chronicle* for coming back so soon. The *Morning Herald* of 9 September 1851 reported the finding of the graves and cautioned its readers not to be alarmed, since some deaths were to be expected on such an undertaking. The article added heartlessly, 'only three lives (*perhaps bad ones*, for none but sound constitutions will stand for this work) had been lost' [my italics]. The *Spectator* declared that 'Even yet the hopes for Franklin's party are not quite extinguished'.

It is now known that this was where Franklin spent his first winter. With nothing to tell them what happened after that, and the season coming to an end, the British ships sat out the winter themselves and recommenced their efforts in the spring of 1851 (when Jane had the *Prince Albert* sent back out) by land and sea, but to no avail. In September Jane wrote to regular American confidante Henry Grinnell:

> I write to you in much agitation and confusion of mind, which you will not wonder at when you hear that Captain Penny with his two ships has returned, and announcing the approaching return of Captain Austin's squadron, after being out for only half the period for which they were equipped. How Captain Austin will explain this abandonment of further search I know not...[25]

Captain Austin did indeed have to explain himself to the Admiralty. It emerged that there had been both a falling-out and a misunderstanding between himself and Penny, and as a consequence Austin had not followed up an opportunity to carry out further searches. The affair soon blew over, and the Admiralty fitted out a new expedition to follow up the findings on Beechey Island, though there were divisions as to whether it was still possible to find anyone alive. In response to a question put to them by the Arctic Committee, Ommanney opined that they 'cannot be alive'; John Ross agreed: 'I do not think British born officers and men could withstand the effects of six winters...'; Captain Kellet said there was a *possibility* that some were still alive; and Richardson thought it *probable* that part of the crews may still survive.[26] The sailing ships *Assistance*, *Resolute* and *North Star*, and the steamers *Pioneer* and *Intrepid* departed in the spring of 1852 under the command of Sir Edward Belcher. Despite the size of his squadron, he returned in 1854 none the wiser as to Franklin's fate.

Speculation mounted not only concerning the whereabouts of the missing men, but also what could have gone wrong, and a series of letters appeared in *The Times* and other publications querying the condition of the tinned meat taken on the expedition. John Barrow – son of Sir John who had died in 1848 – wrote to say that although some tins recently had been found to contain 'disgusting materials',[27] * Goldner's preserved meats had been in constant use by the navy for a number of years, and it was only lately that any problems had been experienced. He felt sure that Commander Fitzjames would have been diligent enough to spot any problems before the *Barretto Junior* had left Disco. This was followed up by a letter from Edward Griffiths, the Lieutenant who had commanded that transport, backing Barrow. He had joined the officers for dinner two days before leaving them, where tinned food was opened as a trial, and he had found it to be 'of a very good kind'.[28]

Meanwhile, a curious report reached London concerning one Adam Beck, an interpreter with Sir John Ross (who had gone out at his own expense at the age of seventy-three). The statement Ross provided was described as an English version of a German translation of an 'Esquimaux-Greenlandish' document. Not a promising start:

> They said sailing ships they came on land... The People followed these sailing ships it is said howling at them being frightened... At Ammanak they lived well clothed...and fires they lighted... They amused themselves and they pleased the women...and the fiddles sounded and they shot with guns and they fished with nets. Many people to Ammanak thronged and combined and darkly they came in the dark and they threw spears and they hit...and they are in heaps overpowered. They die and slaughtered they suffered evil. Twenty-six people remained lately in the neighbourhood of Ammanak.[29]

The Admiralty gave no credence to this tale; Ross believed it, and his First Officer wrote to the Admiralty confirming it. His interpretation was that the two ships were wrecked in 1846, the crews came on shore and were eventually killed by Eskimos, who burnt the white men's clothes. But where? No one seemed to know where Ammanak (or Ommanak) was. There was further debate as to whether anything useful could be made of this tale, but the sceptics won the day.

* Admiralty examiners at Portsmouth had recently condemned hundreds of cans of meat. The opening of one in particular created such a stench as to cause them to 'beat a hasty retreat from the room'. Most was thrown into the sea at Spithead, while some was declared good enough to give to the poor!

A great deal of speculation in the press took place over a sighting by Edward Coward of the brig *Renovation*, of two three-masted vessels trapped on an iceberg off Newfoundland in April 1851. But this was a highly improbable place for a sighting of Franklin's ships, to say the least; Penny wrote to *The Times* saying they were 'probably "country ships" as we whalers call them – formations upon an iceberg which deceive even practised eyes'.[30] (They almost certainly were not the *Erebus* and *Terror*, but professional pride spurred the master of the *Renovation* to reply that they had been sighted by 'spyglasses' as well as the naked eye, and standing rigging and unbent sails were definitely made out.)

Jane, by this time, was not well. We hear of 'giddiness in the head', of being too unwell to receive visitors, and even the phrase 'seriously ill', in letters written on her behalf by companion Sophia Cracroft during the early 1850s. She would have been around the age of sixty by now. She was also feeling the pinch financially, and Sophia felt constrained to warn, for example, the 'Nursing Sisters' Institution' that Lady Franklin would no longer be able to avail them – and many other of the worthy causes she took an interest in – with her financial support. 'You are aware that her resources are economised in order to apply them to a course which appears to her to be a higher duty…'[31] This particularly applied now that Lady Franklin was planning to fund yet another private expedition to the Arctic.

Richardson was against this idea, and Parry told Sophia:

I need not say – indeed how <u>can</u> I say, what I feel after a <u>sixth</u> winter! I think we shall have some of the searching vessels home in the Autumn. I may also say to <u>you</u> that I am very sorry Lady Franklin means to spend more money upon Prince Regent's Inlet. I cannot conceive of any scheme less likely to be attended with success. At the same time you will I am sure believe that I will do <u>anything</u> and <u>everything</u> in my power to render the effort efficient.[32]

Another avenue Jane tried in her desperation was to sound out the services of the redoubtable Hepburn who was back home in Scotland. When nothing was heard for a while, Sophia had a word with Richardson, who told her that the old boy was 'not a good correspondent'; besides which, 'If the letter fell into his wifes [*sic*] hands, I suspect that it never reached him, as I think she would prevent him from going'.[33] But dependable as ever, Hepburn *did* reply (though at what cost to matrimonial harmony we do not know): 'I will most readily strain every nerve in search of my worthy chief'. He was on his way to London.[34]

'He was when we were together worth 3 or 4 people', said Richardson, but pointed out that a lot of time had passed since then. When Hepburn did arrive Richardson gave him a quick 'physical' and pronounced him fit enough to keep up with men carrying baggage – but not up to carrying a burden himself on the march. He would be a useful man to have along. This virtual green light from the learned doctor caused his spirits to soar, and Hepburn duly called on Jane and Sophia 'looking the picture of radiance'.

Jane may have been under great stress and, generally speaking, a fairly serious-minded woman, but she had not quite lost her sometimes mischievous sense of humour. When she heard that Captain Inglefield, who was to command her next private search on the *Isabel*,* was due to dine at the Goldsmith's Company, she wrote observing that 'they include many merchants, bankers and commercial men of all sorts...you might rouse them to a Goldsmith's Expedition... Be sure to tell them that the missing men are still to be found and found alive, at least some of them... Engage them over their Champagne and claret to pledge themselves to this noble feat, or at least pledge themselves to a handsome subscription'.[35]

The *Isabel* expedition, which had benefited from £1700 in subscription raised in Van Dieman's Land, was no more successful than any of the others Jane had sent out. Then in January 1854 she received a further blow when she opened a letter from the Admiralty:

---

* This was to have been commanded by a Captain Beatson of the merchant navy. Sadly, not only did he not have access to the funding he had led Jane to believe was available, but he was 'on the contrary under threats of arrest from various parties who waited till the last moment to enforce their claims'. The Admiralty helped her out.

It is my painful duty to announce to you the decision of the Board of the Admiralty, that at the termination of the present financial year, the names of Sir John Franklin and of the officers of the Erebus and Terror will be removed from the list of the Royal Navy...

No wife ever made more unremitting exertions or greater personal sacrifices to afford aid to a lost husband in the last extremity of his distress; and long as the name of Sir John Franklin will be remembered, the conduct of his wife will be remembered also as worthy of him.[36]

Jane wrote back from Brighton, where she was probably convalescing. She apologised that she would have replied to their letter sooner, but 'the shock it inflicted on my already shattered health was such as not to permit me any mental exertion till now'.[37] She queried the fact that the Admiralty was taking this action while the search was still being continued under their direction, and Barrow the younger agreed with her that this decision seemed 'premature'.[38] Nor had the public given up on Franklin and his men. During the early 1850s the Admiralty had almost one hundred petitions from all over the country (including Spilsby, Franklin's birthplace) urging them not to slacken their efforts.[39]

And then, in the middle of 1854, news of a major breakthrough in the search was received from the indefatigable if rather supercilious Dr Rae, who had been searching the western shore of Boothia Peninsula. Eskimos there had told him about a party of white men who had starved to death some distance to the west. Rae followed up this story, and bought articles from them 'which places the fate of a portion (if not all) of the then survivors of Sir John Franklin's long lost party beyond a doubt, a fate as terrible as the imagination can conceive'.[40]

The story he managed to piece together was that in the spring of 1850 around forty white men were seen trekking south, dragging a boat and sledges; they managed to make the Eskimos understand that their ship or ships had been crushed by the ice, and they were making their way to where they hoped to be able to hunt deer. They were low on food and bought a seal from the Eskimos. Later that season the Eskimos found around thirty bodies on the mainland and

219

five on an island – some buried, some not. The Eskimos had acquired parts of watches, telescopes, compasses, silver cutlery and suchlike: Rae purchased as many of these as he could.

Rae wrote two versions of this report (both of which reached the Admiralty); the second version:

> From the mutilated state of many of the corpses and contents of the kettles, it is evident that our wretched countrymen had been driven to the last dread alternative as a means of sustaining life...[41]

contained a euphemism not present in the first, written some weeks earlier:

> ...it is evident that our wretched countrymen had been driven to the last resource – cannibalism – as a means of prolonging life.[42]

This report and its conclusion provoked a debate that has rumbled on ever since.

The Eskimos Rae spoke to said they had not personally seen any of the whites or visited the scenes they had described, but had been told by others. 'From what I could learn, there is no reason to suspect that any violence had been offered to the sufferers by the natives', Rae reassured his readers.[43] He was soon to discover that not everyone was content to leave the matter there.

※

Among the articles eventually received in London were monogrammed silver forks: '*H D S G*' (Harry Goodsir, Assistant Surgeon on the *Terror*), '*A McD*' (Alexander Macdonald, Assistant Surgeon on the *Erebus*); a watch engraved '*James Reid*' (the *Erebus*'s tough and jovial Ice Master); a piece of flannel 'undervest' marked '*F.DV*' (Charles Frederick DesVoeux, Mate on the *Erebus*). And there was a small silver plate: '*Sir John Franklin KCB*'.[44]

At first, few seemed to pick up on the implications of Rae's allusion to cannibalism. *The Times* made no mention of it in its initial, rather melodramatic assessment of the latest news ('Wherever they turned their eyes, nothing was to be seen but ice and dreary desert...'). It took the 'Thunderer' two more days to fire its first broadside:

> Is the story by the Esquimaux a true one? Like all savages, they are liars, and certainly would not scruple at the utterance of any falsehood which might, in their opinion, shelter them from the vengeance of the white man.[45]

The article admitted that, for the most part, Arctic explorers had found Eskimos to be harmless apart from petty pilfering; they usually had 'little inclination or energy for deeds of blood'. Could, wondered *The Times*, their timidity have been overcome by the sight of weak and starving whites? The *Woolwich Gazette* said that Rae had not recovered anything 'that could not have been stolen by a thieving Esquimo'. The language used now seems harsh and patronising – yet this is not sufficient reason to dismiss the assessments out of hand, as some modern commentators have been eager to do. It is a well-established fact that Eskimo accounts could not always be relied upon, that they were prone to stealing, and that certain groups were violent towards whites and other Eskimos alike.

The *Morning Herald* spoke of the 'profound sensation' of Rae's reports – it had even replaced the progress of the Crimean War as the main news story. The *Herald* declared that the mutilated bodies could be easily accounted for. 'We should be glad if some of the more revolting circumstances connected with their loss should prove untrue.' A letter from the brother of a *Terror* crewman wanted to know: if the Eskimos and Rae could find food, why not Franklin and his men? Why should starving men encumber themselves with fancy cutlery? Why would they all die in one place and not one by one as they struggled on? The writer, 'EJH', accused Rae of being 'reprehensible' in announcing such a thing without first verifying it.

Rae defended himself in *The Times*. To check on all the facts would have meant staying in the region for another winter – he felt it was more important to bring the news home. Food was *not* easy to come by: the area was 'notoriously the most barren of animal life of any area of the Arctic shores…' Another arena in which Rae felt a need to protect his honour was Charles Dickens' periodical, *Household Words*. Dickens had had his own say about the cannibalism issue, thus sparking a debate with Rae which is remembered to this day, particularly by those who accuse 'Victorian England' of not being able to stomach (for want of a better word) the idea of its heroes eating each other. This is another strand of the 'Franklin Story Stereotype' that bears closer examination.

The idea of respected figures turning to cannibalism would not be easy news to accept for people of any era, past or present, and of any nationality. But by and large the letters in the newspapers of the day, despite some of the dubious phraseology employed, mainly question the *strength of the evidence*. It was a second-hand account, in translation, by people with a different concept from Europeans of what the 'truth' meant. It was not unreasonable that there should be a reluctance to believe this terrible story without some kind of confirmation. This was the main approach taken by Dickens – rather than the defence that the men could not have resorted to cannibalism on the grounds that it would have been dishonourable or 'un-British', as is sometimes imputed to him.

There were several stories circulating at around the same time of Eskimos killing white men. Captain Penny was told one such tale by an Eskimo, which was later retracted. 'I do think the Esquimaux have something to conceal', was his opinion. He also counselled that the cannibalism story should not necessarily be taken literally: 'The story of eating one another is a term of reproach which they often use when they wish to say anything bitter of one another'.[46]

At the beginning of 1856 a report reached England of further traces of the expedition being found on Montreal Island, from where it appeared survivors struggled to reach the mainland, but there were no more bodies and still no written clues as to the cause of the disaster. Jane had by now come to terms with the fact that she was not going to see her husband alive again – and had for many months been wearing mourning clothes – but still she kept up the pressure for further expeditions to uncover the full story. As far as the Admiralty was concerned it had done all it could, and it was not prepared to risk any more lives in search of men for whom there was now no hope. Her relationship with the Admiralty became strained, and not all of her letters were answered: something which drew criticism from Dickens in a long article of support for Lady Franklin and her cause.[47]

She planned to finance yet another private expedition from the proceeds of the sale of land in Australia – a course of action that 'I have been forced to undertake by the shabby treatment of the Admiralty, who, after allowing me to indulge hopes for more than a year, that they might be induced to do it themselves, leave me in the lurch at the last moment'.[48] The steam yacht *Fox* sailed at the beginning of July 1857, twelve years to the month since Captain Martin had had his last view of the *Erebus* and *Terror*, and around the time that Richardson was unveiling a statue to Franklin in his home town of Spilsby. Captain McClintock, who had previously been involved in the search for Franklin, commanded the little vessel. The *Fox* carried a tablet that Jane had had made, and McClintock set it up, in accordance with her instructions, on Beechey Island:

To the memory of
Sir John Franklin
Captain Crozier, Commander Fitzjames
and all the other
gallant brother officers and faithful
companions who have suffered and perished
in the cause of Science and
the Service of their country

This tablet
is erected at the spot where
they passed their first Arctic
winter, and whence they issued forth
to conquer Difficulties or
To Die

To commemorate the grief of their
admiring countrymen and friends,
and the anguish, subdued by faith,
of her who has lost, in the heroic
Leader of this Expedition, the most
Devoted and affectionate of
Husbands

'And so He bringeth them unto
the Haven where they would be'

1855[49]

The *Fox* became stuck in the ice during August 1857 and as winter passed was carried inexorably southwards for nearly 1200 miles. McClintock then made his way down Prince Regent Inlet, and by early 1859 a search of King William Land (Island) began. He bartered for more relics of the Franklin expedition from local Eskimos, and heard stories of two ships – one sinking and the other being forced ashore; he was also told a second-hand story of white men falling down and dying as they walked along. McClintock then came upon a skeleton and, from a pocket book close by, it was identified as the remains of Harry Peglar, Captain of the Foretop on the *Terror*. Lieutenant William Hobson, who had been leading another party of searchers, made an even more important discovery.

After picking their way through traces of an encampment near Cape Felix to the north of the island, they made their way down the coast towards Point Victory. Here, many more items were found, including a medicine chest complete with intact phials, and a man-made cairn of the kind built by explorers to draw attention to a message deposited within. Cairns had been found before – Hobson had only recently come across one near Cape Felix, but it had contained only a sheet of paper with nothing written on it (which in itself almost seems like a cryptic message. Was this the last cairn built, the blank paper signifying that they had nothing left to write with – or even that they had literally *nothing left*, including food?) This second cairn was different. A few stones had fallen from the top, and among them was found a cylinder containing, at long last, a written record of the fate of the Franklin expedition.

It was a standard Admiralty form requesting the finder in several languages to forward it to London or the nearest British Consul or port. The appropriate spaces on the form were filled in, but additional writing crowded into all four margins of the page revealed that the cylinder had been opened and the original message added to at a later date.

The first record said:

H.M. Ships Erebus and Terror
    Wintered in 1846-7 at Beechey Island
     in Lat. 70° 5' N Long. 98° 23' W
28 of May 1847

Having wintered in 1846-7 at Beechey Island
in Lat 74° 43'.28" N. Long 91° 39'.15" W after having
ascended Wellington Channel to Lat 77° and returning
by the West side of Cornwallis Island.

Sir John Franklin commanding the Expedition
All well

Party consisting of 2 Officers and 6 men
Left the ships on Monday 24th May 1847

Gm. Gore Lieut
Chas F Des Voeux Mate[50]

Commencing in the bottom left-hand corner margin was the additional message:

25th April 1848 H M Ships Terror and Erebus were deserted on the 22nd April, 5 leagues NNW of this having been beset since 12th Sept 1846. The officers and crews consisting of 105 souls – under the Command of Captain F.R.M Crozier landed here – in Lat 69° 37' 42" Long 98° 41'.
  This paper was found by Lt Irving under the cairn supposed to have been built by Sir John Ross in 1832- where it had been deposited by the late Commander Gore in June 1847. Sir James Ross' pillar has not however been found and the paper has been transferred to this position which is that in which Sir J. Ross' pillar was erected – Sir John Franklin died on the 11th June 1847 and the total loss by deaths in the Expedition has been to this date 9 officers and 15 men

James Fitzjames Captain HMS
Erebus

FRM Crozier
  Captain and Senior Offr
and start on tomorrow 26th
for Backs Fish River[51]

And thus was it revealed that Sir John Franklin had been dead for twelve years. No cause of death was stated, and the lack of explanatory detail in general has meant that this solitary document has raised more questions than it answers, including that of the disproportionate number of deaths among the officers compared with the rest of the crew. It should be noted that the date of 1846–7 given for wintering at Beechey Island must be wrong – it would have been 1845–6.

Further down the coast Hobson made another discovery: a large ship's boat containing two further skeletons, one in the bow and the other near the stern, together with books, clothing and pieces of plate bearing the crests or initials of Franklin and other officers. Nearly forty pounds of chocolate, together with a small amount of tea and tobacco, were also found. When McClintock came across this scene, he, like others after him, was incredulous that desperate men should be hauling a heavy boat containing so many useless items – although Roderic Owen has pointed out that some of it could have been intended for trade with the Eskimos in order to obtain food. McClintock was also puzzled that the boat was not in fact pointing south towards the stated destination of the Great Fish River, but in the opposite direction; he surmised that the party had decided to return to the ships, and that the two unfortunate occupants had been unable to keep up. Neither Hobson, who was himself suffering from scurvy by now, nor McClintock saw any signs of the *Erebus* and *Terror*, nor has anyone to this day.

McClintock broke the melancholy news to Jane on his return to England in September 1859, and there was the inevitable excitement in the press. Among Jane's papers is a note by her nephew explaining that after the 'great struggle of her life' between 1845 and 1857, 'Lady Franklin turned to extended world visiting as a change of scene and subject of which she was doubtlessly in great need'.[52] Despite her age and continuing bouts of sickness, her wanderlust had not diminished – and now she had nothing to wait at home for. She was rarely in England during the next few years. But by June 1875 she had come home for the last time, and her failing health became the subject of the kind of daily bulletins in the newspapers normally reserved for royalty. She died the following month at the age of eighty-three. *The Times* said:

> We record to-day the death of one who, among the gifted women of her time, has certainly not been the least remarkable. After a

lifetime extended far beyond the allotted span, the widow of Sir
John Franklin, the renowned Arctic seaman and explorer, died
yesterday evening at 9 o'clock, at her house in Phillimore Gardens.[53]

Writing in 1951, her biographer Frances Woodward reflected, 'Jane
Franklin herself has been forgotten: Jane Griffin – a very charming,
gifted and loveable person – is unknown'.[54] At that time her journals
had been available only for a few years, and happily the situation has
changed. It is rare today for Franklin's name to crop up without
there being a mention – and usually a favourable one – of Jane; most
of those who are familiar with Franklin's career will also have some
appreciation of the part played in it by his second wife and of her own
admirable qualities.

Her funeral was at Kensal Green cemetery, where McClintock,
Richardson, Ommanny and the younger Barrow were among the
pallbearers. She missed by three days the unveiling by the former
midshipman, now Admiral Sir George Back, of Franklin's memorial
at Westminster Abbey. One of the inscriptions on it read:

> This monument was erected by Jane, his widow, who, after long
> waiting and sending many in search of him, herself departed to find
> him in the realms of Light, July 18, 1875, aged 83 yrs

And Franklin's epitaph was composed by his relative Tennyson:

> Not here: the white North has thy bones, and thou
> Heroic Sailor soul
> Art passing thy happier voyage now
> Toward no Earthly Pole

~ 14 ~

A Good Man

WE have already seen that due to incomplete knowledge of the region beyond Prince Regent Inlet, the route Franklin was supposed to take in search of the North West Passage did not exist. Following his Admiralty instructions, Franklin followed the alternative route by sailing up Wellington Channel as far as 77° North, and then, presumably halted by ice, turned back, passed down the opposite side of Cornwallis Island and backtracked eastwards to spend the winter at Beechey Island. It was during this time that the first three deaths occurred: Torrington, Hartnell and Braine. Whether another attempt was made to make westward progress is not known, but eventually they sailed south, probably through Peel Sound and what was to become Franklin Strait, until their final entrapment approximately fifteen miles north-north-west off King William Island.

That the deaths on Beechey, though all occurring within the space of three months, seem not to have been the prelude to any kind of epidemic or fear thereof is indicated by Gore's 'All well' message written here more than twelve months afterwards. By the time Fitzjames wrote his second message a year later, a further twenty-four men had died, including Franklin. It seems reasonable to suppose that these deaths were due to illness, cold or privation, since any kind of violent attack would presumably have been mentioned.

Cyriax calculated that at least three months' worth of food should have been left at this time, yet the virtual absence of empty tins on King William Island indicates that the provisions were almost completely consumed by the time the ships had to be abandoned.[1] We now know that the region experienced some particularly harsh winters at this time, which, combined with the exertions of the men, could have led to an increase in the daily allowance (Cyriax points

228

out that the weekly ration of preserved meat for the men was 'rather small'); it is also possible that an outbreak of scurvy caused an increase in the use of tinned food, since this was believed to prevent or alleviate the condition.

From here on things seem to have gone downhill fairly rapidly; Cyriax and others have pointed to scurvy as the primary cause, and this, together with the extreme temperatures, seems the most likely explanation. Although it had been known for a long time that a 'healthy' diet could prevent scurvy, the very processes that allowed the food on the expedition to be preserved probably led to the loss of much of the all-important vitamin C. Franklin knew from his Flinders days that lemon juice was effective against the disease, but its potency diminished with the passing of time.

The signs are that by the time the party was heading for the Great Fish River on the mainland neared Terror Bay, on the south-west coast of King William Island, a small group turned back for the ships. Probably they were simply unable to go on. Eskimos later spoke of seeing about forty white men struggling south, and even of the last three or four survivors spending a winter with them. A small number managed to make it to the mainland, where they died at Starvation Cove.

Right up to modern times, bones and artefacts from Franklin's expedition continue to be found dotted around King William Island, but although skeletal remains of numerous individuals have been found these still constitute a minority of the 129 men who had served on the *Erebus* and *Terror*.

✻

The modern world of Franklin is, by and large, divided into two camps. There are the Franklin die-hards (*Frankophiles*?), mostly British, who refuse to believe Rae's story of cannibalism and are sceptical of other modern theories relating to the fate of the men, such as lead poisoning (more of which later). Scurvy, starvation and extreme cold are, they say, more than enough to account for the disaster.

The other camp comprises mostly Canadians, Eskimos and anyone (including some British) with a bee in their bonnet about the

British Empire. This latter group has had a much better press in these politically correct days; yet their view of the Eskimos of Franklin's day as innocent people who always told the truth, whose accounts should always be believed in preference to those of the more suspect Victorians who stubbornly refused to conform to twentieth-century mores, contains a significant dose of wishful thinking. During earlier forays in the region, Franklin himself had come across numerous friendly Eskimos – and others who attacked, lied, stole and plotted to kill him.

Whole books have been written about what became of Franklin and his men: some factual, some fiction; some of the purportedly factual ones seem to fall somewhere in between these two categories. But this work was always intended to be the story of John Franklin's life, not an inquest into his death. The claims and counter-claims of the theorists are sufficient to make one's head spin; a brief overview will suffice for the purposes of this book.

Cannibalism

As we have seen, Dr John Rae first raised this subject. The following points should be borne in mind: Rae had something of a grudge against the Royal Navy and its personnel; he is one of the few people in history to have had a bad word to say about Richardson. Even Franklin's critics normally go easy on Richardson. This attitude might not be unrelated to the fact that (among other grudges) he, an undoubted expert on travelling in the Arctic, had to play second fiddle to Richardson during one of the search expeditions. It should be remembered that Rae never saw the bones bearing the marks of cannibalism, and nor did the Eskimos who told him the story. However, the fact that subsequently many bones bearing cut marks have been found backs up the Eskimo testimony to a point, but that is not the end of the matter.

Could the cut marks have been the result of a battle?

Could the cut marks have been the result of cannibalism by the Eskimos?

Much work on the bones from the Franklin expedition has been done by Anne Keenleyside, a physical anthropologist at McMaster University in Canada, with a particular interest in Eskimo culture.

From her researches it appears that at least some of the cut marks could not be attributed to, for example, defensive injuries sustained during a fight – but of course that does not rule out the possibility that *some* of the marks cannot be thus explained.[2] There does, however, appear to be strong evidence for some kind of butchery after death; whether this was carried out by starving sailors or starving Eskimos (bearing in mind evidence that suggests that certain sections of the latter group *were* having difficulty finding food around this time) is impossible to say.

Before Rae could get to the region where this story was told, some Eskimos (who had already stolen various items from him) tried to talk him out of pressing on. And then his native interpreter ran away and had to be chased and caught. Rae was later told by other Eskimos that the man had feared they would be killed by the 'warlike' natives to the west. If Eskimos were responsible for the deaths of some of the sailors, might it not have been the fear of the truth being discovered, and subsequent retribution, that made everyone so wary of Rae reaching the region?

E C Coleman claims that, 'When carving flesh from a bone it is quite difficult to cause cut marks (unless deliberately intended). It is even more difficult to explain how such marks can be found in groups – especially where the marks run at right-angles to the length of the bone'. He reveals that the local Eskimo tribe were an aggressive people who had a tradition of mutilating the bodies of their victims.[3]

Ms Keenleyside leans towards cannibalism but stops short of asserting it as a fact – 'The possibility that cannibalism was practised by these individuals cannot be entirely be discounted...'[4] – but she concedes that the interpretation is 'controversial' and offers only Eskimo testimony as evidence that it was not they but the white men who did the deed, which is something of a circular argument. The balance of evidence seems to be in favour of cannibalism, but there has not been, and probably never could be, proof as to who the perpetrators were. This has not prevented the idea that the British sailors turned to cannibalism from being presented as fact in most modern accounts; even the Franklin section in a current (2000) exhibition at the National Maritime Museum, Greenwich, takes this line. Probably few people today would blame the sailors for resorting to cannibalism in a final desperate attempt to cling to life, but the case is far from proven.

Lead Poisoning

As we have seen, Owen Beattie's team carried out autopsies on bodies from the expedition and found high levels of lead. According to his account, because elevated levels of lead found came from hair samples this proved that contamination had to have occurred during the voyage and could not be attributed to lead from the environment in which they had lived when ashore. His conclusion was that the sailors must have suffered from the debilitating physical and mental effects of lead poisoning. To be fair, he does also make one of the most commonsensical observations in the whole Franklin debate: 'There is no single reason why the expedition failed; it was a deadly combination of factors'.[5] Anne Keenleyside went some way toward confirming Beattie's findings. She found that lead levels in bones tested were higher even than in modern workers subjected to industrial exposure (though presumably modern regulations mean that this is not a particularly high level). But she also concedes that, for the lead in the bones at least, a question remains as to how much can be attributed to environmental factors in Industrial Revolution Britain.[6]

One defence against the lead poisoning theory comes, ironically, from an extremely anti-Franklin website[7] whose stated aim is to show that 'the real cause of the demise of this expedition was sheer failure to adopt local means of survival and the lack of courage from officers to swallow ones [sic] pride and learn from what was [sic] known as "savage" people'. Debatable... *But* this site points out that 'There was only 11% of food in tins on board Erebus and Terror. The ships [sic] water tanks were made of Iron [sic] ... all together [sic] simply not enough poison to go around'. The article goes on to say that lead water pipes were widely used in Britain, and also that low temperatures would have severely retarded the leaching of lead into the food.

E C Coleman believes the lead poisoning theory to be 'riddled with flaws' and points again to environmental conditions in Britain, such as lead paint and other factors.[8]

Botulism

This is the feeblest of the 'single answer' theories, and as such barely warrants a section of its own; but since it is the most recent talking point relating to the mystery it needs to be addressed.

The idea that inadequate preparation and incomplete soldering of the tinned food taken on the expedition caused a deadly outbreak of botulism among the crews is presented with a great deal of melodrama but not quite as much hard evidence in Scott Cookman's *Ice Blink*.[9] Stephen Goldner is the villain of the piece (*'Like most evil men, Stephen Goldner would have passed unnoticed in a crowd'*), but apart from the fact that he was a little late in completing the massive contract for Franklin's expedition, and that after numerous years without problems the navy began to find batches of his tinned food unfit for consumption, there is very little else to justify his demonisation. To show us the depths to which Goldner *could* have sunk, Cookman declares that Goldner's 'Veal Cutlets Tomata' *could* have been the same product as his cheaper 'Veal Cutlets Italian'; his inferior 'Real Turtle Soup' *could* easily be packaged as his 'Superior Clear Turtle Soup', and so on. The blackguard! But was it true? We do not know, and nor does Scott Cookman.

In the same vein, we learn that in the hurry to fulfil the contract, the food was 'almost certainly' not cooked adequately before what has now become the 'deadly stuff' was stowed on the ships – from which supposition we leap to the conclusion that even before the expedition departed, 'the *Clostridium* in them began to reproduce'. (Cookman is equally confident as to cannibalism among the crew – the evidence being 'overwhelming'.)

In keeping with the general trend of the rest of the book, we get a detailed description of how Harry Goodsir *could* have cut up the bodies, the instruments he *would* have used, and even who the cooks *might* have been. (We learn that Goodsir would have felt some shame, but then been cheered by the 'wonderful aroma of fresh meat'!!)

All of this is possible, but there is little in the way of evidence or fact to substantiate it. This is not one of the stronger theories.

✳

233

Scurvy was still, despite Captain Cook showing the way even before Franklin was born, not an uncommon affliction on the longer and more difficult journeys of exploration. The prevention of the disease was still something of a black art, and the role of vitamins in the diet was not fully ironed out until well into the twentieth century. Not all of the types of food thought to ward off scurvy did so; the ones that did might lose their efficacy over time; and anyway there was the ever-present risk that provisions would run out.

Most of the crew of the *Investigator* searching for Franklin in the early 1850s eventually came down with scurvy and might well have died had they themselves not been rescued. And when, as an eager young teenager, Franklin explored Australia on board an earlier *Investigator* under Flinders, who prided himself on following Cook's dietary example, scurvy could not in the end be avoided. (Although it did not kill any of the crew as stated in *Ice Blink*. Dysentery was the culprit.)

Scurvy may not be as fascinating or controversial as lead poisoning or botulism, but it would have been in keeping with this kind of expedition for it to have played a part in its downfall.

For what it is worth, I believe that, as on Franklin's calamitous first overland expedition, a number of factors, none of them necessarily fatal taken in isolation, combined to form a deadly recipe for disaster.

It could be that the food supplies were exhausted sooner than expected: possibly because the daily ration had to be increased, possibly because *some* of the tinned food was found to be unfit, possibly a mixture of the two. Lead in the canned food may have led to or exacerbated illness, but I do not think the whole expedition was brought to its knees because of it.

It has been stated that there was (again, just like in the 1820s) some unusually harsh weather at around the time the *Erebus* and *Terror* became trapped,* and that even the Eskimos were finding

---

* The *Independent* ran an article (9 August 1999) quoting scientists who said that Robert Scott experienced abnormally low temperatures in 1912 which may well have played a far more important role in his downfall than had previously been thought.

food hard to come by. Rae pointed out that the crews had found themselves in one of the worst areas in the region for finding food.

Wandering sailors may well have been aided by Eskimos, but I also suspect that at some stage – probably later on when different groups of survivors became detached from each other – it is possible that at least one group was attacked and killed by Eskimos. Further, that these or other Eskimos coming across such corpses may have resorted to cannibalism is just as likely a scenario as the same act of desperation being perpetrated by surviving expedition members. It is well within the bounds of possibility that starving crewmen turned to cannibalism, but the case that this is less likely is based not on any idea of cultural superiority, but on the undeniable presence of a cultural *barrier*. The average British sailor had probably known poverty and hunger in his life, but the constant exposure to the life-or-death harshness of the climate in which the Eskimos lived brought about a different attitude toward survival altogether. It is pertinent to remember that Franklin almost certainly did *not* turn to cannibalism on his first overland expedition, even though he knew he was slowly starving to death and had ample opportunity to do so.

It would be nice to have a single sensational theory to explain the loss of the 129 men of Franklin's 1845 North West Passage expedition. The mind naturally inclines towards a tidy explanation. To say that some got sick, some starved, some froze, some may have been attacked, seems almost as unsatisfactory as not knowing anything at all. Anyone could have guessed all this without knowing any facts. But herein lies the biggest clue of all – like many clues, invisible when hidden in plain sight – anyone could have guessed the above because it is the most mundane, the most obvious conclusion – and the most obvious answer is usually the correct one.

✳

When I first got the idea for this book I wanted John Franklin to be a hero. Once I commenced the research I began to form an impression of an aloof, humourless, rather limited old sea captain who had got himself mysteriously lost in the Arctic. He was a hero to the Victorians, but then they were prone to turning unworthy people into heroes, were they not? Later, during countless hours of delving into the primary sources – the letters, the journals, the naval records – and learning more about his early career, his private life, his character, I began to realise that there was much more to the man. It eventually became clear to me that many of the general works on exploration and the Arctic in which he featured had done Franklin and his reputation a great injustice; a pattern began to emerge, it seemed to me, whereby a great deal of the damage could be traced back to a few jaundiced writers whose views were being perpetuated unquestioningly.

Sir John Franklin *was* a hero according to normal usage of that word. He was not a titan – a military genius like Nelson, or a paragon of exploration and navigation like James Cook – but then men like these are exceptionally rare. But he did achieve a great deal in his life and it is easy to forget how internationally famous and admired he was for many decades. He achieved *far* more than, for example, better-remembered figures such as Scott or Shackleton. Perhaps this discrepancy is partly due to the exploits of the latter pair being more recent and occurring at the threshold of technological improvements in media communications. Franklin served his country at the battle of Copenhagen; he was in the thick of the action at Trafalgar, a pivotal encounter in European history; the first of his overland expeditions was calamitous in humanitarian terms but this and the following one were genuine achievements scientifically; his diplomatic efforts in the Mediterranean in the 1830s are all but forgotten yet are real and received great praise at the time; his governorship of Van Dieman's Land is, naturally, remembered for the political turmoil, yet he left the island a better place than he found it and was popular with all but that handful of his implacable enemies, and his name is still remembered there today; his search for the North West Passage was a 'failure', yet we know today that it was an impossible task, and even his critics do not attempt to blame him personally for the deaths of the officers and men of the *Erebus* and *Terror*.

As for Franklin himself, I believe he would derive the greatest satisfaction not from any of the above, but from the many testimonials of the people from all walks of life with whom he came into contact: who spoke of a man who was honourable and compassionate, humble and devout, determined and courageous. A good man.

Appendix I

A Selection of Eleanor Anne Porden's Poetry

The Veils; or the Triumph of Constancy (published 1815). Written when Eleanor was only sixteen and comprising six books running to nearly 60,000 words, this is a striking artistic and intellectual achievement.

Introductory verse:
> Of Earth and Air I sing, of Sea and Fire,
> And various wonders that to each belong,
> And while to stubborn themes I tune the lyre,
> 'Fierce wars and faithful loves shall moralize my song.'

Author's foreword:
> A young lady, one of the members of a small society which meets periodically for literary amusement, lost her Veil (by a gust of wind) as she was gathering shells on the coast of Norfolk. This incident gave rise to the following Poem, which was originally written in short cantos, and afterwards extended and modelled into the form in which it is now respectfully submitted to the public. The author, who considers herself a pupil of the Royal Institution, being at that time attending the Lectures given in Albemarle-Street, on Chemistry, Geology, Natural History, and Botany, by Sir Humphry Davy, Mr. Brand, Dr. Roger, Sir James Edward Smith, and other eminent men, she was induced to combine these subjects with her story; and though her knowledge of them was in a great measure orally acquired, and therefore cannot pretend to be extensive or profound, yet, as it was derived from the best teachers, she hopes it will seldom be found incorrect.
>
> The machinery is founded on the Rosicrusian doctrine, which peoples each of the four elements with a peculiar class of spirits, a system introduced into poetry by Pope, and since used by Darwin,

in the Botanic Garden; but the author believes that the ideal beings of these two distinguished writers will not be found to differ more from each other, than from those called into action in the ensuing Poem. She has there endeavoured to shew them as representing the different energies of nature, exerted in producing the various changes that take place in the physical world; but the plan of her Poem did not permit her to exhibit them to any considerable extent. On the Rosicrusian mythology, a system of poetical machinery might be constructed of the highest character; but the person who directs its operations should possess the scientific knowledge of Sir Humphry Davy, and the energy and imagination of Lord Byron and Mr. Scott.

In personifying the metals and minerals, and the agency of fire, the author has generally taken her names from the Greek language; but as it was impossible to avoid the nomenclature of modern chemistry, she requests, on the plea of necessity, the indulgence of her readers for what she fears will be felt as a barbarous mixture.

Opening verses:

THE CASTLE

THE summer sun its setting radiance shed,
And tinged the eastern clouds with rosy red;
While from the west, a flood of amber light
Stream'd thro' the foliage on the dazzled sight;
As in a forest's wildering mazes strayed
A youthful warrior and a blooming maid.

The Maid was fair, as Poets bent on praise
Have often painted in their flattering lays,
When they from Fancy, not from Nature, drew
Their finished forms, yet still to Nature true.

Erewhile her eyes' soft lustre did outshine
The brightest diamonds of Golconda's mine;
But grief had now their native fire deprest;
And frequent sighs burst from her anguished breast.
No guardian veil concealed her charms, but round
Her jetty locks, a wreath of flowers was bound;
Her vesture rivalled the unsullied snow,
A sable scarf declared her inward woe.

The Knight, in prime of youthful vigour, joined
Undaunted courage, and a courteous mind;
Black were his arms–the painting on his shield
The strange occasion of their grief revealed:
Lo ! on the foamy ocean's shingly sands,
Reft of her Veil, a weeping damsel stands,
Beside a yawning gulf a Gnome appears,
Who waves the ravished veil and mocks her tears;
While forms ethereal lightly float in air,
And weep in pity o'er the injured fair.
An azure marge the pictured forms enroll'd,
Where shine these haughty words embost in gold:
'PROUD GNOME, THE VEIL TO ME, THY RIVAL, YIELD,
'OR DARE MY VENGEANCE IN THE LISTED FIELD.'

✢

The Arctic Expeditions (1818)
The poem which acted as the catalyst for Franklin meeting Eleanor.

Introduction:
    The doubtful fate of the Colony believed to have been once
established on the Eastern Coast of Greenland, and the possibility
of a passage to the Pole, are subjects on which for some years my
mind has dwelt with peculiar interest; this feeling was again excited
when I heard of the great revolution in the Polar Seas, which made it
probable that the one might be reached, and the fate of the other
ascertained. The following lines were prompted by a visit to His
Majesty's ships the *Alexander* and *Isabella*, lying at Deptford, on
Monday the 30th instant.
                        Eleanor Anne Porden, March 31, 1818.

The poem commences:
Sail, sail, adventurous Barks! go fearless forth,
Storm on his glacier-seat the misty North,
Give to mankind the inhospitable zone,
And Britain's trident plant in seas unknown.
Go! sure, wherever Science fills the mind
Or grief for man long sever'd from his kind,*

That anxious nations watch the changing gales,
And prayers and blessings swell your flagging sails.

*The inhabitants (if any) of lost Greenland

*

Eleanor's poem about Franklin's literary agonies, December 1822

Heigh-ho! alack! And well-a-day!
   Was ever wight like me distrest?
What shall I write? What can I say?
   Will this or that way read the best?

"Oh! That my foe a book had written!"
   So spoke the wisest of mankind,
Alas! His curse my head has smitten
   And write I must, though ill-inclined.

I've faced the battle o'er and o'er
   From steel and fire I did not shrink
Not ocean in his wildest roar
   Could frighten me like that drop of ink.

A field of snow's but one blank page,
   Bears, icebergs, buffaloes together,
I'd rather all their might engage
   Than touch that one poor goose's feather.

I'm in the tread-mill all the day,
   No rest is mine, and in my dreams
Gaunt imps of darkness round me play
   With ghastly papers filed in reams

And there, oh! There such lines are traced
   Like flints in chalk strata
And at last, one long dire list prefaced
   With that tremendous word "Errata"!

Bright Phoebus! Now thy help bestow
   Though far from thine my cause has laid

Where faint and wan thy summer glow
    Where winter forms in endless shade.

Give me thy smile for once! But how
    Thou wayward Power? 'Tis worse and worse,
I ask thee but for prose; and now
    My thoughts are jangling into verse.

My mind unwanted numbers haunt
    I'm clean bewitched! I'm in a flurry;
Avaunt! Ye crew of rhymes! Avaunt!
    Why what will Barrow say? Or Murray*?

O God of scribblers! Guide my course,
    Assist me (though the phrase be evil)
So turn my offspring out of doors,
    And give it, fairly, to the Devil.

                                        Eleanor Anne Porden

                            *

Coeur de Lion; or The Third Crusade (1822)

Opening verse:
    While Britain's annals shine with many a name,
        Her loftiest Poets might contend to sing;
    While British bosoms feed poetic flame,
        Why should Her Lyre with foreign praises ring?
    Not for my own, but for my country's fame,
        Oh! make me worthy of thy theme, and bring,
    Sweet Muse! thy noblest numbers, while I dare
    To Blazen Richard's deeds, and Richard's Holy War.

                            *

The 'Miss Greenstockings' poem, St Valentine's Day 1823

    Yes! Yes! Thou art gone to the climes of the East
        Thou hast welcomed the Sun as he springs from the Sea

---

* Franklin's publisher.

242

And thou car'st not though sorrow lie cold in my breast
    Though the Night of the Grave may be closing on me,
Yet though bright are his beans in those changeable skies
Where he dawns but to set, and descends but to rise
Though on wonders I dream not, his lustre may shine
He warms not one bosom more constant than mine

And what if the daughters of Albion be fair
    With their soft eyes of azure and tresses of Gold
To the flowers of their meadow and their charms I compare
    They bloom in the sunshine, but shrink from the cold;
But I through the snow & the Forest would guide thee
On the ice covered lake I would gambol beside thee
With the thongs of the Reindeer they buskins would weave
And dress thy light meal as thou slumber'st at Eve.

Nay frown not! Thou knows't that such moments have been
    Though cruel as false, thou coulds't calmly depart
Thy Comrade too truly has pictured the scene,
    And my form – but thine own, it is drawn on my heart!
Nor think in thy Green Isle some fair one to woo,
For in tempest and snow shall my vengeance pursue
My bidding at noonday shall darken the air,
And the rage of my climate shall follow thee there.

But return! – I have gathered thee dainties most rare,
    The wild birds that soar, and the fish from the sea
The Moose and the Reindeer, the Fox and the Bear,
    In a snow mantled grotto I guard them for thee.
How happy our long day of Summer shall prove
And our long night of Winter, when brighten'd by Love,
When the Moon and the Stars are abroad in the sky
And the brisk Northern Meteors are dancing on high.

Return! And the tempest shall pause in his wrath;
    I will breathe out my spells on the land and the sea.
Return! And ice shall be swept from thy path,
    Not the winds nor the waves dare be rebels to thee.

Spread thy canvass once more, keep the Pole Star before thee
'Tis Constancy's type and thy Beacon of Glory,
By the Lake, by the Mountain, the Forest, the River,
In the wilds of the North, I am thine, and forever.

Coppermine River
Feb 14 1823

Appendix II

1845 North West Passage Expedition – Officers and Crews of *Erebus* and *Terror*

HMS *Erebus*

Officers

Captain Sir John Franklin
Commander James Fitzjames*
Lieutenant Graham Gore*
Lieutenant Henry Thomas Dundas Le Vesconte
Lieutenant James Walter Fairholme
Mates: Robert Orme Sargent*, Charles Frederick Des Voeux*, Edward Couch*
Second Master: Henry Foster Collins
Surgeon: Stephen Samuel Stanley
Acting Assistant Surgeon: Harry D S Goodsir
Paymaster and Purser: Charles Hamilton Osmer
Acting Ice Master: James Reid

Warrant Officers

Boatswain: Thomas Terry
Carpenter: John Weekes
Engineer: John Gregory

Crew

Carpenter's Mate: Thomas Watson, N Yarmouth, Norfolk (aged 40)
Boatswain's Mate: Samuel Brown [alias Hardy], Hull, Yorkshire (27)
Quartermasters:
Daniel Arthur, Aberdeen, Scotland (35)
William Bell, Forfar, Scotland (36)

* Promoted after setting sail.

John Downing, Plymouth, Devon (34)
Sailmaker: John Murray, Glasgow, Scotland (43)
Caulker: James W Brown, Deptford, Kent (28)
Caulker's Mate: Thomas Dixon, Llanelly, S Wales (25)
Blacksmith: William Smith, Thib, Norfolk (28)
Leading Stoker: William Mark, Hampstead, Middlesex (33)
Cook: Richard Wall, Hull, Yorkshire (45)
Captain's Coxwain: James Ridgen, Upper Deal, Kent (32)
Captain's Steward: Edmund Hoar, Portsea, Hampshire (23)
Captain of the Forecastle: Philip Reddington, Brompton, Kent (28)
Captain of the Foretop: Robert Sinclair, Kirkwall, Orkney (25)
Captain of the Maintop: John Sullivan, Gillingham, Kent (28)
Captain of the Hold: Joseph Andrews, Edmonton, Middlesex (35)
Gunroom Steward: Richard Aylmore, Southampton, Hampshire (24)
Paymaster and Purser's Clerk: William Fowler, Bristol (26)
Subordinate Officers' Steward: John Bridgens, Woolwich, Kent (26)
Stokers:
John Cowie, Bermondsey, Surrey (32)
Thomas Plater, Westminster, Middlesex (?)
Able Seamen:
Charles Best, Fareham, Hampshire (23)
Thomas Burt, Wickham, Hampshire (22)*
William Closson, Shetland (25)
Charles Coombs, Greenwich, Kent (28)
Robert Ferrier, Perth, Scotland (29)
Josephus Greater, London (32)
John Hartnell, Brompton, Kent (25)
Thomas Hartnell, Chatham, Kent (23)
Robert Johns, Penryn, Cornwall (24)
Henry Lloyd, Kristiansund(?), Norway (26)
Thomas McConvey, Liverpool, Lancashire (24)
John Morfin, Gainsboro', Lincs (25)
William Orren, Chatham, Kent (34)
Thomas Pocock, Upnor, Kent (24)
Abraham Seeley, Gravesend, Kent (34)

---

* Returned to England on supply ship *Barretto Junior*, 11 Aug 1845.

John Strickland, Portsmouth, Hampshire (24)
Thomas Tadman, Brompton, Kent (28)
George Thompson, Staines, Berkshire (27)
George Williams, Holyhead, Anglesey (35)
Thomas Work, Kirkwall, Orkney (41)
Royal Marines
Sergeant: Daniel Bryant, Inverness, Scotland (31)
Corporal: Alexander Paterson, Inverness, Scotland (30)
Privates:
William Braine, Oakhill, Somerset (31)
Joseph Healey, Manchester, Lancashire (29)
Robert Hopcroft, Nottingham, Nottinghamshire (38)
William Pilkington, Kilrush, Co Clare (28)
William Reed, Bristol (28)
Boys
George Chambers, Woolwich, Kent (18)
David Young, Sheerness, Kent (18)

HMS *Terror*

Officers
Captain Francis Rawdon Moira Crozier
Lieutenant Edward Little*
Lieutenant George Henry Hodgson
Lieutenant John Irving
Mates: Frederick John Hornby,* Robert Thomas*
Second Master: Gillies Alexander Macbean
Acting Surgeon: John Smart Peddie*
Assistant Surgeon: Alexander Macdonald
Clerk in Charge: Edwin James Howard Helpman
Acting Ice Master: Thomas Blankey
Warrant Officers
Boatswain: John Lane
Carpenter: Thomas Honey
Engineer: James Thompson

* Promoted after setting sail.

Crew

> *Boatswain's Mate:* Thomas Johnson, Wisbech, Cambridgeshire (28)
> *Carpenter's Mate:* Alexander Wilson, Holy Island, Co Durham (27)
> *Quartermasters:*
> John Kenley, St Morance, Scotland (44)
> David Macdonald, Peterhead, Scotland (46)
> William Rhodes, Redingstreet, Kent (31)
> *Caulker:* Thomas Darlington, Plymouth, Devon (29)
> *Blacksmith:* Samuel Honey, Portsmouth, Hampshire (22)
> *Leading Stoker:* John Torrington, Manchester, Lancashire (19)
> *Cook:* John Diggle, Westminster, London (36)
> *Captain's Coxwain:* John Wilson, Portsea, Hampshire (33)
> *Captain's Steward:* Thomas Jopson, Marylebone, Middlesex (27)
> *Subordinate Officers' Steward:* William Gibson, London (22)
> *Captain of the Forecastle:* Reuben Male, Woolwich, Kent (27)
> *Captain of the Maintop:* Thomas R Farr, Deptford, Kent (32)
> *Captain of the Foretop:* Harry Peglar, London (37)
> *Captain of the Hold:* William Goddard, N Yarmouth, Norfolk (39)
> *Caulker's Mate:* Cornelius Hickey, Limerick, Ireland (24)
> *Gunroom Steward:* Thomas Armitage, Chatham, Kent (40)
> *Stokers:*
> William Johnson, Kirton Lindsay, Lincolnshire (45)
> Luke Smith, London (27)
> *Armourer(?):* Robert Thomas Carr, London (22)
> *Sailmaker:* James Elliott,* Woolwich, Kent (20)
> *Paymaster & Purser's Steward:* Edward George, Gosport, Hampshire (21)
> *Able Seamen:*
> John Bailey, Leyton, Essex (21 years)
> John Bates, London (24)
> Alexander Berry, S Ferry, Bedfordshire (32)
> George J Cann, Battersea, Middlesex (23)
> Samuel Crispe, Lynn, Norfolk (24)
> John Handford, Sunderland, Co Durham (28)
> William Jerry, Pembroke, Wales (29)

---

* Returned to England on supply ship *Barretto Junior*, 13 Aug 1845.

Charles Johnson, Halifax, Nova Scotia (28)
George Kinnaird, Hastings, Sussex (23)
Edwin Lawrence, London (30)
David Leys, Montrose, Scotland (27)
Magnus Manson, Shetland, Scotland (28)
Henry Sait, Bognor, Sussex (23)
William Shanks, Dundee, Scotland (29)
David Sims, Gedney, Lincolnshire (24)
William Sinclair, Galloway, Scotland (30)
William Strong, Portsmouth, Hampshire (22)
James Walker, South Shields, Co Durham (29)
William Wentzall, London (33)

Royal Marines
Sergeant: Solomon Tozer, Axbridge, Somerset (34)
Corporal: William Hedges, Bradford, Wiltshire (30)
Privates:
William Aitkin, Kenilworth, Surrey (37)
James Daly, Suberclue(?), Westmeath (30)
John Hammond, Bradford, Yorkshire (32)
William Heather, Battersea, Surrey (35)
Henry Wilkes, Leicester, Leicestershire (28)

Boys
Thomas Evans, Deptford, Kent (18)
Robert Golding (19)

Appendix III

A Franklin Chronology

1786. Born in Spilsby, Lincolnshire, 16 April.

1792. Jane Griffin born, Bedford Square, London.

1795. Eleanor Anne Porden born, Devonshire Street, London, 14 July.

1800. Joined HMS *Polyphemus* as Midshipman, March.

1801. Battle of Copenhagen, April. Joined HMS *Investigator*, July.

1803. Wreck of the *Porpoise*, August.

1804. Engaged French battle squadron on *Earl Camden*, January. Joined HMS *Bellerophon*, August.

1805. Battle of Trafalgar, 21 October.

1807. Joined HMS *Bedford* as Master's Mate, October. Made Acting Lieutenant, 5 December.

1808. Promotion to Lieutenant confirmed, 11 February.

1815. Attack on New Orleans. Transferred to HMS *Forth* as First Lieutenant, June.

1818. North Pole Expedition in command of HMS *Trent*, April. Returned to England, October.

1819. Left England on first overland expedition, May; promoted to Commander during expedition.

1822. Returned to England, October. Promoted to Post Captain, 21 November. Made Fellow of the Royal Geographical Society, November.

1823. Married Eleanor Anne Porden, 19 August.

1824. Daughter Eleanor born, 3 June.

1825. Left on second overland expedition, 16 February. Death of Eleanor Anne, 23 February.

1827. Returned to England, 1 September.

1828. Married Jane Griffin, 5 November.

1829. Received knighthood, April. Awarded Gold Medal of the Paris Geographical Society.

1830. Joined HMS *Rainbow*, August; stationed in Mediterranean.

1833. Returned to England.

1834. Paid off from HMS *Rainbow*, January. Awarded Golden Cross of the Order of the Redeemer by King Otho of Greece.

1836. Made Knight Commander of the Guelphic Order. Sailed on *Fairlie* for Van Dieman's Land, 26 August.

1844. Arrived back in England, June.

1845. Departure on HMS *Erebus* for North West Passage expedition, 19 May.

1847. Died, 11 June.

1854. Rae's first news of Franklin's expedition, April.

1859. Hobson finds only written records belonging to expedition.

1875. Death of Jane, 18 July.

Appendix IV

The North West Passage and the North Pole in the Twenty-First Century

There is a realistic chance that the conditions Franklin needed to accomplish two of his feats of exploration may be realised within the lifetime of today's children – thanks to the cumulative effects of global warming.

The *Daily Express* of 16 June 2000 carried an article quoting Art Dyke of the Canadian Geographical Society about the effects of the steadily receding ice in the Arctic region. He believes that within a few decades a North West Passage will be open to ships for several months during the summer. (To underline one of the points made in the final chapter of this book, the article baldly states that Sir John Franklin's expedition ended with the crew 'indulging in cannibalism', a revelation 'missing from the early histories' according to the journalist. The first point is conjecture and the second untrue.)

Then, on 20 August 2000, the *Sunday Times* carried further warnings about the effects of climate changes. Apparently, a 'mile-wide' area of sea has been discovered at the North Pole by oceanographer James McCarthy – Barrow's 'temperate sea' has finally become a reality! There is a prediction that the ice cap could melt completely within a century unless industrialised countries reduce their 'greenhouse' emissions in the near future. The United States of America is the major culprit, and is expected to *increase* its emissions.

Bibliography

Beattie, Owen, & Geiger, John, *Frozen in Time – The Fate of the Franklin Expedition* (Bloomsbury, 1987, 1993)

Beechey, F W, Captain, *A Voyage of Discovery Towards the North Pole* (Richard Bentley, 1843)

Bennet, Geoffrey, *The Battle of Trafalgar* (B T Batsford, 1977)

Berton, Pierre, *The Arctic Grail – The Quest for the North West Passage & the North Pole, 1818–1909* (Viking Penguin, 1988)

Brown, Anthony J, Ill-Starred Captains – Flinders & Baudin (Chatham Publishing, 2001)

Church, Clive H, *Europe in 1830* (George Allen and Unwin, 1983)

Conefrey, Mick & Jordan, Tim, *Icemen – A History of the Arctic & its Explorers* (Boxtree, 1998)

Cookman, Scott, *Ice Blink* (John Wiley & Sons, New York, 2000)

Cyriax, R J, *Sir John Franklin's Last Expedition* (Methuen, 1939)

Delgado, James, *Across the Top of the World* (British Museum Press, 1999)

Evans, Eric, *The Birth of Modern Britain 1780–1914* (Longman, 1997)

Fitzpatrick, Kathleen, *Sir John Franklin in Tasmania* (Melbourne University Press, 1949)

Flinders, Matthew, *A Voyage to Terra Australis; Undertaken for the Purpose of Completing the Discovery of that Vast Country, and Prosecuted in the Years 1801, 1802 and 1803* (G & W Nichol, 1814)

Franklin, Sir John, *Narrative of a Journey to the Shores of the Polar Sea in the Years 1819, 20, 21, & 22* (John Murray, 1823)
 – *Narrative of a Second Expedition to the Shores of the Polar Sea, in the Years 1825, 1826 & 1827* (John Murray, 1828)
 – *Narrative of Some Passages in the History of Van Dieman's Land During the Last Three Years of Sir John Franklin's*

Administration of its Government [Facsimile] (Platypus Publications, Hobart, 1967)

Fraser, Edward, *Bellerophon, Bravest of the Brave* (Wells Gardner, Darlton, 1909)

Garrett, Richard, *The Story of Britain* (HarperCollins, 1983, 1991)

Gell, E M, *Sir John Franklin's Bride* (John Murray, 1930)

Grocott, Terence, *Shipwrecks of the Revolutionary and Napoleonic Eras* (Chatham Publishing, 1997)

Herbert, Wally, *Hunters of the Polar North – The Eskimos* (Time-Life Books, 1981)

Hibbert, Christopher, *Nelson, A Personal History* (Viking Penguin, 1994)

Holland, Clive (ed), *Manuscripts in the Scott Polar Research Institute, Cambridge, England* (Garland Publishing, 1982)

Houston, C Stuart (ed), *Arctic Ordeal – The Journal of John Richardson, Surgeon – Naturalist with Franklin, 1820–1822* (McGill-Queens University Press, 1984)

Howarth, David, *Trafalgar, The Nelson Touch* (Collins, 1969)

Hughes, Robert, *The Fatal Shore* (Collins Harvill, 1987)

Jerdan, William, *Men I Have Known* (Geo Routledge & Sons, 1866)

King, Dean, & Hattendorf, John (eds), *Every Man Will Do His Duty* (Conway Maritime Press, 1997)

Lamb, G F, *Franklin – Happy Voyager* (Ernest Benn, 1956)

Lambert, Richard S, *Franklin of the Arctic* (The Bodley Head, 1954)

Mackenzie, Gordon, *Marylebone – Great City North of Oxford Street* (MacMillan, 1972)

Masefield, John, *Sea Life in Nelson's Time* (Conway Maritime Press, 1984)

Maxtone-Graham, John, *Safe Return Doubtful – The Heroic Age of Polar Exploration* (Patrick Stephens, 1988)

McGoogan, Ken, *Fatal Passage* (HarperCollins, 2001)

Owen, Roderic, *The Fate of Franklin* (Hutchinson, 1978)

Padfield, Peter, *Nelson's War* (Granada Publishing, 1976)

Porden, Eleanor Anne, *The Arctic Expeditions* (John Murray, 1818)
– *Coeur de Lion; or the Third Crusade* (John Murray, 1822)

– *The Veils; or The Triumph of Constancy* (John Murray, 1815)

Porter, Roy, *English Society in the Eighteenth Century* (Penguin, 1982, 1990)

Pugh, Martin, *Britain Since 1789, A Concise History* (MacMillan Press, 1999)

Reid, Alan, *Discovery and Exploration: A Concise History* (Gentry Books, 1980)

Richards, Dennis & Hunt, J W (eds), *An Illustrated History of Modern Britain 1783–1980* (3rd Edn, Longman, 1983)

Robinson, D N, *The Book of Louth* (Barracuda Books, 1979)

Rodger, N A M, *Naval Records for Genealogists* (Public Record Office Handbooks No 22, HMSO, London, 1988)
– *The Wooden World – An Anatomy of the Georgian Navy* (Fontana Press, 1986)

Savours, Ann, *The Search for the North West Passage* (Chatham Publishing, 1999)

Thompson, David, *Europe Since Napoleon* (Longmans, 1957; Rev Edn, Penguin, 1990)

Traill, H D, *The Life of Sir John Franklin* (John Murray, 1896)

Watt, J, Freeman, E J & Bynum, W F (eds), *Starving Sailors – The Influence of Nutrition Upon Naval & Maritime History* (National Maritime Museum, 1981)

Whipple, A B C, *Fighting Sail* (Time-Life Books, 1978)

Woodcock, George, *A Social History of Canada* (Viking Penguin, 1988)

Woodman, David C, *Unravelling the Franklin Mystery – Inuit Testimony* (McGill-Queens University Press, 1991)

Young, G M (ed), *Early Victorian England* (Oxford University Press, 1934, 1951)

Other Resources

Unpublished Documents at:
British Library, London
Derbyshire Public Record Office, Matlock, Derbyshire
Lincolnshire Archive, Lincoln
National Maritime Museum, Greenwich, London

Public Record Office, Kew, London
Royal Geographical Society, London
Scott Polar Research Institute, Cambridge

Websites

Canada's Digital Collections, *John Franklin – 1891–22, 1825–27*
  (http://collections.ic.gc.ca/arctic/explore/franklin.htm)
Church of Jesus Christ of Latter-day Saints, *International
  Genealogical Index* (http://www.familysearch.org/)
Coleman, E C, *Parson's World of Sir John Franklin*
  (http://homepages.enterprise.net/rogerp/franklin.html)
Davidson, Wayne, *Sir John Franklin Was Here*
  (http://www.vif.com/users/Inularit.Resolute/)
Irish Antarctic Explorers
  (http://www.iol.ie/south-aris/irishexp.htm)
Franklin in the Public Eye: 1818–1859
  (http://www.ric.edu/rpotter/publiceye.html)
The Franklin Trail
  (http://www.franklintrail.com/)
Mullington, David & Phillips, Michael, *Sir John Franklin*
  (http://www.cronab.demon.co.uk/frank.htm)
National Maritime Museum, *Sir John Franklin 1786–1847*
  (http://www.nmm.ac.uk/education/fact_franklin.html)
Parks and Wildlife Service, Tasmania, *Guide to Tasmania's Historic
  Places* (http://www.parks.tas.gov.au/hostoric/visguide/eagleh/
  hist.html)
Phillips, Michael, *George Back RN, Arctic Explorer*
  (http://www.w.cronab.demon.co.uk/frank.htm)
Potter, Russell A, *The Fate of Franklin*
  (http://www.ric.edu/rpotter/sjfranklin.html)

Miscellaneous Publications

Chatham Historic Dockyard Trust, *World Naval Base – The
  Historic Dockyard, Chatham, Kent* (Chatham Historic
  Dockyard and Jarrold Publishing, 1999) [Pamphlet]

Cotton-Smith, Rev H, *A History of Spilsby* (The Spilsby Printing Co) [Pamphlet]

Keenleyside, Anne, *An Analysis of Recently Discovered Human Skeletal Remains from the Last Expedition of Sir John Franklin* (McMaster University) [report]

Lowles, W J, *Greenhithe – Local History Leaflet No 7* (Kent County Library) [Leaflet]

Periodicals

Arctic
Daily Express
Equinox
Geographical Journal
Geographical Magazine
Journal of Archaeological Science
Polar Record
The Times

Notes and References

Chapter One – *Every Inch an Honest Tar*

1   H D Traill, *The Life of Sir John Franklin* (John Murray, 1896).
2   LA – Misc DON 447/2.
3   D N Robinson, *The Book of Louth* (Barracuda Books, 1979).
4   SPRI – MS 248/368: C T D'Eyncourt to Lady Franklin, 3 Nov 1865.
5   BL – Franklin 56233.
6   LA – *Flinders* 2/fol 103v.
7   N A M Rodger, *The Wooden World* (Fontana Press, 1986).
8   DPRO – DD3311/121.
9   C Hibbert, *Nelson, A Personal History* (Viking Penguin, 1994).
10 J Masefield, *Sea Life in Nelson's Time* (Conway Maritime Press, 1984).
11 DPRO – op cit.
12 M Flinders, *A Voyage to Terra Australis…* (G & W Nichol, 1814).
13 Ibid.
14 DPRO – op cit.
15 Flinders – op cit.
16 W Jerdan, *Men I Have Known* (Geo Routledge & Sons, 1866). Jerdan knew Franklin, Parry and several other of the main players in this story.
17 DPRO – op cit.
18 DPRO – DD3311/104.
19 Ibid.
20 Ibid.
21 SPRI – MS248/202.
22 G F Lamb, *Franklin – Happy Voyager* (Ernest Benn, 1956).
23 SPRI – MS 249/394.
24 Ibid.
25 Ibid.
26 SPRI – MS 249/394.
27 Flinders – op cit.
28 Ibid.
29 Ibid.
30 Ibid.
31 DPRO – DD3311/104.
32 SPRI – MS 296/1–20.

Chapter Two – *Bellerophon – Death or Glory*

1   SPRI – MS 269.
2   DPRO – DD3311/121.
3   D Howarth, *Trafalgar, The Nelson Touch* (Collins, 1969).
4   DPRO – op cit.
5   Ibid.
6   Ibid.
7   E Fraser, *Bellerophon, Bravest of the Brave* (Wells Gardner, Darlton & Co, 1909). The overall picture of the battle of Trafalgar and the *Bellerophon*'s part in it has been drawn from the wide range of published accounts.
8   Ibid.
9   Ibid.

10 G F Lamb, *Franklin – Happy Voyager* (Ernest Benn, 1956).
11 BL – Franklin 56233.
12 SPRI – MS 286.
13 DPRO – op cit.
14 BL – op cit.
15 Ibid.
16 Ibid.
17 Ibid.
18 Ibid.
19 Ibid.
20 Ibid.
21 Ibid.
22 DPRO – op cit.
23 LA – Misc Don 756/1/1/1.
24 SPRI – MS 248/383/7/D.
25 SPRI – MS 248/394.
26 R Owen, *The Fate of Franklin* (Hutchinson, 1978).
27 SPRI – MS 296.
28 SPRI – MS 248/435: Sir John Lambert wrote to Vice-Admiral Cochrane to tell him how much 'the Army is indebted to the active cooperations and zealous Services of the Navy', and Franklin was one of the few singled out by name as being recommended for promotion.
29 Ibid.
30 Ibid.

Chapter Three – *The Most Northern Point*

1 LA – Misc Don 756.
2 DPRO – DD3311/121.
3 DPRO – DD3311/101.
4 *The Times*, 27 Mar 1818.
5 DPRO – DD3311/101.
6 F W Beechey, Capt RN, *A Voyage of Discovery Towards the North Pole* (Richard Bentley, 1843).
7 Ibid.
8 Ibid. Spinks subsequently volunteered to go with Franklin on his next expedition, where his ability and spirit was greatly appreciated. After later being promoted to Gunner, he died on active service in Gibraltar.

Chapter Four – *Akaitcho*

1 E A Porden, *The Arctic Expeditions* (John Murray, 1818).
2 SPRI – MS 248/50: Lady Franklin's Journals.
3 E A Porden, *The Veils; or The Triumph of Constancy* (John Murray, 1815).
4 According to Eleanor's obituary in *The Monthly Magazine*, Apr 1825.
5 SPRI – MS 248/35.
6 Ibid.
7 Ibid.
8 DPRO – DD3311/90.
9 Ibid.
10 Ibid.
11 P Berton, *The Arctic Grail...* (Viking Penguin, 1988).
12 Ibid.
13 Ibid.
14 J Franklin, Capt RN FRS, *Narrative of a Journey to the Shores of the Polar Sea...* (John Murray, 1823).
15 SPRI – MS 248/107.
16 DPRO – DD3311/101.
17 SPRI – MS 248/50.
18 DPRO – DD3311/101.
19 PRO – CO 6/6/5.
20 Ibid.

21 DPRO – DD3311/121.
22 Franklin, op cit.
23 F Fleming, *Barrow's Boys* (Granta Books, 1998).
24 Franklin – op cit.
25 DPRO – DD3311/121.
26 Franklin – op cit.
27 Ibid.
28 Ibid.
29 Ibid.
30 Ibid.
31 Ibid.
32 Ibid.
33 Ibid.
34 Ibid.
35 Ibid.
36 Ibid.
37 Ibid.
38 Ibid.
39 Ibid.
40 Ibid.
41 Ibid.
42 Ibid.
43 Ibid.
44 Ibid.
45 Ibid.
46 Ibid.
47 Ibid.
48 Ibid.
49 Ibid.
50 DPRO – DD3311/121. Letter from Fort Enterprise to Rev J Wright, 18 Oct 1820.
51 Franklin – op cit.
52 Ibid.
53 Ibid.
54 Ibid.
55 Ibid.
56 Ibid.
57 Ibid.
58 Ibid.
59 Ibid.
60 Ibid.

Chapter Five – *Que Nous Sommes Maigres!*
1 J Franklin, Capt RN FRS, *Narrative of a Journey to the Shores of the Polar Sea...* (John Murray, 1823).
2 Ibid.
3 Ibid.
4 Ibid.
5 Ibid.
6 Ibid.
7 Ibid.
8 Ibid.
9 Ibid.
10 Ibid.
11 Ibid.
12 Ibid.
13 Ibid.
14 Ibid.
15 Ibid.
16 C Stuart Houston (ed), *Arctic Ordeal – The Journal of John Richardson, Surgeon...* (McGill-Queens University Press, 1984).
17 Franklin – op cit.
18 Ibid.
19 Ibid.
20 Ibid.
21 Ibid.
22 Ibid.
23 Ibid.
24 Ibid.
25 Ibid.
26 Ibid.

Chapter Six – *The Throne of Mercy*
1 J Franklin, Capt RN FRS, *Narrative of a Journey to the Shores of the Polar Sea...* (John Murray, 1823).
2 Ibid.

3 Ibid.
4 Ibid.
5 Ibid.
6 Ibid.
7 Ibid.
8 Ibid.
9 Ibid.
10 Ibid.
11 Ibid.
12 Ibid.
13 C Stuart Houston, *Arctic Ordeal – The Journal of John 1*
14 Franklin – op cit.
15 P Berton, *The Arctic Grail...* (Viking Penguin, 1988).
16 Houston – op cit.
17 Ibid.
18 Franklin – op cit.
19 Houston – op cit.

Chapter Seven – *I Am Far From Well*

1 DPRO – DD3311/84.
2 Ibid.
3 DPRO – DD3311/85.
4 Ibid.
5 Ibid.
6 Ibid.
7 H D Traill, *The Life of Sir John Franklin* (John Murray, 1896).
8 E M Gell, *Sir John Franklin's Bride* (John Murray, 1930).
9 DPRO – DD3311/84.
10 Ibid.
11 Ibid.
12 Ibid.
13 Ibid.
14 DPRO – DD3311/90.
15 DPRO – DD3311/115.
16 Ibid.
17 Ibid.
18 J Franklin, Capt RN FRS, *Narrative of a Journey to the Shores of the Polar Sea...* (John Murray, 1823).
19 DPRO – DD3311/101.
20 SPRI – MS 248/56.
21 DPRO – DD3311/115.
22 DPRO – DD3311/115.
23 SPRI – MS 248/50.
24 DPRO – DD3311/115.
25 Ibid.
26 Ibid.
27 Ibid.
28 Ibid.
29 Ibid.
30 Ibid.
31 Ibid.
32 Ibid.
33 Ibid.
34 Ibid.
35 Ibid.
36 Ibid.
37 Ibid.
38 DPRO – DD3311/89.
39 DPRO – DD3311/115.
40 DPRO – DD3311/86.
41 Ibid.
42 SPRI – MS 248/308.
43 SPRI – MS 248/394.
44 SPRI – MS 248/388/2 to S Cracroft, 17 Mar 1824.
45 Ibid.
46 DPRO – DD3311/84.
47 Ibid.
48 SPRI – MS 248/50.
49 SPRI – MS 248/389/1.
50 DPRO – DD3311/86.
51 DPRO – DD3311/89.
52 DPRO – DD 3311/84.
53 Ibid.
54 Ibid.
55 PRO – ADM 7/199 (from letter in *Morning Herald*, 2 Sept 1854).

56 DPRO – DD3311/84.
57 SPRI – MS 248/56.
58 Ibid.
59 DPRO – DD3311/121.
60 Ibid.

Chapter Eight – *Fort Franklin*
1   J Franklin, Capt RN FRS, *Narrative of a Second Expedition to the Shores of the Polar Sea...* (John Murray, 1828).
2   SPRI – MS 248/377.
3   SPRI – MS 248/388.
4   Franklin – op cit.
5   SPRI – MS 248/50.
6   Franklin – op cit.
7   DPRO – DD3311/101.
8   DPRO – DD3311/97.
9   Ibid. One of the Franklin myths is that this postscript is in 'shaky' or 'agitated' handwriting, but an examination of the original letter does not bear this out.
10 SPRI – MS 248/56.
11 DPRO – DD3311/95.
12 DPRO – DD 3311/88.
13 *The Times*, 25 Feb 1825.
14 DPRO – DD3311/134.
15 SPRI – MS 248/56.
16 F Fleming, *Barrow's Boys* (Granta Books, 1998).
17 SPRI – MS 248/388.
18 DPRO – DD3311/95.
19 Franklin – op cit.
20 Ibid.
21 Ibid.
22 DPRO – DD3311/121
23 Ibid.
24 Franklin – op cit.
25 Ibid.
26 DPRO – DD3311/44.

27 Ibid.
28 Ibid.
29 Ibid.
30 Ibid.
31 Ibid.
32 Ibid.
33 Ibid.

Chapter Nine – *A Woman of Most Excellent Sense*
1   International Genealogical Index – GEDCOM 5.5.
2   SPRI – MS 248/56.
3   SPRI – MS 248/50.
4   SPRI – MS 248/56.
5   DPRO – DD3311/59
6   F J Woodward, *Portrait of Jane – A Life of Lady Franklin* (Hodder & Stoughton, 1951).
7   G F Lamb, *Franklin – Happy Voyager* (Ernest Benn, 1956).
8   SPRI – MS 248/50.
9   Ibid.
10 Ibid.
11 Ibid.
12 RGS – SJF7/2.
13 Ibid.
14 SPRI – MS 248/285.
15 Woodward – op cit.
16 Ibid.
17 SPRI – MS 248/68.
18 SPRI – MS 248/286.
19 DPRO – DD3311/121.
20 Woodward – op cit.
21 SPRI – MS 248/287.
22 SPRI – MS 248/286.
23 SPRI – MS 248/172.
24 DPRO – DD3311/121
25 BL – Franklin 56233
26 SPRI – MS 248/287.
27 PRO – ADM 7/199. This story appeared in the *New York Municipal Gazette*

(extract undated) and was
sent to Barrow in Oct 1855.
28 BL – op cit.
29 Ibid.
30 DPRO – DD3311/121.
31 Woodward – op cit.
32 Woodward – op cit.
33 DPRO – DD3311/121
34 Ibid.
35 Ibid.
36 Ibid.
37 SPRI – MS 248/303.
38 Ibid.

Chapter Ten – *Hearts of Stone*
1 SPRI – MS 248/303.
2 E M Gell, *Sir John Franklin's Bride* (John Murray, 1930).
3 K Fitzpatrick, *Sir John Franklin in Tasmania* (Melbourne University Press, 1949).
4 SPRI – MS 248/84.
5 Ibid.
6 Fitzpatrick – op cit.
7 Ibid.
8 J Franklin, Capt RN FRS, *Narrative of Some Passages in the History of Van Dieman's Land During the Last Three Years of Sir John Franklin's Administration...* (Platypus Publications [facsimile], 1967).
9 Ibid.
10 Fitzpatrick – op cit.
11 Franklin – op cit.
12 W A Newman, *Biographical Memoir of John Montagu* (1855), quoted in Fitzpatrick – op cit.
13 Fitzpatrick – op cit.
14 Ibid.

15 Ibid.
16 SPRI – MS 248/85.
17 Fitzpatrick – op cit.
18 Ibid.
19 Ibid.
20 Franklin – op cit.
21 Ibid.
22 G F Lamb, *Franklin – Happy Voyager* (Ernest Benn, 1956).
23 Fitzpatrick – op cit.
24 Ibid.
25 Ibid.
26 Ibid.

Chapter Eleven – *The Basest of Actions*
1 J Franklin, Capt RN FRS, *Narrative of Some Passages in the History of Van Dieman's Land During the Last Three Years of Sir John Franklin's Administration...* (Platypus Publications [facsimile], 1967).
2 Ibid.
3 SPRI – MS 248/157.
4 Franklin – op cit.
5 Ibid.
6 Ibid.
7 SPRI – op cit.
8 Franklin – op cit.
9 Ibid.
10 Ibid.
11 K Fitzpatrick, *Sir John Franklin in Tasmania* (Melbourne University Press, 1949).
12 Franklin – op cit.
13 Ibid.
14 Ibid.
15 Ibid.
16 Ibid.
17 Ibid.

18 G F Lamb, *Franklin – Happy Voyager* (Ernest Benn, 1956).
19 Fitzpatrick – op cit.
20 Franklin – op cit.
21 Ibid.
22 Ibid.
23 Fitzpatrick – op cit.
24 SPRI – op cit.
25 Fitzpatrick – op cit.
26 Franklin – op cit.
27 Fitzpatrick – op cit.
28 Franklin – op cit.
29 SPRI – MS 248/321.
30 Franklin – op cit.
31 Ibid.
32 Ibid.
33 Ibid.
34 SPRI – MS 248/321.

Chapter Twelve – *I Wish You Could See This Ship*
1 A Savours, *The Search for the North West Passage* (Chatham Publishing, 1999).
2 PRO – ADM 7/187.
3 Ibid.
4 R J Cyriax, *Sir John Franklin's Last Expedition* (Methuen, 1939).
5 K Fitzpatrick, *Sir John Franklin in Tasmania* (Melbourne University Press, 1949).
6 Ibid.
7 SPRI – MS 248/303.
8 F Fleming, *Barrow's Boys* (Granta Books, 1998).
9 SPRI – op cit.
10 Ibid.
11 Ibid.
12 Ibid.
13 R Owen, *The Fate of Franklin* (Hutchinson, 1978).
14 Much of the following

background on the officers under Franklin comes from Cyriax – op cit. He in turn obtained most of the information from *A Naval Biographical Dictionary* (London, 1849).
15 *Arctic Matters*, Mar 1852.
16 Ibid.
17 SPRI – MS 248/364.
18 *World Naval Base – The Historic Dockyard, Chatham, Kent* (Chatham Historic Dockyard & Jarrold Publishing, 1999).
19 Ibid.
20 Owen – op cit.
21 LA – Misc Don 447/1.
22 *Arctic Matters*, Mar 1852.
23 Ibid.
24 Cyriax – op cit.
25 SPRI – MS 1372/1–4; D.
26 LA – op cit.
27 DPRO – DD 3311/134.
28 SPRI – MS 248/364.
29 LA – op cit.
30 DPRO – DD3311/133.
31 LA – op cit.
32 DPRO – DD3311/107.
33 *Arctic Matters*, Apr 1852.
34 *Arctic Matters*, Mar 1852.
35 Ibid.
36 Ibid.
37 Ibid.
38 LA – op cit.
39 Ibid.
40 Ibid.
41 Ibid.
42 Ibid.

Chapter Thirteen – *The Haven Where They Would Be*
1 PRO – ADM 7/187.

2   Ibid.
3   Ibid.
4   Ibid.
5   LA – Misc Don 447/1.
6   PRO – op cit.
7   Ibid.
8   Ibid.
9   LA – op cit.
10 Ibid.
11 Ibid.
12 PRO – op cit.
13 SPRI – MS 248/10.
14 PRO – ADM 7/189.
15 LA – op cit.
16 PRO – op cit.
17 PRO – ADM 7/608.
18 PRO – ADM 7/189.
19 SPRI – MS 248/103: One of several examples from Lady Franklin's journals is an entry for 26 Feb 1848 – 'Capt. Maconochie came to breakfast in order to accompany us afterwards into the City...'
20 F J Woodward, *Portrait of Jane – a Life of Lady Franklin* (Hodder & Stoughton, 1951).
21 R Lloyd-Jones, The Paranormal Arctic: Lady Franklin, Sophia Cracroft, and Captain and 'Little Weesy' Coppin (*Polar Record*, 37 [200], 2001).
22 PRO – ADM 7/189.
23 LA – op cit.
24 O Beattie & J Geiger, *Frozen in Time* (Bloomsbury, 1987).
25 LA – op cit.
26 PRO – ADM 7/612.
27 PRO – ADM 7/192.
28 Ibid.
29 Ibid.
30 PRO – ADM 7/193.
31 SPRI – MS 248/106.
32 Ibid.
33 Ibid.
34 Ibid.
35 LA – op cit.
36 Ibid.
37 Ibid.
38 Ibid.
39 PRO – ADM 7/611.
40 PRO – ADM 7/199.
41 Ibid.
42 Ibid.
43 Ibid.
44 Ibid.
45 *The Times*, 26 Oct 1854.
46 SPRI – MS 248/113.
47 LA – Misc Don 447/2.
48 Ibid.
49 Ibid.
50 DPRO – DD3311/133.
51 Ibid.
52 LA – op cit.
53 *The Times*, 18 July 1875.
54 Woodward – op cit.

Chapter Fourteen – *A Good Man*

1   R J Cyriax, *Sir John Franklin's Last Expedition* (Methuen, 1939).
2   A Keenleyside, The Final Days of the Franklin Expedition: New Skeletal Evidence (*Arctic*, 50 [1], Mar 1997).
3   C Coleman, *Parson's World of Sir John Franklin* – http://homepages.enterprise.net/rogerp/franklin.html.
4   A Keenleyside, An Analysis of Recently Discovered Human Skeletal Remains from the Last Expedition of

Sir John Franklin (McMaster University, 10 Jan 1994 [report]).

5 O Beattie & J Geiger, *Frozen in Time* (Bloomsbury, 1987).

6 A Keenleyside, The Lead Content of Human Bones from the 1845 Franklin Expedition (*Journal of Archaeological Science*, 1966).

7 W Davidson, *Sir John Franklin Was Here* – http://www.vif.com/users/inularit.resolute/.

8 Coleman – op cit.

9 S Cookman, *Ice Blink* (John Wiley & Sons, New York, 2000)

Index